The Signature of God

ASTONISHING BIBLE CODES

GRANT R. JEFFREY

Best-selling author of *Creation*

WATERBROOK
PRESS

THE SIGNATURE OF GOD
PUBLISHED BY WATERBROOK PRESS
12265 Oracle Boulevard, Suite 200
Colorado Springs, Colorado 80921
A division of Random House, Inc.

10 Digit ISBN: 0-921714-74-2
13 Digit ISBN: 978-0-921714-74-3

This book is copublished with Broadway Books, a division of Random House, Inc.

The Signature of God was originally published by Frontier Research Publications in 2002.

Library of Congress Cataloging-in-Publication Data
Jeffrey, Grant R.
The Signature of God

1. Apologetics   2. Eschatology   3. Bible Science
1. Title

Printed in the United States of America
2008

10 9 8 7 6 5 4

"Grant Jeffrey has written an extraordinary new book, *The Signature of God*, that provides astonishing proof that the Bible was inspired by God. Grant is recognized as the leading researcher in Bible Prophecy today."

Hal Lindsey, Hal Lindsey Ministries

"The *Prophecy Study Bible* is a phenomenal publishing effort by one of America's premier prophecy experts. Comprehensive, understandable, and powerful. A great work!" *Dr. Ed Hindsen, Editor – Jesus Study Bible*

"The *Prophecy Study Bible* is the most comprehensive, contemporary, and in-depth study of the most relevant prophecies in the Bible — A must addition to every serious student of the Word of God."

Dr. Chuck Missler – Koinonia House Ministries

"*Prince of Darkness* was written by acclaimed Bible Prophecy teacher Grant R. Jeffrey. This unequaled masterpiece is the result of 30 years of intense research. It will stir you and inspire you as few books have. . . . It is extremely well written — extraordinarily researched and fascinatingly presented . . . this is the best book I have ever read on this subject." *Jack Van Impe, Jack Van Impe Ministries*

"*Armageddon: Appointment With Destiny* has been our hottest single religious title. . . . We took it on with tremendous enthusiasm because there was something very exciting about the way Grant wrote, and it was something that we thought might go beyond the traditional religious audience." *Lou Arnonica, Vice President,*
Bantam Books, New York Times, October 22, 1990

"We are excited about Grant Jeffrey's new book. . . . Now the book with the latest information on prophetic fulfilment, the book of the nineties, is *Armageddon: Appointment With Destiny*. It will show that God is in control and, most importantly, it will also prove to be a powerful witnessing tool to those who need Christ." *David Mainse: Host, 100 Huntley Street*

Table of Contents

Acknowledgments

The Signature of God – Astonishing Bible Codes is an enlarged and revised edition of the original best selling 1996 book *The Signature of God* that has sold over 500,000 copies in twenty-four languages around the world. In addition to numerous examples of new research that I have uncovered in the last six years this new edition includes remarkable new Bible Code discoveries that relate to the tragic events of September 11, 2001. This book answers the questions raised by critics of the Bible Codes phenomenon and further explores this extraordinary discovery.

Many of the greatest scholars in the last two thousand years have explored the Scriptures and concluded that they are truly inspired by God. During the last few decades, I completed many research trips to the Middle East and Europe. In addition I communicated with bookstores throughout the world acquiring numerous old and often rare books written by these great men of God from past generations. These volumes contain tremendous archeological, historical and scientific evidence that confirms the inspiration and authority of the Word of God. I am greatly indebted to the work of countless Bible scholars who have labored to find the wealth of evidence that proves the inspiration of the Scriptures. The Internet and major libraries have provided invaluable assistance in completing the research that established the overwhelming evidence that the Bible is the inspired Word of God.

This book is the result of forty years of research involving literally thousands of books, Bible commentaries, and countless hours of detailed study of the Scriptures. As this book demonstrates, our faith and hope for the future is grounded upon a strong conviction in the inspiration of the Scriptures and a confidence in the promises of Jesus Christ to return and establish His kingdom.

My parents, Lyle and Florence Jeffrey, have inspired me through their lifelong commitment to Bible study. Their profound love for Jesus Christ and the prophetic truth of the Scriptures regarding His Second Coming motivated their lifetime of ministry. Special thanks to my editorial assistant, Adrienne Jeffrey Tigchelaar, whose excellent editorial services have provided invaluable assistance.

I dedicate *The Signature of God* to my loving wife Kaye. She continues to inspire my research and writing as well as being my faithful partner in the ministry of Frontier Research Publications, Inc. Without her encouragement and constant assistance this book would never have been completed. I trust that the research revealed in the following pages will inform, inspire, and encourage you to personally study the Bible. If this book renews in the hearts of my readers a new love and appreciation for the Word of God, I will be well rewarded.

Dr. Grant R. Jeffrey
Toronto, Ontario
July, 2002

"The Bible is the greatest of all the books ever penned by men; to study it diligently is the most worthy of all possible pursuits; to clearly understand what the Lord is saying to us through its pages is truly the most noble and the highest of my goals. The application to my heart, mind, and spirit of the truths of the Word of God through the Holy Spirit's gift of understanding and my subsequent obedience to that revelation is my supreme purpose and duty."

Author Unknown
Inscription Found in an old Bible in England

Introduction

Is there a God? Does my life have any meaning or does everything in this universe happen solely by chance? How can I find the truth about life and death? What will happen to me when I die? Is the Bible truly the "inspired" Word of God or is it just the philosophical writings of a group of ancient men? These questions occur to everyone of us at some point in our life. Our answers to these questions are vitally important because they will affect our goals, our relationships, our peace of mind and, ultimately, our eternal destiny. The Bible claims to be the inspired Word of God and declares repeatedly that its message is absolutely true. Therefore, it is of utmost importance that each of us determine for ourselves whether the Bible is truly the Word of God or not.

If the Bible is literally true and God does exist, then everyone of us will someday stand before Almighty God to be judged by Him as to our eternal destiny-heaven or hell. The Scriptures tell us that, following our death, we will give an account to God about how we have responded to Jesus Christ and His offer of personal salvation through His death on the Cross. On the other hand, if the Bible is not true and God does not exist, then we are free to live as we please and experience the consequences of our choices solely in this world. The philosophy of "Eat, drink and be merry for tomorrow we die" is a logical response if man lives in a universe that has no God and no purpose. The answer to this question, "Is the Bible truly the Word of God?" is of the greatest possible importance to every human being whether we admit it or not. Our fundamental beliefs are the most important factor in our life because they determine our decisions and the ultimate course of our life. If we change our deeply held beliefs we will inevitably change our actions, our decisions, and the direction of our life.

Is there some way to determine the truth about God and the Bible? This book, *The Signature of God*, will examine exceptional scientific, medical, historical, and prophetic discoveries that prove that the Bible is authoritative and inspired by God. Some people are content to follow a blind faith based on the religious convictions of their forefathers. However, many of us want to examine these matters for ourselves to determine the answers to these vital questions.

How Would God Reveal Himself to Mankind?

Let's conduct an experiment to examine the question of how God would reveal Himself to humanity if He truly exists. After creating this universe and mankind, how would God reveal Himself and convey His instructions to His creatures? He could choose to speak to every single one of the billions of humans living in every generation, but that would be somewhat impractical. On the other hand, God could choose a number of men living in various generations over a period of years and inspire them to faithfully record in writing His instructions for the rest of mankind. Obviously, the second option is the most practical.

However, there is another problem that God would face in revealing His will and instructions to mankind. How would God prove that the Bible was His legitimate revelation to mankind? The challenge would be to find a method to differentiate the genuine inspired Scriptures of God from the many other religious books produced by religious philosophers over the centuries. I believe the solution is quite obvious: God would authenticate His own true revelation by writing His "signature" on the pages of His Scriptures. This "signature of God" would consist of evidence, prophetic knowledge, and phenomenon located in the text of the Bible that no unaided human could possibly have written. In other words, the genuine Scriptures from God should contain supernatural evidence within its text that no one apart from a divine intelligence could possibly create. Interestingly, the Scriptures do contain a direct statement from God that He has provided precisely this type of supernatural evidence as unmistakable proof of the Bible's inspiration and His divine powers to foretell future events through His prophets. Twenty-five centuries ago the prophet Isaiah recorded this amazing declaration from God: "Remember the former things of old: for I am God, and there is none else; I am God, and there is none like me, Declaring the end from the beginning, and from ancient times the things that are not yet done, saying, My counsel shall stand, and I will do all my pleasure" (Isaiah 46:9,10).

In this passage God declared that fulfilled prophecy provides absolute proof that the Scriptures are inspired by the Lord. It is impossible for any human, or even, Satan himself, to predict future events with precise accuracy. Only God knows the future. It is significant that none of the hundreds of religious books outside of the Bible contain detailed predictions about future events. The reason is simple. Any attempt by humans to precisely predict the future always ends in abject failure. The writers of other religious books knew that they could not accurately know what would occur in the future. They wisely refrained from exposing themselves to ridicule by creating prophecies that would inevitably prove to be false predictions. God is the only one who knows the future as well as the past.

My thesis in *The Signature of God*, is that the Bible contains fascinating evidence that absolutely authenticates the Scriptures as the inspired and authoritative Word of God. The evidence from hundreds of fulfilled prophecies regarding the life and death of Jesus Christ provide the strongest and most obvious proof of the Bible's divine inspiration. However, there are a number of other intriguing prophecies and undeniable facts that prove that only God could have inspired the ancient writers to record His message in the Scriptures.

Evidence that the Bible is a Genuine Revelation from God

How would God authenticate His message so that naturally skeptical men and women could be assured that the Scriptures were truly from God and not simply the speculations of religious philosophers? How would the Lord identify His presence, His divine nature and His commands to mankind and provide proof that this communication was truly from God?

1. The written revelation of God's nature and commands was progressively revealed step-by-step to a series of carefully chosen men over a period of sixteen centuries. The recipients were closely connected by race and faith to facilitate their gathering, assembling, preserving, and distributing God's written revelation throughout this time. The Lord chose the Jewish people, a small defined race that has maintained its identity over the centuries, as the faithful guardian of His written revelations.

2. Although His divine communications were transmitted by inspiration to individual Jews, it was recorded in a permanent written form capable of being examined and read by the writer's contemporaries as well as generations to follow.

3. These divine communications were occasionally accompanied by supernatural miracles to authenticate its divine origin.

4. This revelation contains internal evidence that proves that God is the ultimate author. The Bible includes information that could not have been written by men without divine inspiration.

5. The Bible contains thousands of detailed prophecies concerning events that were precisely fulfilled many years after the predictions were made. Their fulfillment proves that God inspired the Bible. No one but God can prophesy accurately.

6. God inspired biblical writers to record His profound wisdom and truth that transcend all of man's wisdom.

7. God's Holy Spirit supernaturally transforms the lives of millions who commit themselves to the Bible's revelation.

8. The primary purpose of the Bible is to reveal God's plan

of salvation. However, whenever the Scriptures deals with history, archeology, nature, or science, it reveals advanced knowledge that is true and verifiable. Such biblical statements are far in advance of the knowledge of the time of the original human writer.

9. The Bible's wisdom, knowledge, and ethics clearly proclaim its supernatural origin to anyone who is truly seeking answers to life's profound questions. The wisest people of all cultures and times are committed to its truths.

10. The Scriptures contain advanced medical and sanitation knowledge that was thousands of years ahead of its time. This medical knowledge from the Bible has saved countless millions of lives of those who followed its divine precepts over the centuries since the Bible was written. In addition, its lifesaving commands still prove their worth in this century.

11. A careful examination of the names and numbers in the Bible's text reveals special mathematical designs and codes that are so complex that no human or super-computer could have produced these features. Many of these designs are not obvious and occur throughout a series of biblical books written by different biblical authors over several centuries. There is no human explanation for this phenomenon except for divine inspiration.

12. In the 1990s Jewish computer scientists in Israel and the U.S.A. discovered a series of remarkable Hebrew words encoded at equally spaced intervals hidden within the Hebrew text of the first five books of the Bible, the Torah. Later researchers proved that this phenomenon, called Equidistant Letter Sequence, existed throughout the Old Testament Hebrew text. God inspired the writers to unconsciously use specific words and letters to produce the most intriguing and incredibly complicated mathematical and letter codes ever found. These features were carefully hidden from the eyes of everyone until this century and the development of mathematical and super-computer analysis. The discovery of these complex patterns of "wheels within wheels" provides compelling evidence that constitutes a powerful argument for the divine inspiration of the Bible. The scientists declared that these patterns are so complex that they could not have been produced by humans. Furthermore,

while these intricate patterns exist in the Hebrew text of the Old Testament, none of the apocryphal Hebrew texts such as *I Maccabees* display this complex pattern; nor have researchers found clusters of complex codes in any other Hebrew religious or secular texts such as the *Talmud*. This incredible phenomenon provides compelling evidence that the author of the inspired Scriptures was certainly God.

13. In normal human literature, authors naturally try to present themselves in the best light possible. However, the Bible presents these men "warts and all" revealing them often as weak, afraid, and lacking in wisdom. It runs contrary to human experience to find authors revealing themselves with such candor. Additionally, biblical revelation contains many intricate details and unintended coincidences in its stories that, while easily overlooked, prove the overall truthfulness of the historical accounts.

14. Although written by forty-four men over sixteen centuries, the complete text of the Bible reveals a coherent unity and progressive revelation from Genesis to Revelation that develops God's plan of redemption for mankind. The books of the Old Testament continuously point to the coming of a Messiah-King to redeem His people. The New Testament displays the fulfillment of these divine prophecies in the life, death, and resurrection of Jesus the Messiah. The unity of theology and the focus on the message of redemption throughout the Bible argues strongly that a single author created this text. The combined evidence presented in this book reveals that the single author who inspired the writers of the Bible was God.

Three thousand years ago King David, the great king of Israel, wrote these words revealing the nature of God's inspired Word:

> The law of the Lord is perfect, converting the soul: the testimony of the Lord is sure, making wise the simple. The statutes of the Lord are right, rejoicing the heart: the commandment of the Lord is pure, enlightening the eyes. The fear of the Lord is clean, enduring for ever: the judgments of the Lord are true and righteous altogether.

More to be desired are they than gold, yea, than much fine gold: sweeter also than honey and the honeycomb. Moreover by them is thy servant warned: and in keeping of them there is great reward" (Psalm 19:7-11).

The Inspiration of Scripture

The early Christians, Jewish scribes, and generations of Christian believers shared an unshakable conviction that the Scriptures contain the infallible, inspired, and authoritative words of God. The Bible itself claims that "All scripture is given by inspiration of God, and is profitable for doctrine, for reproof, for correction, for instruction in righteousness" (2 Timothy 3:16). The Greek word translated "inspired" literally means "God breathed" indicating the Lord's direct supervision of the writing by the biblical writer. The Bible claims that its words were not written by men in an ordinary manner but that God actually inspired men to record His direct words as His revelation to mankind for all time. Just as God created only one sun to provide light to our planet, He gave us only one book, the Bible, to enlighten our world spiritually.

Tragically, during this past century many pastors, professors, and laymen have lost their faith and confidence that the Bible is truly the inspired and reliable Word of God. Dr. Kennedy, a Regius Professor of Classics at Cambridge University in the early decades of this last century, warned of the relentless battle that was about to begin over the authority of the Bible. "The inspiration of Scriptures will be the last battle ground between the Church and the world." Unfortunately, many in our churches and seminaries today have abandoned this battlefield too easily and accepted defeat at the hands of sceptics that hate the authority of the Word of God. This widespread rejection of the truthfulness of the Scriptures reveals the folly of men who "have forsaken me the fountain of living waters, and hewed them out cisterns, broken cisterns" of vain philosophy (see Jeremiah 2:13). Jeremiah the prophet spoke these words twenty-five centuries ago.

The Bible itself declares in numerous passages that it is the inspired Word of God. The prophet Jeremiah declared, "Then the Lord put forth His hand and touched my mouth, and the Lord said to me: 'Behold, I have put My words in your mouth'" (Jeremiah 1:9). God confirmed that He directly inspired His servants, the prophets, to record His words and instructions "word for word." In the New Testament the apostle Peter declared that "Knowing this first, that no prophecy of Scripture is of any private interpretation, for prophecy never came by the will of man, but holy men of God spoke as they were moved by the Holy Spirit" (2 Peter 1:20,21). One of the strongest statements found in the Bible records the inspired words of Jesus Himself who declared, "The Scripture cannot be broken" (John 10:35).

We will examine the overwhelming scientific evidence that proves the inspiration and authenticity of the Bible as the Word of God. The evidence provided in *The Signature of God* will establish the credibility and authority of the Scriptures for both non-believers and Christians as a reliable foundation for faith in God's inspired revelation. The book is divided into sections that will examine the various areas in which the Scriptures can be tested as to their authenticity and authority. The evidence we will explore includes the following areas:

1. Fascinating ancient inscriptions and manuscripts that prove the historical accuracy of the Scriptures.

2. Little known archeological discoveries that provide overwhelming confirmation of the biblical accounts, including the Tower of Babel and the Exodus.

3. The tremendously accurate scientific statements in the Bible that cannot be explained apart from God's inspiration.

4. The precise fulfillment of prophecies in our generation that authenticate the Scriptures.

5. The staggering phenomenon of hidden codes and mathematical patterns found in the text of the Bible that could not have been produced by human intelligence.

6. Biblical "coincidences" that confirm the divine inspiration of the Scriptures.

7. The phenomenon of the transformed character and lives of the writers of the Bible.

8. The unprecedented influence of the Bible on the lives of individuals, the culture, and history of the Western world.

While many of the topics we will explore in this book are fascinating in and of themselves, their true value for a Christian lies in their ability to confirm and illustrate the events, personalities, and statements of the Word of God. Alexander Knox once wrote about the relationship between human and sacred knowledge as follows: "If in the rills which trickle down amidst these intellectual Alps and Apennines, I could discern no connection with that river which maketh glad the city of God, I own that I should look upon them with as little interest as upon the rocky fragments through which they passed."[1]

As a researcher and writer I feel a tremendous responsibility to carefully check the accuracy of every statement because of the exceptional importance of prophecy and scriptural truths. Those who write about the truths of the Scriptures are like the scribes of ancient Israel. The Scriptures declare that, "every scribe which is instructed unto the kingdom of heaven is like unto a man that is an householder, which bringeth forth out of his treasure things new and old" (Matthew 13:52). When we seek as writers to explore the wonderful truths of the Bible we also "bring forth out of his treasure things new and old" in our attempt to reveal the deeper truths of the Word of God.

The Accuracy of the Bible Manuscripts

Over the last four thousand years, Jewish scribes, and later, Christian scribes, were very careful to correctly copy and transmit the original manuscripts of sacred Scriptures without any significant error. The Jewish scribes who carefully copied out by hand the manuscripts of the Old Testament were called "Masoretic," from the Hebrew word for "wall" or "fence." Their extreme care in meticulously counting the letters of the Bible created a "fence around the Law" to defend its absolute accuracy. For example out of the 78,064 Hebrew letters in the Book of Genesis, they counted precisely 4,152 ב letters and 8,448 ש letters. These sages were so precise in counting the exact number of letters in the Scriptures, that they were able to pinpoint the middle verse of Genesis which is: "And by thy sword shalt thou live, and shalt serve thy brother; and it shall come to pass when thou shalt have the dominion, that thou shalt break his yoke from off thy neck" (Genesis 27:40). When a scribe completed his copy, a master examiner would painstakingly count every individual letters to confirm that there were no errors in the newly copied manuscript. If an error was found, the corrupted copy was destroyed to prevent it ever being used as a master copy in the future.

As proof of the incredible accuracy of this transmission through the centuries, consider the Masoretic and Yemenite translations of the Torah. Over a millennium ago, Yemenite Jews were separated from their brother Jews in the Middle East and Europe. Despite separate transmissions and copying of their Torah manuscripts, a thousand years later only nine Hebrew letters, out of some 304,805 letters in the Yemenite Torah manuscript, differ from the accepted Hebrew Masoretic text of the Torah. Nine letters changed in over 300,000 Hebrew letters – a variation of .002 or 1/500th of one percent![2] Not one of these nine variant letters in the Yemenite Torah change the meaning of a significant word. This astonishing fact proves how exceptionally careful, over a thousand year period, Jewish scribes were in copying their original Torah manuscripts. God has carefully preserved the original text of His sacred Scriptures throughout the last three and a half thousand years, enabling us to have confidence that we still possess the inspired Word of God. The prophet Isaiah declared that the Word of God is eternal: "The grass withereth, the flower fadeth: but the word of our God shall stand for ever" (Isaiah 40:8). In the New Testament, Jesus Himself confirmed the indestructibility of His Holy Word. "For verily I say unto you, Till heaven and earth pass, one jot or one tittle shall in no wise pass from the law, till all be fulfilled" (Matthew 5:18).

Back in the 1700s the famous English critic and conversationalist, Dr. Samuel Johnson, made this timeless and valuable suggestion, "Keep your friendships in repair." This is excellent advice regarding our relationship to our Bible as well as for our human relationships. Our personal relationship with the Word of God needs to be cared for just as much as our friendships. We need to respect God's Holy Word and handle it with care and love. We can enjoy the unchanging companionship of God expressed through His divine Word even when we are separated from human friends by distance or death. Our Bibles that show signs of wear and tear reveal our love and use of them. While our experiences, our possessions, and our relationships constantly undergo change throughout the years we can return again and again to the unchanging Word of God as a solid foundation for our faith that will never change. Unlike human friends who sometimes misunderstand or fail to communicate when we need them, our Bible will always be there to speak to our heart with God's words of wisdom, comfort, and love.

The Oldest Biblical Inscription Ever Found

Several years ago archeologists found more than one thousand items of jewelry and pottery in nine burial caves across the Hinnom Valley opposite the southern walls of the Old City of Jerusalem. The treasures from the past included two silver charms with remarkable biblical inscriptions. The cave where these charms were found was about nine hundred yards south of where Solomon's Temple stood three thousand years ago. While most of the burial caves had previously been cleaned out by grave robbers, these fascinating silver inscriptions were still there in 1979, as confirmed to the *Associated Press* by Tel Aviv archeologist Gabriel Barkay. The items of jewelry were composed of thin pieces of pure silver that were rolled up like tiny scrolls to be worn as charms around the neck. While part of the text was lost, the remaining portion revealed that these silver charms contained the oldest biblical inscription ever found. The remaining text recorded the priestly blessing from the Book of Numbers. It reads, "The Lord bless thee, and keep thee: The Lord make his face shine upon thee, and be gracious unto thee: The Lord lift up his countenance upon thee, and give thee peace" (Numbers 6:24-26). I had the privilege of examining this inscription in the Israel Museum. The archeologists found that this ancient biblical text was inscribed by some Jewish craftsman over 2,600 years ago in the seventh century before Christ, over four hundred years before the writing of most of the Dead Sea Scrolls.

It is worthwhile noting that the Bible records only one

statement made by God to the atheist or agnostic who claims, "There is no God." This sole declaration and verdict of God in response to those who deny His existence is, "The fool hath said in his heart, There is no God" (Psalm 14:1). When I attended school I used to engage in debates with atheists and agnostics about the existence of God. However, as I began to analyze the underlying attitude of those I debated I came to realize that debates of this kind were futile. Now when I get into a discussion with an atheist or agnostic I simply respond as follows: I will not debate you about whether or not God exists for the same reason that I would not debate someone about whether or not the world was round. I believe that those who claim "There is no God," in the face of overwhelming evidence of design found throughout nature, are either fools or liars. Any person who honestly believes that all of the marvelous complexity of this universe simply happened by chance is a fool. If he is not a fool, yet still claims to believe that this incredibly complex universe is a result of random chance, then I must conclude that he is not being honest. In either case it is clearly a waste of time to argue the obvious.

The wonders of creation reveal God's awesome creative power to anyone whose eyes are open to see the truth. God's marvelous providence reveals His wisdom; God's Law revealed in the Old Testament shows us His great justice; the Gospels reveal His overwhelming love for mankind through the person of Jesus Christ.

The Supreme Value of the Bible

Sir Walter Scott (A.D. 1771-1832) was the brilliant poet and author of more than sixty popular books. When he was finally approaching the moment of death, Scott asked his son-in-law and biographer, John G. Lockhart, to bring "the book" from his huge library. When Lockhart naturally asked, "Which book, Sir Walter?" Scott answered, "There is only one book," pointing to the Holy Bible. In his final deathbed conversation, Sir Walter Scott, one of the greatest writers of his day, correctly assessed the supreme value of the Holy Scriptures far above the other great books in his large library, including his own classics.

The most important event in the history of man is the life, death, and resurrection of Jesus Christ. The most important fact in the life of mankind is the reality of God and His divine revelation to us through His Holy Word. The most important decision in the life of any human is the choice they must make in regard to their personal faith in Jesus Christ. Another great man, President Abraham Lincoln, wrote the following comment in a "Reply to Loyal Colored People of Baltimore upon Presentation of a Bible": "I believe that the Bible is the best gift God has ever given to man. All the good from the Savior of the world is communicated to us through the book."[3]

The Pony Express Bible

The history of the Pony Express forms a fascinating part of the history of the American West. These dedicated and resourceful riders carried the mail from St. Joseph, Missouri, over nineteen hundred miles through dangerous Indian country, to Sacramento, California. The Pony Express acquired five hundred of the strongest and fastest horses the company could find. Forty brave men rode these magnificent horses in relays with each man riding fifty miles to the next station. Using four relays per day, the Pony Express riders travelled up to two hundred miles a day. A letter could be delivered in relays covering the complete nineteen hundred miles in only ten days.

To cut down on any unnecessary weight the riders would use the lightest saddles made, with very small, flat leather bags holding the mail. Amazingly, to cut down on the weight the riders carried no rifles. Mail carried by the Pony Express was written on very thin paper. However, the postage rate was $5 an ounce (equal to $200 per letter in today's currency). The managers of the Pony Express believed that the Holy Scriptures were so important that they presented a special full size Pony Express Bible to each rider when they signed up to join this unusual company. Surprisingly, despite their overwhelming concern for reducing the weight of their rider's equipment, every one of the riders carried a full size Pony Express Bible as part of his regular gear. Every Pony Express took their traditional oath: "I do hereby swear before the great and living God that during my engagement with Russell, Majors and Waddell [Pony Express management], I will under no circumstances use profane language, that I will drink no intoxicating liquors, that I will not quarrel or fight with other employees of the firm, and that in every respect I will conduct myself honestly, be faithful in my duties, and so direct all my acts as to win the confidence of my employers. So help me God."[4]

Stanley and Livingstone

The famous Christian missionary and explorer, David Livingstone, had disappeared without a trace during his trip into the vast previously unexplored regions of central Africa. The last reliable news of his expedition reported that Livingstone was sick, without supplies and that he had been deserted by his native guides. Many in Europe gave Livingstone up as lost forever after more than a year with no news from Africa. However, a small group of supporters in London and America believed that they must launch a rescue mission in an attempt to save "Scotland's finest son." In 1869, *The New York Herald* outfitted the brilliant reporter and intrepid explorer, Henry M. Stanley, to mount an expedition to find Dr. Livingstone. Stanley embarked on an arduous journey across the deep jungles and dangerous rivers of the unknown continent of Africa in his valiant attempt to locate David Livingstone.

When he commenced his journey Stanley carried very extensive baggage that included several cases containing seventy-three of his favorite hard-bound books weighing one hundred and eighty pounds. However, as Stanley and his African carriers began to succumb to fatigue after three hundred miles of arduous travel through the jungle, Stanley reluctantly began to abandon or burn his precious books to provide fuel for the campfires every night. As they continued through the jungle, Stanley's initially large library dwindled in size until there was only one book left, his precious Bible. With God's supernatural assistance Stanley finally found the great man of God and greeted him with the famous words, "Dr. Livingstone, I presume?" The two explorers shared their deep personal faith in Jesus Christ. Livingstone told Stanley about the wonderful conversions of many tribes to faith in Christ although they had previously engaged in cannibalism. When he returned from his extraordinary journey Stanley reported that he had read his beloved Bible three times from Genesis to Revelation during his long and arduous journey.

As you read *The Signature of God* I hope you will experience the same thrill of discovery and wonder that I have felt as the Lord led me to research the powerful evidence for the inspiration of the Scriptures that I share in this book. I hope this book will be a great resource for pastors and families to help them provide those who are seeking the truth about the Bible with the latest exciting research proving the authority of the Word of God. My prayer is that the information I share in these chapters will enable many readers to restore their confidence in the Bible as God's inspired Word. Then, they can confidently study the Scriptures knowing that God has provided the proof that the Bible is truly the Word of God because the evidence of His signature appears throughout its pages. The apostle Paul wrote to all Christians as follows, "All scripture is given by inspiration of God, and is profitable for doctrine, for reproof, for correction, for instruction in righteousness" (2 Timothy 3:16).

Notes

1. Charles Forster, *Sinai Photographed*, London: Richard Bentley, 1862.
2. Jeffrey Satinover, *Cracking the Bible Code* (New York: William Morrow and Co., Inc., 1997) 51.
3. Abraham Lincoln, "Reply to Loyal Colored People of Baltimore upon Presentation of a Bible" Internet site: http://www.warroom.com/testfaith.htm.
4. Internet site: http://gorp.com/gorp/publishers/fulcrum/pony-exp.htm.

1

The Battle for the Bible

Our modern world has departed so far from the religious faith that governed the founding fathers of both the United States and Canada that it is almost impossible for the average citizen to recognize the vast gulf that exists between the beliefs of our current society and the beliefs of those who founded our nations. The colonists who came to North America centuries ago were determined to escape the religious oppression of Europe. They wanted to create a free nation on this continent where men and women could worship God freely without restriction. The founders of the United States of America determined to create an educational system based on Christianity and the inspired Word of God. A close examination of the lives and the writings of the framers of the American Constitution clearly reveals that their intent was to create in America a "freedom for religious expression; not a freedom from religious expression."

The writer Frederick Rudolph wrote in his book, *The American College and University*, that within a generation of their landing on Plymouth Rock the original Puritan settlers laid the foundations of an educational system dedicated to training "a

learned clergy and a lettered people." These Christians created Harvard College in 1636 as a Christian college dedicated
to upholding the truths of the Bible. In fact, during the first
century of Harvard University's existence, every single one
of its professors was a minister of the Gospel. The initial 1636
Charter of Harvard College, its Rules and Precepts proclaimed
the following essentials:

> Every one shall consider the main end of his life and
> studies to know God and Jesus Christ which is eternal
> life. Seeing the Lord giveth wisdom, every one shall seri-
> ously by prayer in secret seek wisdom of Him. Every
> one shall so exercise himself in reading the Scriptures
> twice a day that they be ready to give an account of their
> proficiency therein, both in theoretical observations of
> languages and logic, and in practical and spiritual
> truths. . . . Everyone shall consider the main end of his
> life and studies to know Jesus Christ which is eternal
> life."[1]

It has been calculated that 87 percent of the first one hundred and nineteen colleges built in America were established
by Christians to educate young people in their faith. Most
major universities in the eastern United States were created as
Christian institutions of learning-including Harvard, Princeton,
Yale, and Columbia. More than twenty-five percent of the 1855
graduating class of these universities became ministers of the
Gospel.

Although our society is increasingly agnostic, millions still
seek the truth by studying the Word of God. *The Dallas Times
Herald* in October 24, 1983, found in one study that over forty-
three million Americans are involved in regular Bible study
groups.[2]

The Attempt to Destroy the Bible

Throughout history there has been a continual and relentless
conflict between acceptance of God and an open rebellion
against His rule. This continuing struggle can be correctly
described as a tale of two cities: the ongoing war between the

City of God and the City of Man. For two thousand years the battleground has revolved around the Bible. Satan hates the Word of God because it reveals the truth about Jesus Christ, our hope of salvation and the eternal destiny facing each of us between heaven and hell. A close examination of the history of Christianity over the last two thousand years reveals that the greatest attacks that occurred during the first centuries following Christ came from the pagans outside the Church. However, during the last one hundred and fifty years, the most effective enemies of the Cross arose from those false Christians who profess to follow Christ while denying the authority of the Bible and His identity as the Son of God.

The Roman emperors did everything in their power to destroy the new faith of Christianity by burning both Christians and the manuscripts of the Bible throughout their vast empire. As an example, in A.D. 303, the Emperor Diocletian issued an official command to kill Christians and burn their sacred books. Professor S. L. Greenslade, the editor of the *Cambridge History of the Bible*, recorded the history of this persecution: an imperial letter was everywhere promulgated, ordering the razing of the churches to the ground and the destruction by fire of the Scriptures, and proclaiming that those who held high positions would lose all civil rights, while those in households, if they persisted in their profession of Christianity, would be deprived of their liberty"[3]

However, the Christian's enthusiasm and dedication to the Scriptures in those first centuries following Christ motivated them to produce numerous manuscripts that were widely copied, distributed, and translated throughout the empire. The New Testament is the most widely quoted book in history from the moment of its writing by the apostles until today. Ignatius, the Bishop of Antioch in A.D. 70, the minister responsible for several churches in Syria, quoted extensively from the New Testament in his writings. Clement, the Bishop of Rome in A.D. 70 (mentioned by Paul in Philippians 4:3) also quoted extensively from the New Testament only forty years after Christ's resurrection.

According to Professor J. Harold Greenlee the quotations

from the New Testament "are so extensive that the N. T. could virtually be reconstructed from them without the use of New Testament manuscripts."[4] Historians have recovered almost *one hundred thousand manuscripts and letters* from the first few centuries of this era that were composed by Christian writers. Their love and devotion to the inspired Scriptures was so overwhelming that these letters contain an enormous number of direct quotations from the New Testament. This was the primary way that the truths of Scripture were transmitted throughout the Roman Empire, despite the rampant persecution and burning of Bibles by the Roman emperors. If the Roman government had been successful in totally destroying every New Testament throughout the Roman Empire, the survival of these one hundred thousand letters from early Christians guaranteed the survival of the Word of God. These numerous letters by the early Christians contain an astonishing 98 percent of the New Testament. In other words, even if the Romans had succeeded in destroying the New Testament manuscripts, we could still reliably reconstruct 98 percent of the New Testament text from these numerous quotations. This fact shows the absolute integrity of the text of the New Testament as it exists today as well as demonstrating the passion the early Christians possessed for the Holy Word of God.

Despite the efforts of the pagan emperors to burn every copy of the Bible during the first three centuries after Christ, Christianity became the official state religion of the Roman Empire following the conversion of the Emperor Constantine in A.D. 325. Centuries later, however, the medieval church fell into apostasy from biblical truth and compromised with the kings and aristocracy of Europe. After many centuries, laws were issued that made possession of the Bible illegal for any Christian layman. During those centuries of the Inquisition in Europe after A.D. 1199 there were appalling penalties, including burning at the stake, for anyone found to possess a copy of the Scriptures. During the Dark Ages even priests in the medieval church of Rome were usually unable to read the Latin manuscripts of the Bible for themselves. As a result of their ignorance of the Bible, both priests and laypeople were unable to compare the false doctrines that were widespread in the medieval Roman church against the doctrines of the Word of God. Few Christians today realize that, in Italy, it was illegal to possess a Bible until 1870 due to the hatred of apostate church officials for the truth of the Scriptures.

John Lea reported in his book, *The Greatest Book in the World*, that a French king once proposed to his court that they should launch a new wave of persecution against the Christians within his realm. However, a wise counselor and general replied to the king's proposal in these words, "Sire, the Church of God is an anvil that has worn out many hammers."[5] The enemies of the Bible have attacked the Scriptures without respite for almost two thousand years. However, the Bible still stands unshaken as the most widely read and published book in history, while the philosophies of the enemies of the Scriptures are buried with their spokesmen. The survival of the Scriptures against these unrelenting attacks by Satan provides irrefutable evidence that it is truly inspired by God.

Finally, after almost a thousand years of virtual spiritual darkness, in A.D. 1520 the Protestant Reformation under the leadership of Martin Luther opened the flood gates of biblical truth to the European population through the translation and printing of the Bible in contemporary languages such as German, French, and English. The revolution in religion and spiritual freedom surpassed anything ever seen in the history of mankind. The spiritual rallying cry of the Protestant Reformation was *Sola Scripture* meaning "solely Scripture." In opposition to the medieval Roman church's position that church councils, tradition and papal decrees could supersede the teaching of Scripture, the Protestant Reformers insisted that every doctrine taught in the Church must be drawn from the clear teaching of the Bible. This absolute reliance on the actual words of the inspired Word of God placed the Reformation on the strongest possible spiritual foundation. The stronghold of Scripture motivated the Reformers to preach the Gospel of Jesus Christ everywhere, leading to the greatest influx of souls into the Kingdom of God in the history of the Church.

While most people in our Western culture in past centuries

accepted the truth of God's existence and His creation of the universe, a growing number of people in our modern world deny the existence of God and His creative role. Those who accept evolution[6] as the answer as to how human life was formed have rejected the concept of a divine creator who created this earth in all of its awesome complexity. In addition, large numbers of people today totally reject the inspiration and authority of the Scriptures in the false belief that the Bible has somehow been proven to be "full of errors and contradictions." The unrelenting attack by agnostic scholars and the media against the authority of the Bible during the last century is unprecedented in Western history. The attack launched on the accuracy and reliability of the Scriptures and the resurrection of Jesus Christ has come not only from academics outside the Church but also from countless pastors and theologians who have lost their personal confidence and faith in the authority of the Word of God.

Professor E. B. Pusey, in his brilliant 1800s defense of the authenticity of the book of Daniel against the higher critics of his day, wrote about the continual attacks on the inspiration of Scripture from those who claimed to be ministers of the Gospel:

> The faith can receive no real injury except from its defenders. Against its assailants, those who wish to be safe, God protects. If the faith shall be (God forbid!) destroyed in England, it will not be by open assailants, but by those who think that they defend it, while they have themselves lost it. So it was in Germany. Rationalism was the product, not of the attacks on the Gospel but of its weak defenders. Each generation, in its controversies with unbelief, conceded more of the faith, until at last it was difficult to see what difference there was between assailants and defenders. Theology was one great graveyard; and men were disputing over a corpse, as if it had life. The salt had 'lost its savour.' The life was fled[6]

There are few things in life so spiritually ineffective or

pathetic as a preacher or seminary professor who has lost his faith in the authority and inspiration of the Scriptures, yet continues to preach or teach about the Bible. People who refuse to accept the authority of the Word of God will never learn the truth about life and death from such unbelieving teachers. Jesus Christ Himself declared: "If they hear not Moses and the prophets, neither will they be persuaded, though one rose from the dead" (Luke 16:31).

Loss of Faith by Mainline Protestant Religious Leaders

After a century and a half of continuous assault on the authority and reliability of the Scriptures many pastors and seminary professors have lost their confidence in the inspiration of the Word of God. The sociologist Jeffrey Hadden completed a survey of the beliefs of ten thousand Protestant ministers in May 1982, (as reported in a magazine published by *Christ For The Nations*).[7]

In response to the survey, ten thousand mainline Protestant pastors answered as follows:

1. *Was Jesus born of a virgin?*

Over 50 percent of the ministers would not say "Totally Agree"

2. *Was Jesus the Son of God?*

Over 80 percent of the ministers would not say "Totally Agree"

3. *Is the Bible the Inspired Word of God?*

Over 80 percent of the ministers would not say "Totally Agree"

More than half of these pastors could not answer "Totally Agree" to these questions. A majority of the pastors surveyed qualified their answers to these questions ranging from partial agreement to total disagreement. Significantly, a century ago, the vast majority of pastors would have answered "Totally Agree" to these questions.

Is there any doubt as to why many church leaders and denominations are spiritually weak and without conviction? When pastors and teachers lose their faith in the Word of God, they would be more honest if they openly left the Christian ministry rather than lead a whole generation of laymen in their congregations to an eternity without Christ and without hope of salvation based on the Word of God.

The widespread agnosticism and atheism in our modern government, media, universities, and seminaries has resulted in the moral collapse of our society. The philosopher Thomas Hobbes (1588–1679) wisely described the inevitable effects on our society of the growing agnosticism and the gradual abandonment of the authority of Scriptures in the life of our nations. Hobbes predicted the terrible results that would follow the loss of a national religious faith in Christ in these insightful words. "No arts, no letters, no society, and which is worst of all, continual fear and danger of violent death, and the life of man solitary, poor, nasty, brutish and short."[8] Tragically, the results of our national apostasy were accurately predicted in his writings.

A century and a half later, North America has publicly abandoned the Bible as the moral anchor of our society and education. It should surprise no one that, after decades of teaching our children that their are no absolute rights and wrongs, we face an appalling breakdown in public morality, widespread corporate and government corruption, as well as growing fear of violent crime. President Andrew Jackson strongly believed in the central position of the Scriptures to the life of his nation. As he lay on his deathbed President Jackson pointed to the Bible on the table by his bed and said to his companion, "That Book, Sir, is the rock on which our Republic rests."[9]

The Authenticity of the Old Testament

Dr. Robert Dick Wilson was the professor of Semitic Philology at Princeton Seminary for many decades. He was an expert in forty-five languages and dialects. He was considered the greatest expert alive in the Hebrew Old Testament. Dr. Wilson contributed numerous scholarly works confirming the accuracy of the Old Testament throughout his career of fifty years. His brilliant criticism of errors and weaknesses in the positions of the higher critical school were so powerful they were never answered. The liberal critics simply ignored his devastating arguments against their dismissal of the Bible's accuracy because they could not refute his position.

Over the years a series of authorities, including R. D. Wilson, James Orr, Oswald Allis, and Edward J. Young, thoroughly refuted the anti-Bible claims of the higher critics. Dr. Wilson summarizes the situation as follows:

> In conclusion, we claim that the assaults upon the integrity and trustworthiness of the Old Testament along the line of language have utterly failed. The critics have not succeeded in a single line of attack in showing that the diction and style of any part of the Old Testament are not in harmony with the ideas and aims of writers who lived at, or near, the time when the events occurred that are recorded in the various documents. . . . We boldly challenge these Goliaths of ex-cathedra theories to come down into the field of ordinary concordances, dictionaries, and literature, and fight a fight to the finish on the level ground of the facts and the evidence.[10]

Old Testament Statements Regarding its Inspiration

The Scriptures themselves clearly and repeatedly declare that the Bible is inspired by God. Moses closed his ministry with this command to the Children of Israel affirming inspiration: "Set your hearts unto all the words which I testify among you this day, which ye shall command your children to observe to do, all the words of this law" (Deuteronomy 32:46). The Book of Proverbs also states: "Every word of God is pure: he is a shield unto them that put their trust in him. Add thou not unto his words, lest he reprove thee, and thou be found a liar" (Proverbs 30:5,6).

The Authority of the Old Testament Confirmed by Jesus Christ

One of the most important evidences regarding the accuracy and inspiration of the Old Testament Scriptures is that both Jesus Christ and the apostles absolutely confirm the authority of these writings as being inspired directly by God. Jesus Christ declared that "the scripture cannot be broken" (John 10:35). In another passage Jesus stated, "And it is easier for heaven and earth to pass, than one tittle of the law to fail" (Luke 16:17). In addition, the Lord confirmed that Moses was the writer of the first five books of the Law (Luke 24:27; John 5:46,47). Christ also stated that Isaiah was the author of the Book of Isaiah (Matthew 13:14, citing Isaiah 6:9,10).

One of Jesus' most significant statements was His declaration that Daniel had written the Book of Daniel (Matthew 24:15) thereby contradicting those critics who claim that Daniel was written by someone pretending to prophesy in 165 B.C. Jesus spoke of Adam, Eve and their son Abel as real personalities (Matthew 19:4,5; 23:35). In Luke 17:26,28, Jesus referred to both Noah and Lot. According to John 8:56-58, the Lord confirmed the Bible's narrative about Abraham. Perhaps, most importantly, Jesus confirmed the accuracy of the Genesis account about the creation (Mark 10:6-9) and the worldwide flood (Matthew 24:37-39).

Christ affirmed his belief in the Old Testament miracles when He talked about the supernatural judgment on Sodom and Gomorrah (Luke 17:29) including the death of Lot's wife (v. 32). In other passages Jesus described the feeding of manna to the Israelites during the Exodus (John 6:32), and the miraculous healing of the serpent's bites (John 3:14). The Gospels record Christ's confirmation of the miraculous events in the life of Elijah and Elisha (Luke 4:25-27), and the supernatural swallowing of Jonah by a great fish (Matthew 12:39,40). Jesus settled all doubts for Christians in His declaration: "For verily I say unto you, Till heaven and earth pass, one jot or one tittle shall in no wise pass from the law, till all be fulfilled" (Matthew 5:18). Jesus Christ rebuked Satan by quoting Deuteronomy 8:3: "Man doth not live by bread only, but by every word that proceedeth out of the mouth of the Lord doth man live" (Matthew 4:4; also Luke 4:4). In His discussion with the Pharisees, Jesus won His argument based on the presence of a single word in the Scriptures. The Lord asked the Jewish scholars, "If David then call him Lord, how is he his son?" (Matthew 22:45).

In light of these absolute confirmations by Jesus Christ of

historical events and miraculous occurrences in the Old Testament, it is astonishing that some preachers and Christians dare to deny the truthfulness of these biblical events. Those who accept Jesus Christ as truly God should find it quite easy to accept His divine verdict that the Old Testament is absolutely truthful and inspired directly by God. If I accept Jesus as my God and Savior then I will accept His confirmation that I can safely trust in the authority of the Old Testament.

Statements from the Apostles

The apostles constantly affirmed the verbal inspiration of the Bible. The apostle Paul described the Scriptures as the very "oracles of God" (Romans 3:2; Hebrews 5:12). Later, in Galatians 3:16, Paul said: "Now to Abraham and his seed were the promises made. He saith not, And to seeds, as of many; but as of one, And to thy seed, which is Christ." Notice that in this passage, Paul based his entire argument to his readers on the presence of a single word and noted the fact that the word was the singular word "seed" and not the plural word "seeds." Paul's doctrine regarding the inspiration of Scripture is absolutely clear: "All scripture is given by inspiration of God, and is profitable for doctrine, for reproof, for correction, for instruction in righteousness: That the man of God may be perfect, thoroughly furnished unto all good works" (2 Timothy 3:16,17).

The Early Date of the Writing of the New Testament

It is now acknowledged, even by many liberal scholars, that the New Testament Gospels and Epistles were written and widely circulated throughout the Christian communities of the Roman Empire within forty or fifty years of the events they describe. This fact is of overwhelming importance in verifying the absolute historical accuracy of these documents. Thousands of people who personally witnessed the events of Jesus Christ's life, teaching, death, and resurrection were still alive when the disciples composed and distributed the Gospels and Paul's Epistles to the various churches. These carefully copied manuscripts were read in hundreds of Christian assemblies every Sunday, by millions of Gentile and Jewish believers, from the cold northern shores of Britain to the hot deserts of Syria and North Africa.

In addition to Christian testimony about the enormous number of new believers, even the enemies of Christ, such as the Roman historians Tacitus and Pliny, acknowledged that there were vast multitudes of Christians throughout the Roman Empire.[11] If the New Testament actually contained factual errors regarding the events of Christ's life, His teaching, or the miracles He performed, there would have been an enormous split within the early Church as witnesses to these historical events would have debated and contested any inaccurate historical records.

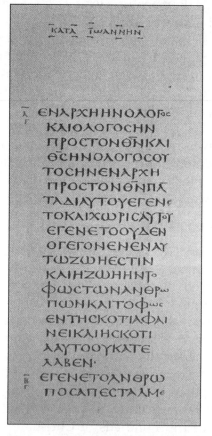

A New Testament Greek Manuscript.

Although the Christians were subject to the most terrifying tortures and martyrdom conceivable, there is no record that any Christian *ever* declared that the Gospel account of Jesus Christ was in error. If they had denied the reality of the life, death, and resurrection of Jesus, the Roman judges would have been delighted to set them free. Rome would have widely published such a denial of the Gospels' statements about Jesus Christ's death and resurrection. However, despite the fact that a large number of Roman official records and a much larger number of Christian writings have survived until today, we cannot find evidence of a single eyewitness to these Gospel events about Christ ever denying their truthfulness. This fact is of outstanding importance in assessing the reliability and truthfulness of the Gospel records as any judge or lawyer would confirm.

The early Church had many enemies among the pagans. During the second and third century of this era some pagans and gnostics infiltrated the Church. In response to the warnings of our Lord and the apostle Paul about false teachers and "teachers having itching ears," the Church leadership was vigilant in detecting and rejecting any spurious writings that counterfeited the genuine New Testament inspired writings. As an example, two important early Church writers, Tertullian and Jerome, tell us that a presbyter from Asia (Turkey) published a counterfeit epistle that he claimed the apostle Paul had written. Church leaders instantly instigated an ecclesiastical trial to examine this claim.

They subsequently convicted this counterfeiter and repudiated his spurious forgery. Their rejection of this forgery was widely published to other churches throughout the empire. Is it probable that people who were so vigilant to establish the truth of the Gospel and to preserve the genuine Scriptures would blindly accept the New Testament record of Christ's miracles and resurrection unless they had overwhelming proof of its truthfulness? When you consider that millions of these converts died horribly as martyrs rather than deny their Lord it stands to reason that they were convinced with all their mind, soul, and spirit that the Gospels spoke the truth about Jesus Christ as the Son of God.

The Universal Distribution of the New Testament

All scholars acknowledge that the New Testament was widely copied and translated into many other languages during the first few decades following the resurrection of Christ. Numerous ancient manuscripts of the New Testament have survived in different languages. These manuscripts confirm that there were no differences in the text regarding doctrine or factual matters. The libraries of Europe and North America contain many ancient copies and translations of the Greek New Testament, including the Syriac, Egyptian, Arabic, Ethiopian, Armenian, Persian, Gothic, Slavonic, and Latin translations. This widespread publication assisted greatly in the effective distribution of the Gospels and Epistles into "Judea, and Samaria and the uttermost parts of the earth." In addition, the widespread copying and translation of the Scriptures made it absolutely impossible for anyone to corrupt the legitimate text of the New Testament by introducing an invented story of a miracle or a false doctrine into a counterfeit copy. Due to their overwhelming love of the Scriptures, the early Christians constantly quoted from these texts.

If anyone was so foolish as to attempt to introduce a spurious text with an invented story, miracle, or doctrine, this counterfeit alteration would have been instantly detected and denounced throughout the hundreds of churches. Once the original Greek manuscript of the New Testament was translated faithfully into Hebrew, Syriac, Egyptian, Coptic, Latin, and other languages between A.D. 60-70, it would have been impossible for anyone, even a corrupt high Church official, to impose a counterfeit text on the Christians. A counterfeit text's alterations would be compared against the countless other widely available genuine Greek manuscripts and the additional translations in other languages. Any textual differences would instantly identify a counterfeit text as a forgery. The profound love of the saints for the New Testament during the first centuries of the Church age assure us that they were vigilant in their defense and preservation of the integrity of the Scriptures. This fact allows us to have total confidence that we possess today the same New Testament that was given to the Church by the inspired writers.

The Survival of the Bible

The famous French writer Voltaire, an anti-biblical skeptic, often wrote expressing his contempt for the Bible and Christianity. He had an intense hatred of the Word of God, probably because it reminded him that he would someday stand before the Great White Throne to be judged by Almighty God. His sinful arrogance expressed itself in his utter contempt for the Scriptures and Christians who followed the words of Jesus Christ. Voltaire wrote a prediction about the future of the Bible more than two centuries ago from his library in Paris: "I will go through the forest of the Scriptures and girdle all the trees, so that in one hundred years Christianity will be but a vanishing memory."[12] Despite Voltaire's prediction, there are more Christians alive today than any other time in history. Those who study the statistics have found that more than 115,000 people accept Jesus Christ as their personal Savior every day around the world. Ironically, despite Voltaire's confident prediction about the imminent death of Christianity, his library, in which he wrote his false prediction, was acquired years later by the British and Foreign Bible Society. His library was soon filled from floor to ceiling with thousands of copies of the Bible he hated, but could not destroy

Despite the opposition of Satan and his followers to the Scriptures the Bible remains triumphant as the most widely read, published, and influential book in the history of man. The truths found in its pages have changed the lives and destiny of untold billions. The Scriptures have profoundly influenced the course of history for nations and empires. When an ambassador of an African prince was introduced to Queen Victoria, the greatest queen of England, he asked her the question his monarch had requested he present to her. "What is the secret of your country's power and success throughout the world?" Queen Victoria picked up the Bible on her table and answered, "Tell your prince that this book is the secret of England's greatness."

Notes

1. Internet site: http://www.forerunner.com/forerunner/ X0101_Christians_Started_I.html.
2. Roy Abraham Varghese, *The Intellectuals Speak Out About God*, (Chicago: Regenery Gateway, Inc., 1984), p.xxii-xxiii.
3. Stanley L. Greenslade, *Cambridge History of the Bible* (Cambridge: Cambridge University Press, 1963).
4. J. Harold Greenlee, *Introduction to New Testament Textual Criticism* (Grand Rapids: William B. Eerdmans Publishing Company, 1964).
5. John Lea, *The Greatest Book in the World*, Philadelphia: 1929.
6. E. B. Pusey, *The Prophet Daniel* (Plymouth: Devonport Society, 1864) xxv, xxvi.
7. Internet site: http://giftsforhim.speedyweb.com/ templepublishing/Chapter%20One.htm.
8. Internet site: http://www.rjgeib.com/thoughts/nature/ hobbes-bio.html.
9. Andrew Jackson, *Encyclopedia of 7700 Illustrations* (Hong Kong: Nordica International, Ltd., 1991) 192.
10. Robert Dick Wilson, *A Scientific Investigation of the Old Testament*, (Chicago: Moody Press, 1959) 130.
11. Tacitus, *Annals* XV. 44.
12. David John Donnan, ed. *Treasury of the Christian World* (New York: Harper Brothers, 1953).

2

Incredible Evidence From Historical Documents The Awesome Accuracy of the Old Testament

Although the Bible has been relentlessly attacked by unbelieving scholars for more than a century it still stands as the most accurate and authoritative book ever written. Despite the continuing media assaults on the Bible's claim to be a supernatural revelation from God, evidence from historical inscriptions and manuscripts discovered in the last century proves that the Word of God is inspired. Although we will never be able to verify every one of the thousands of historical personalities, events, and places recorded in the Bible, the overwhelming evidence presented in this chapter will provide any intelligent reader with the confidence that we have established the credibility of the greatest book ever written.

My library has hundreds of books containing accounts from numerous historians of the ancient world including Herodotus, the so-called "Father of History." However, a Roman historian titled Herodotus "the Father of Lies" in recognition of the factual inaccuracy of his fanciful accounts of the past. Any examination of these secular histories reveals a multitude of gross errors regarding details such as dates, locations, people, sequence and duration of events. To state that ancient secular historians were casual in their approach to accuracy is an understatement. An example of this casual attitude regarding factual accuracy is revealed in Herodotus's own history where he wrote, "My business is to record what people say. But I am by no means bound to believe it-and that may be taken to apply to this book as a whole."[1]

However, when we closely examine the evidence found in the Bible we discover that the writers are extremely careful and accurate in their recording of historical facts. The writers of the Bible were contemporaries of the times and events they recorded. A comparison of the discoveries during the last century of historical and archeological research with the statements of the Bible reveals forty-one different kings of Israel and surrounding nations that are confirmed by contemporary inscriptions and documents. The whole body of ancient literature does not reveal a single report from secular historians that can be confirmed by archeology with the same degree of confidence by which we can prove thousands of biblical statements, personalities, and events.

In the last one-hundred-and-fifty years many critics of the Bible upheld the so-called Documentary Hypothesis that denied the biblical claim that Moses was the author of Genesis and the rest of the first five books of the Bible. They claimed that the different names for God that appeared in Genesis (Elohim, Jehovah, Adonai, etc.) indicated that five different authors composed portions of this book. They believed that an editor later recompiled the five records into one book approximately six hundred years before Christ. However, this widely taught theory is absurd when you carefully consider the history of the Jewish people. Remember that in a court of law a judge and jury place great weight on evidence that is acknowledged to be factual by both sides, the prosecutor and the defense, for the simple reason that if both sides agree, it is extremely likely that it is true.

The Jewish people are known for their brilliance and their willingness to debate at great length any issue involving their religion and history. Ask yourself if it is credible that the Jews would universally adopt the complicated and onerous religious regulations of Passover, Pentecost, and the Feast of Tabernacles unless their forefathers had begun celebrating these feasts to commemorate the miraculous events of the Exodus. Obviously, such national festivals were transmitted from generation to generation through the ages. How could this happen if the original miraculous deliverance from Egypt had never occurred? Moses, the great Lawgiver of Israel, reminded the Jews that they had personally witnessed with their own eyes these miracles and supernatural acts by God to deliver them from the bondage of Egypt. "Know today that I do not speak with your children, who have not known and who have not seen the chastening of the Lord your God, His greatness and His mighty hand and His outstretched arm-His signs and His acts which He did in the midst of Egypt, to Pharaoh king of Egypt, and to all his land; what He did to the army of Egypt, to their horses and their chariots: how He made the waters of the Red Sea overflow them as they pursued you, and how the Lord has destroyed them to this day; what He did for you in the wilderness until you came to this place; . . . but your eyes have seen every great act of the Lord which He did" (Deuteronomy 11:2-7).

If an unknown editor had created the five books of the Torah a thousand years later and tried to get the Jewish people, scattered in diverse communities from Iran to Spain, to universally adopt these festivals of Passover, etc., when no one had ever celebrated them before, he would have been denounced as an impostor. At the very least, Jewish rabbis and sages would have conducted strong debates opposing the introduction of such a book that no one had ever seen before. However, there is no record whatsoever that such debates or discussions ever occurred. The critics' theory of an unknown editor creating the Torah is absurd. The Samaritans were a group of colonists imported into the West Bank of Israel around 700 B.C., by the Assyrians to repopulate the area after they took the Israelite population of the ten northern tribes in chains back to Assyria (modern Iraq-Iran).

One of the oldest manuscripts in the world is the Samaritan Pentateuch, an ancient copy of the first five books of the Law, which contained virtually every single word found in the Hebrew text of the Torah. From the moment the Samaritan colonists moved into the center of Israel, they found themselves in opposition to the Jewish people who returned from the Babylonian Captivity, which continued into the time of Christ's ministry. Although the Samaritans accepted the five books of the Torah as genuine, their own version was jealously guarded and preserved for thousands of years until today. Why would the Samaritans, who hated the Jews, accept the historical accuracy and authority of the Torah of the Jews if they knew these books were not authoritative and true? The fact that the Samaritans, the enemies of the Jews, agree with them in accepting the genuineness of the five Books of Moses should prove to any unbiased mind that we have the original unaltered writings of Moses, the great Lawgiver of Israel.

In addition, critics denied that Moses could have written his account in the fifteenth century before Christ because they claimed that writing was not yet invented. However, the discovery by archeologists of numerous ancient written inscriptions, including the famous black stele containing the Laws of Hammurabi written before 2000 B.C., have conclusively proven that writing was widespread for many centuries before the time of Moses.

The Greek historian Herodotus discussed the Exodus in his book *Polymnia*: "This people [the Israelites], by their own account, inhabited the coasts of the Red Sea, but migrated thence to the maritime parts of Syria, all which district, as far as Egypt, is denominated Palestine."[2] It is interesting to note that Strabo, a pagan historian and geographer who was born in 54 B.C., also confirmed the history of the Jews and their escape from Egypt under the leadership of Moses. He wrote, "Among many things believed respecting the temple and inhabitants of Jerusalem, the report most credited is that the Egyptians were the ancestors of the present Jews. An Egyptian priest named Moses, who possessed a portion the country called lower Egypt, being dissatisfied with the institutions there, left it and came to Judea with a large body of people who worshipped the Divinity."[3]

Food and Water in Sinai

Many critics have suggested that such a dry desert area as Sinai could never have supported the huge flocks of sheep of the Israelites as recorded in Exodus. In 1860, W. Holland explored most of the Sinai Peninsula. Despite the present desolate and dry condition of the barren land, he found that some areas would still support large flocks of sheep. If the temperature or level of rainfall was only slightly changed, the amount of available pasturage would have been much greater than today's conditions would indicate.

In his book, *Recent Explorations in the Peninsula of Sinai*, Holland wrote, "Large tracts of the northern portion of the plateau of the Tih, which are now desert, were evidently formerly under cultivation. The Gulf of Suez (probably by means of an artificial canal connecting it with the Bitter Lakes) once extended nearly fifty miles further north than it does at present, and the mountains of Palestine were well clothed with trees. Thus there formerly existed a rain-making area of considerable extent, which must have added largely to the dews and rains of Sinai. Probably, also, the peninsula itself was formerly much more thickly wooded. The amount of vegetation and herbage in the Peninsula, even at the present time, has been very much underrated; and a slight increase in the present rainfall would produce an enormous addition to the amount of pasturage. I have several times seen the whole face of the country, especially the wadies, marvelously changed in appearance by a single shower."[4]

It is fascinating to note that numerous biblical personalities (including Nebuchadnezzar, Belshazzar, and Darius), who were totally repudiated by higher critics in past decades, have now been reliably verified by recent historical and archeological discoveries. In the past, critics of the Bible's accuracy contemptuously rejected the story of the defeat of the confederation of five kings from the East by the small army of Abraham as found in Genesis 14. These critics claimed that there was no evidence to support this biblical account, and therefore denied the story. However, the continuing archeological research in the Middle East has found ample evidence proving that the story is credible in all its particular details.

Dr. Nelson Glueck, considered by many to be the leading Palestinian archeologist in this century, was the president of the Hebrew Union College. Reporting on the newly discovered evidence about this invasion, Glueck wrote the following report in his book *Rivers in the Desert*: "Centuries earlier, another civilization of high achievement had flourished between the 21st and 19th centuries B.C., till it was savagely liquidated by the Kings of the East. According to the Biblical statements, which have been borne out by the archaeological evidence, they gutted every city and village at the end of that period from Ashtaroth Karnaim, in southern Syria through all of Trans-Jordan and the Negev to Kadesh-Barnea in Sinai (Genesis 14:1-7)."[5] Dr. Glueck spent many years of his life exploring the land of Israel in his search for archeological records. As a result of his many discoveries he concluded that the Bible was totally reliable in every area where he could examine the evidence.[6]

The explorations and excavations in the Middle East during the last century and a half have thrown remarkable light on the accuracy and reliability of the words of the Holy Scriptures. With each additional discovery we find new exciting confirmations of the most remarkable statements from the Word of God. In this chapter I will share some of the most fascinating of these discoveries and their implications for the authority of the Bible.

King Nebuchadnezzar's Inscription About the Tower of Babel

From the time of Adam and Eve, "The whole earth had one language and one speech" (Genesis 11:1), before the dispersion of the population following God's supernatural act causing the confusion of their languages at the Tower of Babel. God purposely confounded the language of all the people on the earth (Genesis 11:9) so they could not understand the speech of their neighbors to force them to disperse throughout the earth. The people had gathered together in sinful pride against God in their attempt to build a tower that would reach to the heavens. Moses recorded God's subsequent judgment and destruction of the Tower of Babel and the city of Babylon. The remains of the Tower of Babel are vitrified (melted to form a kind of rough glass) which indicates that God used a huge amount of heat to destroy this tower that was erected at the dawn of time by men in their sinful pride to reach up to the heavens in defiance of God.

Scientists who study the origin of languages, known as philologists, have concluded that it is probable that the thousands of dialects and languages throughout the planet can be traced back to an original language in man's ancient past. Professor Alfredo Trombetti claims that he can prove the common origin of all languages. Max Mueller, one of the greatest oriental language scholars, declared that all human languages can be traced back to one single original language.[7]

The French government sent Professor Oppert to report on the cuneiform inscriptions discovered in the ruins of Babylon. Oppert translated a long inscription by King Nebuchadnezzar in which the king referred to the tower in the Chaldean language as *Barzippa*, which means "Tongue-tower." The Greeks used the word *Borsippa*, with the same meaning of tongue-tower, to describe the ruins of the Tower of Babel. This inscription of Nebuchadnezzar clearly identified the original tower of Borsippa with the Tower of Babel described by Moses in Genesis.

King Nebuchadnezzar decided to rebuild the base of the ancient Tower of Babel, built over sixteen centuries earlier by Nimrod, the first King of Babylon. He also called it the Temple of the Spheres. During the millennium since God destroyed it, the tower was reduced from its original height and magnificence until only the huge base of the tower (four hundred and sixty feet by six hundred and ninety feet) standing some two hundred and seventy-five feet high remained within the outskirts of the city of Babylon. Today the ruins have been reduced to about one hundred and fifty feet above the plain with a circumference of 2,300 feet. Nebuchadnezzar rebuilt the city of Babylon in great magnificence with gold and silver, and then decided to rebuild the lowest platform of the Tower of Babel in honor of the Chaldean gods.

King Nebuchadnezzar resurfaced the base of the Tower of Babel with gold, silver, cedar, and fir, at great cost on top of a hard surface of baked clay bricks. These bricks were engraved with the seal of Nebuchadnezzar. (A photograph of one of these Babylonian bricks created by Nebuchadnezzar is included in the photo section.) In this inscription found on the base of the ruins of the Tower of Babel, King Nebuchadnezzar speaks in his own words from thousands of years ago confirming one of the most interesting events of the ancient past.

King Nebuchadnezzar's Inscription
Found on Base of the Tower of Babel

The tower, the eternal house, which I founded and built.

I have completed its magnificence with silver, gold, other metals, stone, enamelled bricks, fir and pine.

The first which is the house of the earth's base,

the most ancient monument of Babylon; I built and finished it.

I have highly exalted its head with bricks covered with copper.

We say for the other, that is, this edifice, the house of the seven lights of the earth,

the most ancient monument of Borsippa.

A former king built it, (they reckon 42 ages) *but he did not complete its head.*

Since a remote time, people had abandoned it, without order expressing their words.

Since that time the earthquake and the thunder had dispersed the sun-dried clay.

The bricks of the casing had been split, and the earth of

the interior had been scattered in heaps. Merodach, the great god, excited my mind to repair this building.
I did not change the site nor did I take away the foundation.
In a fortunate month, in an auspicious day,
I undertook to build porticoes around the crude brick masses, and the casing of burnt bricks.
I adapted the circuits, I put the inscription of my name in the Kitir of the portico.
I set my hand to finish it. And to exalt its head.
As it had been in ancient days, so I exalted its summit.
(Italics added for emphasis)[8]

This inscription was initially translated by Professor Oppert. In addition, Mr. William Loftus translated this fascinating inscription in his book, *Travels and Researches in Chaldea and Sinai.* This ancient inscription confirms the biblical accuracy of one of the most fascinating stories in the Book of Genesis. The pagan king Nebuchadnezzar confirms in his own words the incredible details that "a former king built it, but he did not complete its head," confirming the truthfulness of the Genesis account that God stopped the original builders from completing the top of the Tower of Babel. Most significantly, King Nebuchadnezzar's inscription declares that the reason the original king could not complete the tower was because, "Since a remote time, people had abandoned it, without order expressing their words." In other words, *they lost their ability to control their language and communications.*

The Bible's Account of the Tower of Babel

And it came to pass, as they journeyed from the east, that they found a plain in the land of Shinar, and they dwelt there. Then they said to one another, 'Come, let us make bricks and bake them thoroughly.' They had brick for stone, and they had asphalt for mortar. And they said, 'Come, let us build ourselves a city, and a tower whose top is in the heavens; let us make a name for ourselves, lest we be scattered abroad over the face of the whole earth.' But the Lord came down to see the city and the tower which the sons of men had built. And the Lord said, 'Indeed the people are one and they all have one language, and this is what they begin to do; now nothing that they propose to do will be withheld from them. Come, let Us go down and there confuse their language, that they may not understand one another's speech.' So the Lord scattered them abroad from there over the face of all the earth, and they ceased building the city. Therefore its name is called Babel, because there the Lord confused the language of all the earth; and from there the Lord scattered them abroad over the face of all the earth. (Genesis 11:2-8)

Compare the biblical statement with the words engraved on the ancient inscription of King Nebuchadnezzar, "A former king built it, but he did not complete its head. Since a remote time, people had abandoned it." The words of Moses in Genesis 11:7 declare; "So the Lord scattered them abroad from there over the face of all the earth, and they ceased building the city." Even more startling is the phrase of the pagan king where he declared that the reason they could not complete the top of the "tongue-tower" was that the "people abandoned it, without order expressing their words." This expression by Nebuchadnezzar clearly confirms the remarkable historical event recorded in Genesis when God supernaturally "confused the language of all the earth" and He "scattered them abroad over the face of all the earth" (Genesis 11:2-8). This inscription by King Nebuchadnezzar provides compelling evidence that the Bible gives us an accurate record of the historical events it describes.

Joseph and the Seven Years of Famine

An intriguing inscription confirms the Bible's account of the "seven years of great plenty" followed by the "seven years of famine" when Joseph served Pharoah in Egypt (Genesis 41: 29,30). This inscription was discovered during the nineteenth century in southern Saudi Arabia. This inscription was found on a marble tablet in a ruined fortress on the seashore of

Hadramaut in present-day Democratic Yemen. An examination of the writing suggests that it was written approximately eighteen hundred years before the birth of Christ, a time that corresponds with the biblical narrative about Jacob and his twelve sons. This inscription was first rendered in Arabic by Professor Schultens and was later translated into English by Rev. Charles Forster in William Harris Rule & J. Corbet Anderson' book, *Biblical Monuments*:

We dwelt at ease in this castle a long tract of time;
nor had we a desire but for the region-lord of the
vineyard.
Hundreds of camels returned to us each day at
evening,
their eye pleasant to behold in their resting-places.
And twice the number of our camels were our sheep,
in comeliness like white does, and also the slow
moving kine.
We dwelt in this castle seven years of good life
–how difficult for memory its description!
Then came years barren and burnt up:
when one evil year had passed away,
Then came another to succeed it.
And we became as though we had never seen a
glimpse of good.
They died and neither foot nor hoof remained.
Thus fares it with him who renders not thanks to God:
His footsteps fail not to be blotted out from his
dwelling.
                    (Italics added for emphasis)[9]

This ancient poem records the devastation of the years of famine and barrenness that followed the seven years of plenty. The language of the poem implies that the famine also lasted seven years. This account from ancient Arabia provides independent evidence confirming the accuracy of the biblical account of the seven years of plenty in the Middle East followed by seven years of famine that occurred during the rule of Joseph as prime minister of Egypt.

Moses recorded the history of the Egyptian famine and the wise preparations that Joseph made to gather up the surplus grain during the seven years of plenty to provide for the coming years of famine. "So he gathered up all the food of the seven years which were in the land of Egypt, and laid up the food in the cities; he laid up in every city the food of the fields which surrounded them" (Genesis 41:48). Again, Moses recorded: "Then the seven years of plenty which were in the land of Egypt ended, and the seven years of famine began to come, as Joseph had said. The famine was in all lands, but in all the land of Egypt there was bread. . . . The famine was over all the face of the earth, and Joseph opened all the storehouses and sold to the Egyptians. And the famine became severe in the land of Egypt. So all countries came to Joseph in Egypt to buy grain, because the famine was severe in all lands" (Genesis 41:53-57).

Explorers during the last century discovered a number of other interesting ancient inscriptions in the Middle East that provided confirmation of facts recorded in the sacred Scriptures. Ebn Hesham, an Arab from Yemen, showed the English explorer, Mr. Cruttenden, a rich tomb of a wealthy Yemenite woman who had died during the time of the Egyptian famine recorded in Genesis 41. This Yemenite tomb was fortunately discovered around 1850 after being exposed following a flood that uncovered the grave site.[10]

The tomb contained the body of a rich noblewoman who was covered in beautiful jewels. Seven collars of pearls surrounded her neck; her hands and feet were covered with seven bracelets, armlets, rings, and ankle-rings displaying costly jewels. In addition, her tomb contained a coffer filled with rich treasure.

However, the greatest treasure of all was an engraved stone tablet bearing her final inscription which appears to confirm the biblical account of Joseph's careful management of the remaining food reserves during the seven years of famine in Egypt. The original engraving was photographed and appeared in Professor Niebuhr's *Voyage en Arabie* (Plate LIX).

A Yemenite Inscription About a Famine
During the Time of Joseph

In thy name O God, the God of Hamyar,
I Tajah, the daughter of Dzu Shefar, *sent my steward to*
Joseph,
And he delaying to return to me, I sent my hand maid
With a measure of silver, to bring me back a measure of
flour:
And not being able to procure it, I sent her with a
measure of gold:
And not being able to procure it, I sent her with a
measure of pearls:
And not being able to procure it, I commanded them to
be ground:
And finding no profit in them, I am shut up here.
Whosoever may hear of it, let him commiserate me;
And should any woman adorn herself with an
ornament
From my ornaments, may she die with no other than
my death.

(Italics added)[11]

This ancient inscription reveals a Yemenite Arab noble woman's sincere complaint that she could not purchase Egypt's grain with her gold. The tragic history of famines often recorded the bartering of the most precious of metals and luxuries in trade for the smallest amount of food available.

Ancient Histories Confirm the Exodus

The biblical record in the Book of Exodus about the supernatural deliverance of the Jews from their bondage in Egypt is one of the most miraculous accounts in the Bible. Very few Christian pastors or laymen are aware that we have numerous historical records and ancient inscriptions that provide evidence and confirmation for these key events that resulted in the creation of the Jewish people as a distinct nation. Moses recorded the following statement: "And the children of Israel journeyed from Rameses to Succoth, about six hundred thousand on foot that were men, beside children. And a mixed multitude went up also with them; and flocks, and herds, even very much cattle" (Exodus 12:37,38).

It is noteworthy that the Jewish historian Flavius Josephus reported in his book *Josephus Against Apion* that two ancient Egyptian priest-scholars, Manetho and Cheremon, specifically named both Joseph and Moses in their history of Egypt as leaders of the Jews.[12] Josephus recorded that the Egyptians remembered a tradition of an Exodus from their country by the Jews whom they hated because they believed the Israelites were unclean. Manetho wrote that the Jews, "went out of that country afterward, and settled in that country which is now called Judea, and there built Jerusalem and its temple."[13]

It is interesting to note that Manetho and Cheremon stated that the Jews rejected Egyptian customs, including the national worship of Egyptian gods. Manetho declared that *Osarsiph* "Moses" became the lawgiver and leader of the Jewish slaves and that he "made this law for them, that they should neither worship the Egyptian gods, nor should they abstain from any one of those sacred animals which they have in the high esteem, but kill and destroy them all . . . When he had made such laws as these, and many more such as were mainly opposite to the customs of the Egyptians."[14]

Most importantly, these pagan historians acknowledged that the Jews killed the animals which they held as sacred, indicating the Israelite's practice of sacrificing lambs on that first Passover. These historians also confirmed that the Israelites immigrated into the area of "southern Syria" which was the Egyptian name for ancient Palestine. Perhaps the most important confirmation is found in the statement by Manetho that the sudden Exodus from Egypt occurred in the reign of "Amenophis, son of Rameses, and father of Sethos, who reigned toward the close of the 18th dynasty" which places this event between 1500 and 1400 B.C.[15] This evidence confirms the chronological data found in the Old Testament that suggests the Exodus occurred approximately 1491 B.C.

A few years ago, after much searching, I was able to locate a complete set of volumes containing the forty books in the

Library of Diodorus Siculus, a Greek historian from Agyrium in Sicily who lived from 80 B.C., until his death approximately twenty years before the birth of Jesus. Diodorus traveled extensively throughout the Middle East acquiring a vast knowledge of ancient events. He compiled records from various peoples which are quite valuable because they often recorded fascinating historical details that would otherwise have been lost forever. In his book, Diodorus reported:

> In ancient times there happened a great plague in Egypt, and many ascribed the cause of it to God, who was offended with them because there were many strangers in the land, by whom foreign rites and ceremonies were employed in their worship of the deity. The Egyptians concluded; therefore, that unless all strangers were driven out of the country, they should never be freed from their miseries. Upon this, as some writers tell us, the most eminent and enterprising of those foreigners who were in Egypt, and obliged to leave the country . . . who retired into the province now called Judea, which was not far from Egypt, and in those times uninhabited. These emigrants were led by Moses, who was superior to all in wisdom and prowess. He gave them laws, and ordained that they should have no images of the gods, because there was only one deity, the heaven, which surrounds all things, and is Lord of the whole.[16]

The historical records and inscriptions I have included in this chapter are only a small sample of the evidence confirming the historical accuracy of the Old Testament. However, these discoveries provide ample evidence that we can trust the Old Testament writers as accurate historians, even when they describe miraculous events such as the Tower of Babel and the seven-year famine in Egypt.

Notes

1. Alma E. Guinness, ed., *Mysteries of the Bible* (New York: The Reader's Digest Association, Inc. 1988).
2. Herodotus, *Polymnia*, section C. 89.
3. Strabo, *Geography*, lib. xvi., c.2.
4. W. Holland, *Recent Explorations in the Peninsula of Sinai* (1869).
5. Nelson Glueck, *Rivers in the Desert* (New York: Farrar, Straus and Cudahy, 1959) 11.
6. Nelson Glueck, *Rivers in the Desert* (New York: Farrar, Straus and Cudahy, 1959) 31.
7. Joseph Free, *Archeology and Bible History* (Wheaton: Scripture Press Publications, 1969).
8. William Kennett Loftus, *Travels and Researches in Chaldea and Sinai* (London: James Nisbet, 1857) 29.
9. Charles Forster, *Sinai Photographed* (London: Richard Bentley, 1862).
10. William Harris Rule and J. Corbet Anderson, *Biblical Monuments* (Croydon: 1873) 9.
11. William Harris Rule & J. Corbet Anderson, *Biblical Monuments* (Croydon: 1873) 9.
12. Flavius Josephus, *Josephus Against Apion* trans. William Whiston (Grand Rapids: Kregel Publications,1960. I., 26, 27, 32).
13. Flavius Josephus, *Josephus Against Apion* trans. William Whiston (Grand Rapids: Kregel Publications,1960. I., 26).
14. Flavius Josephus, *Josephus Against Apion* trans. William Whiston (Grand Rapids: Kregel Publications,1960. I., 26).
15. Flavius Josephus, *Josephus Against Apion* trans. William Whiston (Grand Rapids: Kregel Publications,1960. I., 26).
16. Diodorus Siculus, *Library of History*, Lib. 1., ap Phot., Loeb Classical Library, trans. C. H. Oldfather, (Cambridge: Harvard University Press, 1993).

3

Startling Archeological Discoveries

Can we trust the Bible? The answer is an overwhelming YES! The reason for this confident statement is that for the past one hundred and fifty years many brilliant scholars have conducted detailed archeological examinations at thousands of sites throughout the Middle East. The results of their discoveries have proven that the Bible is reliable and accurate in every single area where its statements could be tested. In the balance of this chapter I will share some of the wonderful archeological discoveries that provide tremendous proof that the Bible is a true and accurate record of past events in ancient Israel.

Throughout most of the last two thousand years, the majority of men living in the western world have accepted the statements of the Scriptures as genuine. Respected biblical scholars including Rev. David Brown, Rev. Adam Clarke, Rev Robert Jamieson, and Rev. A. R. Faussett, among others, wrote numerous Bible commentaries in the early part of the 1800s. However, despite their best efforts, their knowledge of the history and archeology of the ancient world was limited solely to the Bible and excerpts from classical writings from Greek and Latin writers. Unfortunately, most writers of the classics either exaggerated or failed to differentiate between mythology and historical events. As a result, most Bible commentators in past centuries were unable to add much additional knowledge to confirm the Bible's accounts of events. Fortunately, the field of biblical archeology has exploded in the past century and a half. The discoveries have provided tremendous insight into the life, culture and history of the ancient biblical world. Most importantly, these discoveries have confirmed thousands of biblical statements as true.

Beginning with the higher critical school of biblical critics in Germany and England in the nineteenth century we have witnessed a progressive abandonment of the historic faith in the Word of God. While European seminaries gradually abandoned the authority of the Scriptures, North American seminaries and Bible colleges still upheld the accuracy of the Bible to some degree. In the 1960s most North American seminaries still accepted the basic records of the Old and New Testaments as being historically true. However, in the following decades there occurred a wholesale abandonment of belief in the historical accuracy of the Bible. The attitudes behind these attacks on biblical accuracy and authority were those of complete rejection of God's inspiration of the Scriptures. In addition, many critics approach the Bible with an attitude of outright denial of super-natural events, such as miracles, and biblical prophecy. To these unbelieving critics, the presence of a miracle or prophecy in a biblical text was absolute proof that it was not genuine. Critics rejected the possibility of inspiration, miracles, and prophecy before they began their examination of the evidence.

Despite the overwhelming success unbelieving critics have had in establishing their unbelieving attitudes within the seminaries, textbooks, and popular media, something strange began to occur. Archeologists digging at sites throughout the Middle East continued to discover extraordinary artifacts that contradicted their sceptical attitudes. Many of the new archeological discoveries found in Israel and surrounding nations provided intriguing confirmation of the accuracy of the Word of God. As a result of these continuing discoveries, Dr. Nelson Glueck, the most outstanding Jewish archeologist of the last century, wrote in his great book, *Rivers in the Desert*, this remarkable statement. "It may be stated categorically that no archaeological discovery has ever controverted a Biblical reference. Scores of archaeological findings have been made which confirm in clear outline or in exact detail historical statements in the Bible. And by the same token, proper evaluation of Biblical descriptions has often led to amazing discoveries. They form tesserae in the vast mosaic of the Bible's almost incredibly correct historical memory."[1]

In confirmation of Dr. Glueck's statement, another respected scholar, Dr. J. O. Kinnaman, declared: "Of the hundreds of thousands of artifacts found by the archeologists, not one has ever been discovered that contradicts or denies one word, phrase, clause, or sentence of the Bible, but always confirms and verifies the facts of the biblical record."[2]

The well-known language scholar, Dr. Robert Dick Wilson, formerly professor of Semitic philology at Princeton Theological Seminary, made the following comment,

"After forty-five years of scholarly research in biblical textual studies and in language study, I have come now to the conviction that no man knows enough to assail the truthfulness of the Old Testament. When there is sufficient documentary evidence to make an investigation, the statement of the Bible, in the original text, has stood the test."[3]

The Bible claims that it is the inspired and accurate Word of God. Therefore, it is vital that we compare the scriptural records against the archeological discoveries uncovered at actual sites where many of the thrilling events of the Bible actually occurred. The results of these detailed investigations are available for anyone to examine. The archeological record provides overwhelming confirmation of thousands of detailed statements and facts recorded in the sacred Scriptures. Scholars have not found one single confirmed archeological discovery that absolutely disproves a statement of the Scriptures. To the contrary, as the evidence in *The Signature of God* reveals, the scholars have discovered literally hundreds of objects, inscriptions, and sites that confirm the accuracy of biblical statements in even unimportant areas.

The most important thing for believers in God is that new archeological evidence supports and confirms the accuracy, inspiration, and historical authority of the Word of God. No one should expect that archeology will ever be able to provide detailed confirmation of such personal events recorded in Scriptures such as the sacrifice of Isaac by Abraham. By their personal nature, it is unlikely that such events in the lives of private individuals would ever leave any archeological evidence. The vast majority of personal events in our lives, although they definitely occurred, can never be confirmed archeologically, let alone in a court of law. Most personal events recorded in the Bible would have left little or no evidence that could be discovered thousands of years after the event. However, whenever the Bible dealt with major events such as the rise and fall of kingdoms, cities, buildings, etc., the spade of the archeologist has often been able to discover wonderful confirmation of the truth of the account recorded in the Holy Scripture.

Only fifty years ago many disbelieving scholars totally rejected the historical accuracy of the Bible because they claimed that the Scriptures talked about numerous kings and individuals that could not be confirmed from any other historical or archeological records. Recent discoveries, however, have shown that they should not have abandoned their faith in the Word of God so easily. If they had only trusted in the truthfulness of the Bible or waited a little longer they would have been rewarded with the recent archeological discoveries that confirm many biblical details, events, and personalities.

For example, many scholars contemptuously reject the Bible's statements about King David. Many textbooks used in universities and seminaries openly reject any historical statements in the Scriptures about King David or Solomon. They believe that David is only a myth or literary fiction. Examples of this critical approach include the books *In Search of Ancient Israel*, by Philip R. Davis, and the *Early History of the Israelite People*, by Thomas L. Thompson. Dr. Thompson wrote, "The existence of the Bible's 'United Monarchy' during the tenth-century [B.C.]

is . . . impossible."[4] The so-called "minimalist" scholars accept only the minimum of information found in the Bible, rejecting every biblical statement unless it can be established by other non-biblical evidence. Professor Anson Rainey of the Tel Aviv Institute wrote an significant article in the well respected magazine, *Biblical Archaeology Review*, denouncing the minimalist school as "a circle of dilettantes." He claimed their ideas were a "figment of their vain imaginations" while concluding that the archeological discoveries including the inscription about the "house of David" at Dan in northern Israel should announce the "death knell to their conceit" in reflecting David, Solomon, and numerous other biblical figures.

The minimalist theory of rejecting all biblical statements unless supported by non-biblical sources is a totally biased position and would be ridiculed out of hand in any other area of study. Imagine a student of Plato's Greek philosophy that automatically rejected outright any statement made by Plato himself, his followers, or any Greek philosophical writer in later years who quoted him favorably. This is an absurd way to approach the study of any subject, let alone the Bible, that has been supported by the discoveries of archeology more than any other ancient book. Yet many biblical scholars in the secular universities proudly adopt this "minimalist" approach today. The rational way to study ancient history is to carefully examine every bit of evidence regarding a personality or event considering the evidence from both those who support and those who oppose the particular subject. The true scholar will then carefully weigh the evidence of all sources and come to a balanced conclusion based on the facts.

The House of David

Recent archeological investigations have demolished the position of those who rejected the biblical account of Israel's kings such as King David. In 1993, archeologists digging at Tel Dan in the Galilee in northern Israel found a fragment of a stone inscription that clearly refers to the "house of David" and identifies David as the "king of Israel." This is the first inscription outside the Bible that confirms the Bible's statement that David was the king of Israel in the ninth century before Christ. Many Bible critics who had rejected King David as a myth were upset to discover their position could no longer be defended. Some critics suggested that the fragment was a "fake." The following summer, two additional fragments of the original inscription were found that provided scholars with the whole inscription, confirming that it referred to David as king of Israel. However, another scholar, Professor Andre Lemaire from the College de France, discovered another ninth century B.C. stone inscription created by King Mesha of Moab that also referred to "the House of David." These important inscriptions, recorded a century after King David's death, confirm that David was the king of Israel at the time the Bible stated and that he established a royal dynasty, the "House of David" as the Scriptures reported.[5]

The Merenptah Stela's Reference to Israel

A stone inscription found in Egypt confirms that the Children of Israel were a people known to the Egyptians many centuries before the reign of King David, as the Bible claims. The Merenptah Stela is a seven-and-a-half-foot-high stone inscription discovered in 1895 in the temple of Pharaoh Merenptah at Thebes in Egypt. Scholars believe that Pharaoh Merenptah launched an invasion into the area of the modern-day West Bank in Canaan, defeating the Jewish inhabitants of the land. The second line from the bottom of this Merenptah Stela's inscription refers to *Israil*. The pharaoh's inscription boasts, "Israel is laid waste; his seed is not" as translated by Professor John Wilson in *Ancient Near East Texts*.[6]

Many scholars have assumed that this inscription referred to a military victory over the nation Israel at a point in time after they had conquered the land of Canaan. However, recent work by the archeologist Professor David Rohl suggests that the Merenptah Stele's inscription actually refers to the pharoah's terrible oppression of the Israelite slaves, the descendents of Jacob–Israel. The phrase "his seed is not"probably refers to the genocide of the male Jewish children as recorded in Exodus 1: 22: "And Pharaoh charged all his people, saying, Every son that is born ye shall cast into the river, and every daughter ye shall save alive."

Many scholars have wondered if the Bible's account of the Jewish captivity in Egypt could be true because no other inscriptions referring to the Exodus have been discovered to date. However, there is ample evidence that the Egyptian rulers were very adverse to recording either their defeats or the victories of their enemies. The pharaohs often replaced monuments and inscriptions by their predecessors with their own inscriptions engraved on the same stones. Therefore it is not really surprising that the Egyptians would not want to record their devastating defeat at the hands of Israel's God.

Merenptah – The Pharaoh Who Drowned

Egyptian archeologists discovered the mummified body of Pharaoh Merenptah over a century ago but only completed its medical examination in 1975. His body had been removed from its original burial chamber thousands of years ago following a grave robbery. The priests carefully repaired the damage and reburied Merenptah's mummy in a small room in the new royal tomb of Pharoah Amenhotep II in approximately 1,000 B.C. Fortunately the priests included Merenptah's name in the outermost bandage wrappings of the repaired mummy allowing a definite identification. The mummified body was first discovered, but not identified, by the French archeologist Victor Loret in 1898 together with ten other mummies.

A detailed medical examination of Merenptah's body was completed in 1974-75 with the aid of x-rays and modern forensic techniques provided by a Professor Michel Durigon employed by the Paris Police Forensic Labratory. When Durigon examined the pharaoh's tissue with a microscope he discovered the body had been in water for a short time. Dr. Maurice Bucaille, the former chief of the Surgical Clinic, University of Paris participated in the forensic examination and included the following statement in his 1994 book *The Hebrews in Egypt*: The "conservation of the transversal striations of muscular fibrillae gave evidence of the impossibility for the body to have remained more than a short time in the water, for, otherwise, these striations would not have appeared in the microscopic examination."[7]

Although the internal organs had been removed during the initial mummification process the scientists were amazed to discover that massive injuries had been inflicted on this body. The body had suffered extreme violence from external blows causing massive loss of tissue and bones in three areas: the abdomen, the thorax, and the cranium (skull). The back was also severely damaged from a massive blow. The remarkable violence inflicted on this pharaoh's body was very unusual because most Egyptian pharaoh's died peacefully or by poison. Yet the forensic evidence proved that this particular pharaoh had died during an incredibly violent incident, probably in water. What could account for these injuries? When the waters rushed back, the horses would have panicked as they violently tried to escape their harnesses and the chariots. Certainly the soldiers and pharaoh would have sustained terrible injuries as they drowned.

The book of Exodus records that the Egyptian pharaoh led his army after the departing Jews and was killed with his army and their horses as the waters returned violently to destroy all of them. "And the Lord hardened the heart of Pharaoh king of Egypt, and he pursued after the children of Israel: and the children of Israel went out with an high hand" (Exodus 14:8) In the Psalms we read of the death of Pharaoh and his army: "To him which divided the Red sea into parts: for his mercy endureth for ever: And made Israel to pass through the midst of it: for his mercy endureth for ever: But overthrew Pharaoh and his host in the Red sea: for his mercy endureth for ever" (Psalms 136:13-15).

It is worthwhile to note that Sir Flinders Petrie, one of the greatest Egyptologists, concluded that Pharaoh Merenptah was the pharaoh of the Exodus. Professor Karl-Richard Lepsius also identified Merenptah with the Exodus account.[8] Professor Gaston Maspero claimed that an Alexandrian legend held that Merenptah was the pharaoh of the Exodus "who is said to have perished in the Red Sea."[9]

Critics of the Bible have claimed for decades that the Bible's statements in the book of Joshua about the conquest of the Promised Land in the centuries before the monarchy of King David were pure fiction. In light of this new archeological evidence critics will be forced to relinquish their rejection of the Bible's record of Israel's conquest as stated by Joshua. Critics claimed that the books of Samuel, Kings, and Chronicles were recorded by Jews living in Persia centuries after the events occurred. They suggest that such records contain numerous errors and myths. However, the Bible claims that God's Holy Spirit inspired the writers to correctly record the events. When you compare the Word of God to the accuracy of the ancient historians such as Herodotus, you can quickly see that most ancient histories were nothing more than creative fiction and records of hearsay evidence without careful research or checking of facts. In stark contrast, the Bible is extremely careful and accurate as to events, chronology, sequence, and personalities.

In addition to the archeological evidence for King David, we now have confirmation of other kings of Israel. The name of Omri, king of Israel, is recorded on an inscription known as the Stela of King Mesha of Moab. In addition, Omri's name appears on the rock inscriptions of three kings of Assyria, the annals of both Tiglath-Pileser III and Sargon II, and the Black Obelisk of King Shalmaneser III, who wrote, "I conquered . . . all of the Land of Omri (Israel)." Other Assyrian inscriptions found in Nineveh confirm the Bible's records about these kings of Israel: Ahab, Jehu, Joash, Menehem, Pekah, and Hoshea. In addition, the names of many of the kings of the southern kingdom of Judah are also recorded on inscriptions of the nations that fought against the Jews. The inscriptions found by archeologists also confirm the names of these kings of Judah: Ahaziah, Uzziah, Ahaz, Hezekiah, Manasseh, and Jehoiachin. Scholars found ration records of the army of Nebuchadnezzar, king of Babylon (606 to 562 B.C.) that state, "ten sila of oil to Jehoiachin, king of Judah. . . ." Obviously, the fact that these foreign nations listed the kings of Israel and Judah provides the strongest evidence confirming the accuracy of the Word of God.

In 1846, the explorer Austen Henry Layard discovered an incredible Black Obelisk in the ruins of Nimrud (present-day

Iraq), the ancient capital of the great Assyrian Empire that conquered the northern kingdom of Israel. This six-and-a-half-feet-high Black Obelisk, a four-sided stone inscription, recorded the conquest of the Assyrian King Shalmaneser II over numerous foreign kingdoms including King Jehu of Israel (approximately 841 to 814 B.C.). A detailed examination of the obelisk reveals King Jehu bowing down in obedience to the Assyrian king. The obelisk refers to Jehu as the "son of Omri" indicating their awareness that his dynasty traced back to Omri in confirmation of the Book of Kings.[10]

The Walls of Jericho

During excavations of Jericho between 1930 and 1936, Professor John Garstang found one of the most incredible confirmations of the biblical record about the conquest of the Promised Land. The results were so amazing that he took the precaution of preparing a written declaration of the archeological discovery, signed by himself and two other members of his team. "As to the main fact, then, there remains no doubt: the walls fell outwards so

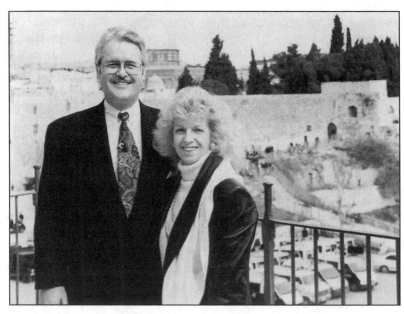

Grant and Kaye Jeffrey in front of the Western Wall.

completely that the attackers would be able to clamber up and over their ruins into the city."[11] This fact is important because the evidence from all other archeological digs around ancient cities in the Middle East reveal that walls of cities always fall inwards as invading armies push their way into a city. However, in the account in Joshua 6:20, we read, "the wall fell down flat, so that the people went up into the city every man straight ahead, and they took the city."[12] Only the supernatural power of God could have caused the walls to fall outward as described in Joshua's account of the conquest of Jericho according to Professor John Garstang in his book *Joshua- Judges.*

Following the fall of East Jerusalem to the Jordanians in the 1948 War of Independence, the Jordanian army dynamited Jewish synagogues and other buildings in the Jewish Quarter of Jerusalem in the years following their conquering of the Old City. Nevertheless, this wanton destruction over a twenty-year period, until Jerusalem was liberated during the 1967 Six Day War, created a unique archeological opportunity. When the Jews recaptured the Jewish Quarter in 1967 they had to rebuild every building because of the Jordanian destruction. However, this made it possible for Israeli archeologists to remove the rubble built up over the last two thousand years and explore the bedrock of this fascinating biblical city.

This was a unique opportunity because the existing modern buildings in most ancient cities prevent large archeological exploration. In addition to numerous discoveries confirming the accuracy of many passages in the Bible, the scholars, under the leadership of the archeologist Nahman Avigad of Hebrew University, found the remains of the wall of King Hezekiah built when the Assyrian army attacked Israel in 701 B.C. The Bible tells us that King Hezekiah built the walls of Jerusalem to resist the Assyrian armies: "And when Hezekiah saw that Sennacherib was come, and that he was purposed to fight against Jerusalem, He took counsel with his princes . . . they did help him. Also he strengthened himself, and built up all the wall that was broken, and raised it up to the towers, and another wall without" (2 Chronicles 32:2-5). The archeologists found that portions of the wall actually cut through walls of recently built houses, indicating the urgency of the defensive actions and the authority of the king. This is confirmed in the Bible's own account, "And ye have numbered the houses of Jerusalem, and the houses have ye broken down to fortify the wall" (Isaiah 22:10).

Dr. Millar Burrows, a professor at Yale University, studied the evidence that indicates the historicity of Abraham and the other patriarchs of Israel as recorded in Genesis. "Everything indicates that here we have an historical individual. As noted above, he is not mentioned in any known archaeological source, but his name appears in Babylonia as a personal name in the very period to which he belongs."[13] Burrows wrote in his book *What Mean These Stones?* about the underlying reason most scholars reject the authority of the Bible, "The excessive skepticism of many liberal theologians stems not from a careful evaluation of the available data, but from an enormous predisposition against the supernatural. . . . On the whole, however, archaeological work has unquestionably strengthened confidence in the reliability of the scriptural record."[14]

·The Discovery of Seals of Biblical Personalities

One of the most fascinating archeological discoveries in the last few years was the finding in Jerusalem of two bullae, or official clay seals, that bear the impression of the actual seal used by the biblical personality, Baruch, the dedicated scribe who transcribed the inspired messages of Jeremiah the prophet to Israel, including the inspired Book of Jeremiah in approximately 606 B.C.

Jeremiah needed an assistant who assisted in recording his inspired messages. Baruch, the son of Neriah, was Jeremiah's friend and scribe in the dangerous years of his master's imprisonment.

The Lord promised the scribe Baruch that he would be spared when the city of Jerusalem was destroyed by the Babylonian army, ". . . behold, I will bring evil upon all flesh, saith the Lord: but thy life will I give unto thee for a prey in all places whither thou goest" (Jeremiah 45:5).

Both of the bullae discovered in Jerusalem bear the

inscription, "Belonging to Berekhyahu, son of Neriyahu, the Scribe." However, the second bullae was found in Jerusalem earlier in this century and purchased by a Jewish collector, Shlomo Moussaieff of London, who owns the greatest private collection of ancient Jewish inscriptions in the world. This second clay seal, bearing the same inscription, also reveals a fingerprint that probably belonged to Baruch.

In 1903 another intriguing seal was discovered in the ruins of Meggido in northern Israel that bore an inscription of a beautiful lion and the words, "Belonging to Shema servant of Jeroboam." This fascinating discovery indicates that the seal originally belonged to an official of King Jeroboam of Israel. Other seals have been discovered confirming the biblical records about King Uzziah (777 to 736 B.C.) and King Hezekiah (726 to 697 B.C.).[15]

Another important seal found in Jerusalem dates from the seventh century before Christ and is inscribed as follows: "Belonging to Abdi Servant of Hoshea." This seal made of orange chalcedony, used to authenticate royal documents for security, belonged to Abdi, a high official of King Hosea, the last king of the northern kingdom of Israel before it was conquered by the Assyrian Empire in 721 B.C.[16] Another large seal on red limestone was found bearing the inscription "Belonging to Asayahu, servant of the king" together with a galloping horse. The name "Asaiah" is a short form of the name "Asayahu." This name occurs twice in the Old Testament in connection with the title "servant of the king." In 2 Chronicles 34:20 we find the name, "Asaiah a servant of the king's" and again in 2 Kings 22: 12, "Asahiah a servant of the king's." It is possible that this seal was owned by "Asaiah, the servant of the king" a high court official who was sent by King Josiah to carefully examine the scroll of the lost Book of Deuteronomy that was found in the Temple by the High Priest Hilkiah in approximately 622 B.C.

Dr. Henry M. Morris concluded his in-depth study of the archeological evidence concerning the Bible entitled *The Bible and Modern Science* with these words. "Problems still exist, of course, in the complete harmonization of archaeological material with the Bible, but none so serious as not to bear real promise of imminent solution through further investigation. It must be extremely significant that, in view of the great mass of corroborative evidence regarding the Biblical history of these periods, there exists today not one unquestionable find of archaeology that proves the Bible to be in error at any point."[17]

Explorers in Iraq in the last century found the ancient inscribed clay cylinder bearing the actual decree of King Cyrus of Persia allowing the various captured natives of many different nations to return freely to their ancient homelands. It was the government policy of the preceding Babylonian Empire of King Nebuchadnezzar to displace whole peoples such as the Jews and resettle them in the far reaches of their empire. However, King Cyrus of Persia, a moderate and God-fearing monarch, reversed the cruel Babylonian policy. Immediately after conquering the Babylonian Empire, King Cyrus issued a decree allowing the Jews to freely return to their homeland in Israel ending their seventy-year-long captivity.

The decree of King Cyrus began with these words, "I am Cyrus, king of the world, great king." After describing his conquests and deeds, the cylinder inscription reads, "I gathered all their former inhabitants and returned to them their habitations." In this incredible discovery we find the confirmation of one of the most astonishing events in the pages of Scripture. "Now in the first year of Cyrus king of Persia, that the word of the Lord by the mouth of Jeremiah might be fulfilled, the Lord stirred up the spirit of Cyrus king of Persia, that he made a proclamation throughout all his kingdom, and put it also in writing, saying, Thus saith Cyrus king of Persia, The Lord God of heaven hath given me all the kingdoms of the earth; and he hath charged me to build him an house at Jerusalem, which is in Judah. Who is there among you of all his people? his God be with him, and let him go up to Jerusalem, which is in Judah, and build the house of the Lord God of Israel, he is the God, which is in Jerusalem" (Ezra 1:1-3).

The Archeological Evidence of the New Testament

Obviously, the entire basis for the faith and hope of Christians depends on the truthfulness of the historical records of the New

Testament. Our hope for heaven and salvation itself depends on the accuracy of the words of Jesus of Nazareth and the apostles as recorded in the pages of the New Testament manuscripts. It is significant that there is a relentless attack on the reliability of the Gospels and the Epistles because those who hate the Bible understand that if they can cause men to doubt the New Testament, then their faith will be immeasurably weakened. Fortunately, the continued archeological discoveries during the last century have provided further evidence that confirms the total reliability of the written documents that form the foundation of the Christian faith.

The English scholar, William Ramsay, traveled as a young man to Asia Minor over a century ago for the sole purpose of disproving the Bible's history as described by Luke in his Gospel and in the Book of Acts. Ramsay and his professors were convinced that the New Testament record must be terribly inaccurate. He believed that Luke could not be correct in his history of Christ or in his account about the growth of the Church during the first decades following Christ. Dr. Ramsay began to dig in the ancient ruins of sites throughout Greece and Asia Minor, searching for ancient names, boundary markers, and other archeological finds that would conclusively prove that Luke had invented his history of Christ and His Church. To his amazement and dismay, William Ramsay discovered that the statements of the New Testament Scriptures were accurate in the smallest detail.

Finally, Dr. Ramsay was convinced by the overwhelming evidence proving the Bible's accuracy. As a result, he accepted Jesus Christ as His personal Savior. He became both a Christian and a great biblical scholar. As a result of his conversion to belief in Jesus Christ, Sir William Ramsay's books became classics in the study of the history of the New Testament. Another great scholar, A. N. Sherwin-White, was a great classical historical scholar at Oxford University who studied the extensive evidence for and against the historical accuracy of the Book of Acts. Sherwin-White wrote his conclusion after studying the evidence, "For Acts the confirmation of historicity is overwhelming . . .

any attempt to reject its basic historicity even in matters of detail must now appear absurd."[18]

Dr. William F. Albright was unquestionably one of the world's most brilliant biblical archeologists. In 1955 he wrote: "We can already say emphatically that there is no longer any solid basis for dating any book of the New Testament after circa A.D. 80."[19] However, additional discoveries over the next decade convinced him that all the books in the New Testament were written "probably sometime between circa A.D. 50 and 75." Significantly, Albright concluded that the writing of the New Testament within a few years of the events it described made it almost impossible that errors or exaggeration could have entered the text. He wrote that the duration between the events of Christ's life and the writing was "too slight to permit any appreciable corruption of the essential center and even of the specific wording of the sayings of Jesus." In other words, Professor Albright, one of the greatest minds in the field of archeology and ancient texts, concluded that the New Testament records the truth about Jesus Christ and his statements.

Dr. John A. T. Robinson was a distinguished lecturer at Trinity College, Cambridge and developed a reputation as a great scholar. Naturally, he accepted the academic consensus universally held since 1900, that denied the disciples and Paul wrote the New Testament and concluded that it was written up to a hundred years after Christ. However, an article in *TIME* magazine, March 21, 1977, reported that Robinson decided to personally investigate for himself the arguments behind this scholarly consensus against the New Testament's reliability because he realized that very little original research had been completed in this field in this century. He was shocked to discover that much of past scholarship against the New Testament was untenable because it was based on a "tyranny of unexamined assumptions" and what he felt must have been an "almost willful blindness." To the amazement of his university colleagues, Robinson concluded that the apostles must have been the genuine writers of the New Testament books in the years prior to A.D. 64. He challenged other scholars to complete original research necessary to truly examine the question fairly.

As a result of such a new analysis Robinson believed that it would necessitate "the rewriting of many introductions to-and ultimately, theologies of the New Testament." Robinson's book, *Redating the New Testament*, published in 1976, suggests that Matthew's Gospel was written as early as A.D. 40, within eight years of Christ.[21]

Notes

1. Nelson Glueck, *Rivers in the Desert* (New York, Grove, 1960) 31.
2. Internet site: http://www.geocities.com/Heartland/7234/quotes.html.
3. Internet site: http://www.geocities.com/Heartland/7234/quotes.html.
4. Thomas L. Thompson, *Early History of the Israelite People* (Brill: 1992).
5. *U. S. News & World Report*, October 25, 1999.
6. John Wilson, *Ancient Near East Texts* (1969) 376.
7. Maurice Bucaille, *The Hebrew in Egypt* (Tokyo: NTT Mediascope Inc., 1994).
8. Karl-Richard Lepsius, Die Chronologie der Aegypter (Berlin: 1849) 388).
9. Gaston Maspero, *Guide to the Visitor of Cairo Museum* (Cairo).
10. Austen H. Layard, *Discoveries among Nineveh and Babylon* (New York: Harper & Brothers, Publ. 1853) 523.
11. John Garstang, *Joshua- Judges* (London: Constable, 1931).
12. John Garstang, *Joshua- Judges* (London: Constable, 1931).
13. Millar Burrows, *What Mean These Stones?* (New York: Meridian Books, 1956) 258-259.
14. Millar Burrows, *What Mmean These Stones?* (New York: Meridian Books, 1956).
15. Internet site: http://www.biblehistory.net/Chap20.htm.
16. Andre Lemaire, *Biblical Archaeology Review*, "Royal Signature: Name of Israel's Last King Surfaces in a Private Collection" (June, 1995).
17. Henry M. Morris, *The Bible and Modern Science* (Chicago: Moody Press,1956).
18. A. N. Sherwin-White quoted by Rubel Shelley, *Prepare To Answer* (Grand Rapids: Baker Book House, 1990).
19. William Albright, *Recent Discoveries in Biblical Lands* (New York: Funk and Wagnalls, 1955) 136; quoted in Josh McDowell, op. cit., p. 65.

20. John A. T. Robinson, *TIME* magazine 21 March, 1977, Internet site: http://members.christhost.com/ResourceCentre/history.htm.
21. John A. T. Robinson, *Redating the New Testament* (Philadelphia: The Westminster Press,1976).

4

The Historical Evidence About Jesus Christ

Many modern scholars dispute the historical accuracy of the Bible. They especially reject the Gospel accounts of the life, death and resurrection of Jesus Christ. As an example of this rejection of biblical authority, the Jesus Seminar, a group of seventy-five New Testament liberal scholars, meet semi-annually to determine whether or not any of the Gospel quotations of Jesus' words meet with their scholarly approval. Incredibly, these liberal scholars examine individual "sayings" of Jesus recorded by the four Gospels and each academic votes to accept or reject these statements of Christ. The Jesus Seminar is sponsored by the Westor Institute, a private California study center, founded by Robert Funk, a liberal New Testament scholar. This group arrogantly pretends to sit in judgment of whether or not a particular biblical statement meets with their approval and is "genuine."

One indication of the underlying attitudes of these seminarians regarding the authenticity of Jesus' words, is found in the comments of Arthur Dewey of Xavier University, a member of the infamous Jesus Seminar. As reported in an article in *TIME* magazine in April 1994, he stated that, while rejecting most of Christ's words, they believed Jesus was occasionally humorous. "There is more of David Letterman in the historical Jesus than Pat Robertson." These particular liberal scholars are openly contemptuous in their rejection of the authority of the Bible based on their own exalted opinions. However, they merely represent the tip of the iceberg of academic scholarship that rejects, in whole or in part, most of Scripture as being the genuine inspired Word of God. These agnostic and unbelieving attitudes have permeated not only the academic world but also modern media. It is virtually the universal opinion today among secular academics that the Bible is without historical accuracy and cannot be relied upon by serious students.

Beginning in 1985, the Jesus Seminar has used a system of colored beads to indicate their vote or determination of the validity of particular statements which Jesus made. If, in their exalted opinion, these scholars think that Jesus would "certainly" have made such a statement, they vote by dropping a red bead in the box. If they believe that Jesus "might" have made a statement close to what the Gospel writer recorded, then they vote by dropping a pink bead. When they believe that the statement may be close to what Jesus thought, but not what He actually stated, they drop a grey bead in the box. Finally, when they reject a given statement in the Gospels as something they believe that Jesus would never have said, the scholars drop a black bead into the box showing that they totally reject the authenticity of the Gospel's statement.

During their meeting in Santa Rosa, California, *TIME* magazine reported in their April 6, 1996 issue that the scholars had decided that the Gospels of Matthew, Mark, Luke and John were "notoriously unreliable: the judges . . . had to throw out the Evangelists' testimony on the Nativity, the Resurrection, the Sermon on the Mount." The article in *TIME* repeats "the assertion, published by the 75-person, self-appointed Seminar three years ago, that close historical analysis of the Gospels exposes most of them as inauthentic." The criteria used by these liberal scholars to judge the Gospel records, reveals clearly why they reject almost everything that Christians have believed during the last two thousand years. The criteria used to reject statements included: any prophetic statements, statements by Jesus on the cross, descriptions of His trial, the Resurrection, and any claims to be the Messiah or the Son of God. Their bottom line rule: "When in sufficient doubt, leave it out."[1] However, if the view of the Jesus Seminar is correct—that almost nothing definite can be known about the life of Jesus of Nazareth—the basis for all Christian belief is destroyed.

Incredibly, this group has chosen to publish a new version of the Gospels which display the "words of Jesus" in various colors of ink reflecting their verdicts on the validity of His words. Not surprisingly, very little of their final Gospel text reveals Christ's words printed in red, indicating that these scholars reject many of Christ's statements. The arrogance of these self-appointed guardians of the validity of the words of Jesus Christ is almost unbelievable. As an example, when these academics examined the text containing the Lord's Prayer, they rejected every word in this prayer as spurious except for two single words, "Our Father." In reality, these liberal scholars declare by their votes whether or not they would have made these Gospel statements if they were Jesus! The cable channel Cinemax 2, ran a program in April of 1996, called "The Gospel According to Jesus," that records people reading from a new version of the Bible created by the author Stephen Mitchell. In this astonishing version, Mitchell eliminated almost all of the statements and most of the miracles by Jesus as recorded in the Gospels.

The brilliant conservative evangelical scholar, Professor Michael Green, of Regent College, rejects the analysis of the Jesus Seminar. Professor Green stated that the Gospels are the best authenticated of all ancient documents from that period some two thousand years ago. Green declared, "We have copies of them going back to well within the century of their composition, which is fantastic compared with the classic authors of the period. And in striking contrast to the two or three manuscripts we have attesting the text of these secular writers, we have hundreds of the New Testament. They give us the text of the New

Testament with astonishing uniformity." In addition, Professor Green noted the remarkable harmony found in the Gospel records: "The artless, unplanned harmony in their accounts is impressive and convincing."

Many people see Jesus as a wonderful moral teacher, but reject the Bible's claims for His deity and that He died on the cross for our salvation. However, this opinion is totally contradicted by historical evidence and logic. The English theologian C. S. Lewis presented his famous trilemma argument which makes the following statements.[2] Any person who did the miracles and spoke the messages ascribed to Jesus could not be a mere human teacher or an uninspired prophet, no matter how enlightened or exalted they might be. Anyone who performed the miracles ascribed to Jesus and made the statements Jesus made about His nature and powers must be the Son of God as He claimed, or a liar, or a lunatic. Anyone who claimed the things that Jesus said must be either insane, a demon from hell, or the true Son of God. As you examine the evidence in this chapter and the overwhelming evidence found in the Gospel records, I believe that every reader will conclude that Jesus Christ could not possibly have been a liar or a lunatic. This analysis leaves us with the final remaining possibility: that Jesus of Nazareth was precisely who He claimed He was, namely, the Son of God.

Historical Documents About Jesus

In this chapter I will share a number of compelling documents and ancient inscriptions that confirm the historical accuracy of the Gospel accounts about Jesus of Nazareth. Obviously, I can only touch on the highlights in this chapter, but the evidence shared will provide ample proof that the Gospel statements can be relied upon to stand the test of historical scrutiny. The evidence presented will prove conclusively that tremendous historical evidence exists both within and outside of the Bible that confirms the details of the life, death, and resurrection of Jesus Christ. Many sceptics contemptuously reject the Bible's claims that Jesus Christ is the Messiah.

They reject out of hand the historical evidence that has survived from the first century which confirms many facts about Jesus that are recounted in the Gospel records. One of the strongest pieces of evidence about Jesus comes from the well-known Jewish historian Flavius Josephus who lived at the time of the apostle Paul. Josephus mentions Jesus twice in his exhaustive history, *The Antiquities of the Jews*. One of these references, known as the *Testimonium Flavianum Passage*, confirms a number of historical facts regarding the life, death and resurrection of Jesus of Nazareth. This testimony will be examined later in this chapter.

After a detailed analysis of the historical evidence for the life and resurrection of Jesus of Nazareth, Professor Simon Greenleaf, the greatest authority in the Western world on the matter of legal evidence and the author of the authoritative work, *The Testimony of the Evangelists*, concluded that the evidence for Jesus was overwhelming.[3]

Sir William Ramsay began his scholarly career as a complete skeptic regarding the historical evidence about Jesus of Nazareth. William Ramsay, possibly the greatest of all New Testament archeologists, completed the most in-depth studies ever completed on the Book of Acts. He wrote, "Luke is a historian of the first rank; not merely are his statements of fact trustworthy; he is possessed of the true historic sense, . . . In short this author should be placed along with the very greatest of historians."[4] Professor Ramsay's comment on Luke's reliability as a historian is of tremendous importance in that not only was Luke the author of the Gospel account that bears his name, he also records the greatest number of details about Christ's virgin birth, career, death and resurrection.[5] If Luke's writing is reliable regarding the Book of Acts, then he is also a worthy historian regarding the details of Christ's life and resurrection.

President Abraham Lincoln was an agnostic until he reached the age of forty. Then he read Dr. James Smith's brilliant examination called *The Christian's Defence* that proved the historical reality of the events in Christ's life. The overwhelming evidence from this book convinced Lincoln with the result that he became a genuine Christian for the rest of his life. "My doubts scattered to the winds and my reason became convinced by the arguments in support of the inspired and infallible authority of the

Old and New Testaments."[6] Daniel Webster, one of the greatest lawyers of his age, declared that "I believe the Scriptures of the Old and New Testaments to be the will and word of God, and I believe Jesus Christ to be the son of God."

Throughout history many men have examined the evidence regarding the life of Jesus of Nazareth. To any unbiased observer who is willing to evaluate it without prejudice, the accumulated evidence proving the Gospel record is truly overwhelming. Otto Betz, a respected scholar, stated in his book, *What Do We Know About Jesus?* that "No serious scholar has ventured to postulate the non-historicity of Jesus."[7]

Some writers have suggested that there is little historical evidence regarding the life of Jesus. For example, the writer Solomon Zeitlin wrote, "Even Paul's epistles have awakened the question, Does he speak of a real historical personage or of an ideal? The main sources for the historicity of Jesus, therefore, are the Gospels."[8] However, Zeitlin dismisses the Gospel historical accounts and concluded: "So we are right to assume that even the Gospels have no value as witnesses of the historicity of Jesus. The question therefore remains: Are there any historical proofs that Jesus of Nazareth ever existed?"[9] Scholars such as Zeitlin casually dismiss the strong historical evidence that validates the Gospel accounts about Jesus because it contradicts the anti-supernatural opinion they tenaciously hold on to that rejects the Bible's accuracy. If liberal scholars applied the same arbitrary rejection of historical evidence to other ancient personages, such as Julius Caesar or Alexander the Great, they would be forced to reject all history as myth.

However, a careful unbiased analysis of the historical sources available will convince most fair-minded readers that Jesus of Nazareth is the Messiah of both history and prophecy. In his book, *The New Testament Documents: Are They Reliable?* the brilliant historian F. F. Bruce wrote, "The historicity of Christ is as axiomatic for an unbiased historian as the historicity of Julius Caesar."[10]

The Reliability of the New Testament
Confirmed by Scholars

During the earlier years of this century many liberal scholars concluded that the Gospels were unreliable as historical evidence, because they believed that they were written almost one hundred years after the events described. They concluded that the Gospel documents were based on hearsay and oral traditions rather than on eyewitness accounts. This prejudice led a whole generation of liberal scholars to reject the Gospels as competent eyewitness history.

The average Christian, believing the Bible to be the inspired Word of God, rejected the liberal argument because the Gospels and the Epistles declare that they are direct eyewitness accounts of the life of Christ. For example, Luke declared that he wrote these truths, "Even as they delivered them unto us, which from the beginning were eyewitnesses, and ministers of the word" (Luke 1:2). Later, in the Book of Acts, Luke confirmed that his reports as written to the Roman officer Theophilus, contained "many infallible proofs," the strongest historical and legal proofs possible. Luke stated that Jesus "showed Himself alive after His passion by many infallible proofs, being seen of them forty days" (Acts 1:3).

Fortunately, the tremendous advances in historical research and biblical archeology in the last century have convinced most scholars in the last two decades that the Gospels and Epistles were written within thirty-five years or less of the events which they describe. The late William F. Albright, the greatest biblical archeologist of his day, declared in an article for *Christianity Today*, January 18, 1963, W. F. Albright wrote: "In my opinion, every book of the New Testament was written by a baptized Jew between the forties and eighties of the first century A.D."[11]

Sir Frederic G. Kenyon, the director of the British Museum, was possibly the most respected New Testament textual scholar in our century. He commented on the significance of the fact that the evidence is overwhelming that the Gospels were composed shortly after the events of Christ's life and that the early Church widely distributed them within its congregations within a relatively short period of time. Kenyon wrote: "The interval, then, between the dates of original composition and the earliest extant evidence becomes so small as to be in fact negligible, and the last foundation for any doubt that the Scriptures have come down to us substantially as they were written has now been removed. Both the authenticity and the general integrity of the books of the New Testament may be regarded as finally established."[12]

After a professional lifetime of in-depth review of the New Testament manuscripts, Kenyon concluded that the present text in our Bible is absolutely reliable. He wrote: "It is reassuring at the end to find that the general result of all these discoveries and all this study is to strengthen the proof of the authenticity of the Scriptures, and our conviction that we have in our hands, in substantial integrity, the veritable Word of God."[13]

Luke's reliability as a historian is unquestionable. Professor Merrill F. Unger declares forthrightly that the recent discoveries of archeology have proven the accuracy and authority of the Gospel accounts as reliable eyewitness accounts. Unger wrote, "The Acts of the Apostles is now generally agreed in scholarly circles to be the work of Luke, to belong to the first century and to involve the labors of a careful historian who was substantially accurate in his use of sources."[14]

Modern scholars now possess more than five thousand manuscript copies of portions of the New Testament in the Greek language. In addition, there are an additional fifteen thousand manuscripts in other languages from the first few centuries of this era. No other important text, whether historical or religious, has more than a few dozen copies that have survived until our generation. The twenty thousand surviving manuscripts of the New Testament reveal numerous individual differences of spelling, et cetera. However, this enormous and unprecedented number of manuscripts provides the strongest evidence possible, allowing scholars to check and trace the origin of the various readings to ascertain with certainty the original text.

Most importantly, it is important to recognize that the vast majority of these variations or discrepancies, usually caused by careless copying, are usually trivial including variant spellings that still leave no doubt regarding the intent of the wording. Not one of these small differences affect a single important fact or doctrine of the Bible.

It is virtually impossible that anyone could have created and introduced significant changes into the authenticated New Testament manuscripts during the few years that elapsed between their original recording by the apostles shortly after the death of Jesus, and the time they were widely distributed among the early churches in the final four decades of the first century. In addition, any significant changes would have been instantly detected and corrected. Many Christians who had personally known and listened to the words of the apostles were still alive at the time these New Testament manuscripts were read in churches every Sunday.

One of the chief followers of Christ, John the Apostle, was still the bishop in charge of seven churches in Turkey until the first few years of the second century (A.D. 105). Obviously John would have instantly detected and denounced as heretical any counterfeit passages that anyone might have attempted to insert into genuine biblical manuscripts. The writings of the early Church confirm that John read the three gospels composed by Matthew, Mark and Luke and confirmed their accuracy. Then he wrote the gospel of John to cover the activities of Jesus during His first year of ministry that had not been covered by the other apostles.

The significance of these scholars' conclusion about an early date for the Gospels is overwhelming. It was impossible to widely distribute a blatantly false story about Christ while thousands of followers and observers were still alive to dispute it. Furthermore, the Greek originals of the Gospels and Epistles were widely copied, distributed and translated immediately into Hebrew, Syriac, Latin, Coptic and other languages. These documents were treasured by the churches and read in their Sunday services. If anyone had wanted to introduce a false miracle, event, or doctrine into the Gospels, they would have faced an impossible task. In order to introduce a false statement, the forger would have to simultaneously forge this counterfeit passage into every single copy of the Gospels in every country and language without being detected or challenged by any Christian. This would have been absolutely impossible. It is significant that the Gospel's historical account about Christ's life, death and resurrection was not denied by the Jews or the Romans critics who lived in the first century. This fact provides strong evidence that the Gospel account is historically true.

To put this in proper perspective, imagine that some writer wanted to create a false story in the 1990s about President Kennedy performing miracles and being raised from the dead for forty days after his tragic assassination in November, 1963. To succeed with his plan the writer would have to accomplish two impossible things: (1) He would have to simultaneously acquire every one of the millions of books and newspaper reports about the president and insert his counterfeit passages in this material without being detected by a single reader. (2) He would have to simultaneously convince millions of people around the world to accept his forgery as true, despite the fact that these people who were alive when Kennedy lived have independent recollections that contradict his invented story.

It is obvious to anyone who considers the problem carefully that it is impossible for anyone to successfully produce such a forgery about President Kennedy's life that would convince anyone, let alone the whole population of the world. However, the liberal scholars who suggest that the Gospel records were altered to introduce new doctrines and statements about Christ's virgin birth and resurrection are proposing something that is just as implausible as the above example. The only reason these scholars have been able to convince many people about their theory is that there is a great desire in the minds of many to reject the truth of the Bible. If they accept the reality of the Bible's accuracy they must admit in their own mind that they will someday have to give an account of their life to God. Their inability to face this reality forces them to reject out of hand the possibility that the Gospel records are true.

However, the evidence proving the historical reality about Jesus is powerful and convincing for anyone who will openly examine the evidence. One of the most convincing proofs of the supernatural nature of Christ's life is found in His absolutely unprecedented influence on the subsequent history and books that have reflected western philosophy, theology and ideas. The brilliant biblical scholar Bernard Ramm described this incredible influence on western literature as a result of the life, death and resurrection of Jesus Christ: "From the Apostolic Fathers dating from A.D. 95 to the modern times is one great literary river inspired by the Bible—Bible dictionaries, Bible encyclopedias, Bible lexicons, Bible atlases, and Bible geographies. These may be taken as a starter. Then at random, we may mention the vast bibliographies around theology, religious education, hymnology, missions, the biblical languages, church history, religious biography, devotional works, commentaries, philosophy of religion, evidences, apologetics, and on and on. There seems to be an endless number."[15]

In his comment on the sustained and overwhelming attacks on the authority of the Bible from the academic community, Bernard Ramm wrote about the total failure of these attacks to make a serious dent in the popularity and influence of the Scriptures. "A thousand times over, the death knell of the Bible has been sounded, the funeral procession formed, the inscription cut on the tombstone, and committal read. But somehow the corpse never stays put."[16]

Confirmation From Non-Christian Sources

The following section is an overview of several Roman and pagan historical manuscripts from the early centuries of the Christian era regarding the life, death, and resurrection as well as the spiritual influence of Jesus Christ that have survived for almost two thousand years.

Cornelius Tacitus – Governor of Asia

Cornelius Tacitus was a Roman historian and governor of Asia [Turkey] in A.D. 112. He referred to the persecution of the Christians caused by Emperor Nero's false accusation that the Christians had burned Rome. "Christus [Christ], the founder of the name, was put to death by Pontius Pilate, procurator of Judea in the reign of Tiberius: but the pernicious superstition, repressed for a time broke out again, not only through Judea, where the mischief originated, but through the city of Rome also."[17] Tacitus, as a careful historian with access to the government archives of Rome, confirmed many details in the Gospels, Acts, and Romans.

Suetonius – Roman Historian

Suetonius was the official historian of Rome in A.D. 125. In his *Life of Claudius* (25.4) he referred to the Christians causing disturbances in Rome which led to their being banished from the city. He identifies the sect of Christians as being derived from "the instigation of Chrestus" which was his spelling of the name Christ.[18]

Pliny the Younger

Plinius Secundus, known as Pliny the Younger, declared that the Christians were "in the habit of meeting on a certain fixed day before it was light, when they sang in alternate verse a hymn to Christ as to a God, and bound themselves to a solemn oath, not to any wicked deeds, but never to commit any fraud, theft, adultery, never to falsify their word, not to deny a trust when they should be called upon to deliver it up."

Pliny was governor of the Roman province of Bithynia [Turkey] in A.D. 112. He wrote to the emperor requesting instructions about the interrogation of the Christians whom he was persecuting. In his *Epistles*, he states that these believers would not worship Emperor Trajan and would not curse their leader, Jesus Christ, even under extreme torture. Pliny described the Christians as people who loved the truth at any cost. It is impossible to believe that these people would willingly die for something they knew was a lie. Their martyrdom was based on the fact that they knew the truth of the statements in the Gospels about Jesus.[19]

Lucian of Samosata

Lucian lived in Samosata a century after Christ. In his book, *The Passing Peregrinus*, he declared that Jesus was worshiped by his followers and was "the man who was crucified in Palestine because he introduced this new cult into the world."[21]

Evidence About Jesus from Flavius Josephus

Now there was about this time Jesus, a wise man, if it be lawful to call him a man, for he was a doer of wonderful works, a teacher of such men as receive the truth with pleasure. He drew over to him both many of the Jews, and many of the Gentiles. He was [the] Christ, and when Pilate, at the suggestion of the principal men among us, had condemned him to the cross, those that loved him at the first did not forsake him: for he appeared to them alive again the third day: as the divine prophets had foretold these and ten thousand other wonderful things concerning him. And the tribe of Christians so named from him are not extinct at this day.[22]

Flavius Josephus was a Pharisee and priest living in Jerusalem. Born in A.D. 37, following the death of Christ, he witnessed first-hand the events leading up to the destruction of Jerusalem and the Temple. He fought as a general of the Jewish rebel forces in Galilee in the war against Rome. Josephus was captured by the Romans at the fall of the city of Jotapata and became friends with the Roman general Vespasian. As a historian, with access to both Roman and Jewish governmental records, he described the events in Israel during the turbulent decades of the first century. In A.D. 94, Josephus published in Rome his definitive study of the history of the Jewish people called *Antiquities of the Jews*. One of the most fascinating passages in his important history concerned the events in the life, death and resurrection of Jesus Christ.

Numerous liberal scholars have declared that this reference to Jesus Christ and another reference to James and John the Baptist must be interpolations or forgeries by later Christian editors. In other words they have concluded that Josephus's reference to Jesus could not possibly be genuine. However, such an assertion of forgery requires significant proof. Yet none of these scholars can produce a single ancient copy of Josephus's

Antiquities of the Jews, that does not contain this passage on Jesus. If they had found dozens of ancient copies of Josephus's book that failed to contain this passage they would have some "evidence" that this was not an original passage by the Jewish historian. However, Phillip Schaff declared in his book, *History of the Christian Church*, that all ancient copies of Josephus's book, including the early Slavonic [Russian] and Arabic language versions, contain the disputed passage about the life of Christ.[23]

Every one of the ancient copies from the fourth and fifth centuries in several different languages contain these passages. No one has ever explained how an editor could have altered each of these widely distributed versions during the centuries following their publication. The real reason why these liberal scholars reject the Josephus passage out of hand is their deeply ingrained prejudice that it could not be genuine because it confirms the historicity of the claims about Jesus Christ. If the events recorded in the Gospels actually occurred, it is only natural that Josephus would mention them at the appropriate place in his narrative of that turbulent century. In fact, it would be astonishing if Josephus had failed to mention anything about the ministry and resurrection of Jesus.

The biblical scholar Craig Blomberg wrote in his 1987 book, *The Historical Reliability of the Gospels*, that "many recent studies of Josephus however, agree that much of the passage closely resembles Josephus' style of writing elsewhere. . . . But most of the passage seems to be authentic and is certainly the most important ancient non-Christian testimony to the life of Jesus which has been preserved." Blomberg concluded his lengthy analysis of the historical evidence for and against Jesus, with this statement; "The gospels may therefore be trusted as historically reliable."[24]

In addition, R. C. Stone, in his article titled "Josephus" wrote the following: "The passage concerning Jesus has been regarded by some as a Christian interpolation; but the bulk of the evidence, both external and internal, marks it as genuine. Josephus must have known the main facts about the life and death of Jesus, and his historian's curiosity certainly would lead him to investigate the movement which was gaining adherents even in high circles. Arnold Toynbee rates him among the five greatest Hellenic historians."[25]

Evidence About James, the Brother of Jesus

In another passage in Flavius Josephus's book, *Antiquities of the Jews*, he described the death of James, the brother of Jesus. "As therefore Ananus (the High Priest) was of such a disposition, he thought he had now a good opportunity, as Festus (the Roman Procurator) was now dead, and Albinus (the new Procurator) was still on the road; so he assembles a council of judges, and brought before it the brother of Jesus the so-called Christ, whose name was James, together with some others, and having accused them as law-breakers, he delivered them over to be stoned." While many liberal scholars reject the historicity of the first passage about Jesus Christ, most modern scholars accept the authenticity of this second passage about James "the brother of Jesus the so-called Christ."[26]

Evidence About John the Baptist

Flavius Josephus described the death of John the Baptist in his respected history as follows:

> "Now, some of the Jews thought that the destruction of Herod's army came from God, and that very justly, as a punishment of what he did against John, that was called the Baptist; for Herod slew him, who was a good man, and commanded the Jews to exercise virtue, both as to righteousness towards one another, and piety towards God, and so to come to baptism; for that the washing [with water] would be acceptable to him, if they made use of it, not in order to the putting away, [or the remission] of some sins [only] but for the purification of the body: supposing still that the soul was thoroughly purified beforehand by righteousness. Now, when [many] there came to crowd about him, for they were greatly moved [or pleased] by hearing his words, Herod, who feared lest the great influence John had over the people might put it into his power and inclination to raise a

rebellion [for they seemed ready to do anything he should advise], thought it best, by putting him to death, to prevent any mischief he might cause, and not bring himself into difficulties, by sparing a man who might make him repent of it when it should be too late. Accordingly he was sent a prisoner, out of Herod's suspicious temper, to Macherus (Masada), the castle I before mentioned, and was there put to death."[27]

These historical descriptions by Josephus, together with the other sources mentioned above, provide ample evidence that Jesus of Nazareth lived in the first century of this era.

Further Confirmation
Julius Africanus and Thallus

Julius Africanus was a North African Christian teacher writing in A.D. 215. He recorded the writing of a pagan historian by the name Thallus who lived in A.D. 52 shortly after the resurrection of Christ. Thallus recorded in his history that there was a miraculous darkness covering the face of the earth at the Passover in A.D. 32. Julius Africanus records, "Thallus, in the third book of his histories, explains away this darkness as an eclipse of the sun-unreasonably, as it seems to me."[28] Julius explained that Thallus's theory was unreasonable because a solar eclipse could not occur at the same time as the full moon and it was at the season of the Paschal full moon that Christ died.

This historical reference by the pagan historian Thallus confirmed the Gospel account regarding the darkness that covered the earth when Jesus was dying on the cross. There are other ancient historical references to this supernatural darkness at the death of Christ. Modern astronomers confirm that Julius Africanus was right in his conclusion that a normal eclipse could not possibly occur at the time of a full moon, which was the time of Passover. The high priest carefully calculated the position of the full moon to the smallest degree because their whole Jewish liturgical calendar, especially Passover, depended on following the lunar position exactly.

It is interesting to note that the ancient Jewish *Targums*, or paraphrases of the Old Testament, contain additional evidence that the Jews expected the Messiah to be born in Bethlehem as prophesied in Micah 5:2. Charles R. Condor discovered that seventy-two of the *Targums* on various passages of the Old Testament contain information about the coming Messiah although the biblical passage itself did not contain the name Messiah. It is intriguing to note that two of these well respected *Targums* indicated clearly that the Messiah would be born at or near Bethlehem. For example, the *Targum* on Genesis 35:21 talks about Israel pitching its tents "beyond the tower of Eder." The *Targum of Jonathan* adds this comment identifying this location, "which is the place where shall be revealed the King Messias in the end of days."[29]

Charles R. Condor noted in his submission to the *Palestine Exploration Fund Report*, April 1875, that "Migdol Eder, or 'the Tower of the Flock' was known in A.D. 700 as about 1,000 paces from Bethlehem," which is the location of the ruins of the Monastery of the Holy Shepherds. Another *Targum*, commenting on the passage, Exodus 12:42, makes a fascinating reference to the area of Nazareth where Jesus was raised by His parents in His father's carpentry shop. This *Targum* states that "Moses cometh forth from the desert and Messias goeth forth from Roma." This "Roma" was a village located near to the town of Nazareth.[30]

Following an exhaustive study of the literature regarding the archeological and historical controversies about the accuracy of the New Testament, the researcher and scientist Henry M. Morris, Ph.D., concluded that we can totally trust the manuscripts as correct records of the events described. Morris wrote, "no statement in the New Testament has to this date been refuted by an unquestioned find of science or history. This in itself is a unique testimony to the amazing accuracy and authenticity of the New Testament records."

The historian Philip Schaff outlined in his book, *The Person of Christ*, the overwhelming influence which the life of Jesus of Nazareth had on the subsequent history and culture of the western world. "This Jesus of Nazareth, without money and arms, conquered more millions than Alexander, Caesar, Mohammed, and Napoleon; without science and learning, He shed more light on things human and divine than all philosophers and scholars combined; without the eloquence of schools, He spoke such words of life as were never spoken before or since, and produced effects which lie beyond the reach of orator or poet; without writing a single line, He set more pens in motion, and furnished themes for more sermons, orations, discussions, learned volumes, works of art, and songs of praise than the whole army of great men of ancient and modern times."[31]

While the historical records provide overwhelming evidence to prove the absolute reliability of the Gospel records about Jesus Christ, the statements of the disciples can only reveal His earthly existence as the Messiah. We have not yet witnessed the reality of His awesome glory that will be revealed when we see Him returning in His glory to take His church home to heaven nor when He will reveal Himself to the population of earth at the Second Coming. The Puritan writer John Owen discussed the glory of Jesus Christ in these words. "Should the Lord Jesus appear now to any of us in His majesty and glory, it would not be to our edification nor consolation. For we are not meet nor able, by the power of any light or grace that we have received, or can receive, to bear the immediate appearance and representation of them. His beloved apostle John had leaned on His bosom probably many a time in His life, in the intimate familiarities of love; but when He afterward appeared to Him in His glory, 'he fell at His feet as dead.' " The men and women living in the first century of this era, who heard the words of Jesus of Nazareth, were amazed at the tremendous wisdom shown by His words. When Jesus Christ finally appears in His revealed glory as Almighty God at the Great Day of the Lord, Matthew prophesied that "then shall all the tribes of the earth mourn, and they shall see the Son of Man coming in the clouds of heaven with power and great glory" (Matthew 24:30).

Extraordinary Evidence About Jesus in the Dead Sea Scrolls

If someone had asked a minister in 1947 to prove that the original Hebrew Scriptures from the Old Testament were reliably copied without error throughout the last two thousand years, he might have had some difficulty in providing an answer. The oldest Old Testament manuscript used by the King James translators was dated approximately A.D. 1100. Obviously, that old manuscript from A.D. 1100 was a copy of a copy of a copy, etc., for over two thousand years. How could we be sure that the text in the A.D. 1100 copy of the Scriptures was identical with the original text as given to the writers by God and inspired by Him? However, an extraordinary discovery occurred in the turbulent year before Israel became a nation. A Bedouin Arab found a cave in Qumran near the Dead Sea which ultimately yielded over a thousand priceless manuscripts dating back before A.D. 68, when the Roman legions destroyed the Qumran village during the Jewish war against Rome.

An Arab shepherd boy discovered the greatest archeological find in history in 1947. When the ancient Hebrew scrolls from these caves were examined by scholars they found that this Qumran site contained a library with hundreds of precious texts of both biblical and secular manuscripts that dated back before the destruction of the Second Temple and the death of Jesus Christ. Once the Bedouins recognized the value of the scrolls they began searching for additional documents in every valley and cave near the Dead Sea. The most incredible discovery was the immense library of biblical manuscripts in Cave Four at Qumran that contained every single book of the Old Testament with the exception of the Book of Esther. Multiple copies of several biblical texts such as Genesis, Deuteronomy and Isaiah were found in Cave Four. Scholars were able to reach back a further thousand years in time to examine biblical texts that had lain undisturbed in the desert caves during all of the intervening centuries.

The scholars discovered that the manuscript copies of the most authoritative Hebrew text, *Textus Recepticus*, used by the King James translators in 1611, were virtually identical to these ancient Dead Sea Scrolls. After carefully comparing the manuscripts they discovered that, aside from a tiny number of spelling variations, not a single important word was altered from the original scrolls in the caves from the much copied A.D. 1100 manuscripts used by the Authorized King James Version translators in 1611. How could the Bible have been copied so accurately and faithfully over the many centuries without human error entering into the text? The answer is found in the overwhelming respect and fear of God that motivated Jewish and Christian scholars whose job was to faithfully copy the text of the Bible. In a later chapter dealing with the Hebrew Codes found in the text of the Bible, I will share how the Masoretic scribes meticulously copied the text of the Scriptures over the centuries.

The Essenes were a Jewish community of ascetics that lived primarily in three communities: Qumran at the Dead Sea, the Essene Quarter of Jerusalem (Mount Zion), and Damascus. They appear to have existed from approximately 200 B.C., until the destruction of their communities in Jerusalem and Qumran by the Roman armies in A.D. 68. During the first century there were three significant Jewish religious communities: the Pharisees, the Sadducees, and the Essenes. The Essenes established their religious community near the shores of the Dead Sea. In their love for the Word of God they faithfully copied each Old Testament scroll in their Scriptorium in the village of Qumran. New evidence suggests that these men of God were aware of the new religious leader in Israel known as Jesus of Nazareth and the group of writings about Him known as the New Testament. The Christian historian Eusebius, who wrote around A.D. 300, believed that the Essenes were influenced in their beliefs by Christianity.

When the scrolls were first discovered, many Christian scholars naturally wondered if they might contain evidence about the new faith of Christianity. Despite overwhelming interest, the vast majority of scrolls were not translated for publication in the intervening forty-nine years. For almost fifty years, the hopes of Christian scholars were frustrated by the decision of the small group of original scroll scholars to withhold publication and release of a significant number of these precious scrolls. Some scholars speculated publicly that there might be evidence about Christ in the unpublished scrolls but the original scroll scholars vehemently denied these claims. While some scroll scholars had published part of their assigned texts, after forty-five years the original team responsible for the huge number of scrolls discovered in Cave Four had published only twenty percent of the five hundred Dead Sea Scrolls in their possession.

Quotes from the New Testament in the Dead Sea Scrolls

Finally, after a public relations campaign led by the *Biblical Archeology Review* magazine demanded the release of the unpublished scrolls to other scholars, the last of the unpublished scrolls were released to the academic world. To the great joy and surprise of many scholars, the scrolls contain definite references to the New Testament and, most importantly, to Jesus of Nazareth. In the last few years several significant scrolls were released that shed new light on the New Testament and the life of Jesus. One of the most extraordinary of these scrolls released in 1991 appears to refer directly to the crucifixion of Jesus Christ.

The Crucified Messiah Scroll

In 1991 the world was astonished to hear that one of the unpublished scroll fragments included intriguing references to a "Messiah" who suffered crucifixion for the sins of men. The scroll was translated by Dr. Robert Eisenman, Professor of Middle East Religions of California State University. He declared, "The text is of the most far-reaching significance because it shows that whatever group was responsible for these writings was operating in the same general scriptural and Messianic framework of early Christianity."[32] Although the original scroll scholars still claimed that there was no evidence about early Christianity in the unpublished scrolls, this new scroll contradicted their statements. This single scroll is earth-shaking in its importance. As Dr. Norman Golb, Professor of Jewish History at the University of Chicago said, "It shows that contrary to what some of the editors said, there are lots of surprises in the scrolls, and this is one of them."

This remarkable five-line scroll contained information about the death of the Messiah. It referred to "the Prophet Isaiah" and his Messianic prophecy (Chapter 53) that identified the Messiah as one who will suffer for the sins of His people. This scroll provides an amazing parallel to the New Testament revelation that the Messiah would first suffer death before He would ultimately return to rule the nations. Many scholars believed that the Jews during the first century of our era believed that, when He finally came, the Messiah would rule forever without dying. The exciting discovery of this scroll reveals that the Essene writer of this scroll understood the dual role of the Messiah as Christians did. This scroll identified the Messiah as the "Shoot of Jesse" (King David's father) the "Branch of David," and declared that he was "pierced" and "wounded." The word "pierced" reminds us of the Messianic prophecy in Psalm 22:16: "They pierced my hands and feet." The prophet Jeremiah (23:5) said, "I will raise unto David a righteous branch."

The scroll also describes the Messiah as a "leader of the community" who was "put to death." This reference pointing clearly to the historical Jesus of Nazareth is creating shock waves for liberal scholarship that previously assumed that the Gospel account about Jesus was a myth. Jesus is the only one who ever claimed to be the Messiah who was crucified. The genealogies recorded in both Matthew and Luke's Gospels, reveal that Jesus was the only one who could prove by the genealogical records kept in the Temple that He was the lineage of King David as the "Son of Jesse." Since the tragic destruction of the Temple and its records in A.D. 70, it would be impossible for anyone else to ever prove their claim to be the Messiah based on their genealogical descent from King David. Additionally, the scroll identified the Messiah as "the sceptre" which probably refers to the Genesis 49:10 prophecy: "The sceptre shall not depart from Judah, nor a lawgiver from between his feet, until Shiloh come; and unto him shall the gathering of the people be." This scroll confirms the historical truthfulness of the New Testament record about Jesus and His crucifixion. The evidence from the scroll suggests that the Jewish Essene writer acknowledged that Jesus of Nazareth was the "suffering Messiah" who died for the sins of His people.

The "Son of God" Scroll Fragment

Another curious scroll fragment discovered in Cave Four, known as 4Q246, refers to the hope of a future Messiah figure. This is another of the scrolls that was unpublished for fifty years. Amazingly, the text in this scroll refers to the Messiah as "the son of God" and the "son of the Most High." These words are an exact parallel to the wording recorded in the Gospel of Luke.

The Text of Scroll 4Q246 – the Son of God Scroll

He shall be called the son of God,
and they shall designate [call] him son of the Most High.
Like the appearance of comets, so shall be their kingdom.
For brief years they shall reign over the earth and shall trample on all;
one people shall trample on another and
one province on another until the people of God
shall rise and all shall rest from the sword.[33]

Compare the words in the scroll 4Q246 text to the inspired words found in Luke 1:32 and 35: "He shall be great, and shall be called the Son of the Highest: and the Lord God shall give unto him the throne of his father David. . . . And the angel answered and said unto her, The Holy Ghost shall come upon thee, and the power of the Highest shall overshadow thee: therefore also that holy thing which shall be born of thee shall be called the Son of God" (Luke 1:32-35).

Anyone comparing these two first century texts will be intrigued by the amazing similarity of concept and wording describing the Messianic leader. One of the great differences between Christian and Jewish conceptions of the promised Messiah revolves around His relationship to God. While the Jews believe the Messiah will be a great man, such as Moses, with a divine mission, the Christians believe that the Bible teaches that the Messiah would be uniquely "the Son of God." The Jewish view usually held that the concept of a "son of God" violated the primary truth of monotheism found in Deuteronomy 6:4, "Hear, O Israel: The Lord our God is one Lord."

The Christians believed that Jesus' claim to be the Son of God was not a violation of Deuteronomy 6:4. Rather, Christians believe in the Trinity, the doctrine that the Father, the Son and the Holy Spirit are revealed in the Bible to be One God, revealed in three personalities. As Christians, we do not believe in three separate gods. Therefore, Christians understand the statements about Jesus as the Son of God to be in complete conformity to the truth of monotheism—there is only one God. It is fascinating in this regard to consider the presence of these statements in this Dead Sea Scroll Jewish text: "He shall be called the son of God, and they shall designate [call] him son of the Most High."

The presence of these statements in the Dead Sea Scrolls suggests the possibility that some of the Essenes either accepted the Messianic claims of Jesus to be the Son of God or anticipated this concept based on the Old Testament prophecies. Either possibility opens up significant new areas for scholarly exploration of these interesting manuscripts from Israel's past.

Another possibility that must be considered is this: Is it possible that this scroll 4Q246 is a direct quote from the Essene writer hearing the words of the Gospel of Luke that was now widely circulating according to early Christian witnesses? Luke, the physician, claimed that he wrote the Gospel of Luke as an eyewitness of the events he personally observed. In Luke 1:1-3, he says: "Forasmuch as many have taken in hand to set forth in order a declaration of those things which are most surely believed among us, Even as they delivered them unto us, which from the beginning were eyewitnesses, and ministers of the word; It seemed good to me also, having had perfect understanding of all things from the very first, to write unto thee in order, most excellent Theophilus."

The discovery of the virtually identical wording "the Son of God" from Luke 1:32 and 35 with the scroll found buried in a cave in A.D. 68, stands as a tremendous witness to the early existence and transmission of the Gospel records within thirty-five years of Christ. If the Gospels were written and distributed within thirty-five years of the events of the life of Jesus (as the

Gospels claim) then they stand as the best eyewitness historical records we could ever hope to possess. In fact, all of these ancient historical records confirm the truth of the Gospels.

Other New Testament Quotes Identified in the Dead Sea Scrolls

In 1971, a Spanish biblical scholar named Jose O'Callaghan studied some of the small fragments of scrolls discovered in Cave Seven at Qumran. He was looking for correspondences between these fragments of Greek scrolls and the Septuagint, the Greek translation of the Hebrew Old Testament that was widely used by Jesus and the apostles.

These fragments are quite small, containing only small portions of each verse. After almost two thousand years, the elements and insects have significantly damaged these manuscripts. In some cases only small fragments containing parts of a verse on three or four lines remain from an original scroll. It required considerable detective work to determine the precise text in these tiny fragments.

One day he carefully examined several small scroll fragments located in a photo in *The Discoveries of the Judean Desert of Jordan*. To his great surprise O'Callaghan noticed that several did not fit any Old Testament text. These fragments were listed as "Fragments not identified." To his amazement, Dr. O'Callaghan found that these Greek language fragments bore an uncanny resemblance to several verses in the New Testament. He read the Greek words "beget" and a word that could be "Gennesaret," a word for the Sea of Galilee. The fragment containing "Gennesaret" appears to be a quotation of the passage referring to the feeding of the five thousand found in Mark 6:52,53, which states: "For they considered not the miracle of the loaves: for their heart was hardened. And when they had passed over, they came into the land of Gennesaret, and drew to the shore."

If these texts are actually portions of these Christian writings they would be the earliest New Testament texts ever discovered. The *New York Times* responded, "If O'Callaghan's theory is accepted, it would prove that at least one of the Gospels, that of

St. Mark, was written only a few years after the death of Jesus."
The *Los Angeles Times* headlined, "Nine New Testament fragments dated A.D. 50 to A.D. 100 have been discovered in a Dead
Sea Cave." It stated that "if validated, [they] constitute the most
sensational biblical trove uncovered in recent times."

Other Scroll Fragments and the New Testament

Dr. Jose O'Callaghan ultimately identified eight different scroll
fragments from Cave Seven that appear to be quotes from New
Testament passages. The scholarly magazine *Bible Review* ran a
fascinating article on Dr. O'Callaghan, these scrolls, and their
possible connection with the New Testament in an article in
December, 1995.[34]

The fragments appeared to O'Callaghan to be portions of
the following verses from the Gospels and Paul's Epistles:
"For the earth bringeth forth fruit of herself . . ."
(Mark 4:28).
"And he saw them toiling in rowing; . . ." (Mark 6:48).
"And Jesus answering said unto them, Render to
Caesar . . ." (Mark 12:17)
"And when they had eaten enough, they lightened the
ship . . ." (Acts 27:38).
"And not only so, but we also joy in God through our
Lord Jesus Christ . . ." (Romans 5:11-12).
"And without controversy great is the mystery of
godliness: . . ." (1 Timothy 3:16).
"For if any be a hearer of the word, and not a doer . . ."
(James 1:23-24).

As one example of Dr. O'Callaghan's study, he examined a
small scroll fragment known as 7Q5 that contained only twenty
Greek letters on five lines of text. Many of the thousands of
scroll fragments that were successfully identified from the
Qumran site are equally small. Another scroll scholar, Carsten
Thiede, agrees with O'Callaghan that portions of the Mark 6:
52,53 passage appears in this scroll fragment. While other scroll
scholars disagree with the identification of this fragment as a
verse from the New Testament they do admit that almost all

of the scrolls found in Cave Seven were written in the period between 50 B.C., and A.D. 50, which is consistent with the time of the writing of the Gospel of Mark.

Naturally, as with other matters connected with the controversial Dead Sea Scrolls, many scholars disagreed with the conclusions of Dr. O'Callaghan. The debate still continues twenty years later. At this stage we cannot be certain that O'Callaghan's conclusion is correct. More work needs to be done. However, the recent publication of the discovery of Scroll 4Q246 and its obvious parallel to "the Son of God" as found in Luke 1:32 and 35, provides strong support for the possibility that these fragments are related to these New Testament passages. In addition, I have great hopes that the new archeological exploration of recently detected caves at Qumran by my friend Gary Collett may provide new evidence including New Testament references. Many of these mysteries will be solved when the four hundred unpublished scrolls are finally published in the next few years. The new dig at Qumran may also uncover additional scrolls that will help us understand more clearly the Messianic beliefs of this group of religious men and women who lived at this desert site during the time when Jesus walked the earth.

When we consider the total amount of evidence that confirms the biblical record about Jesus of Nazareth we can have confidence that we know more about the life, death, and resurrection of Christ than we know about any other person in the ancient world. God has not left us in darkness concerning the truthfulness of the miracles, prophecies and teaching of His Son, Jesus Christ.

Notes

1. Internet site: http://www.songtime.com/sbcsearch.htm
2. C. S. Lewis, *Mere Christianity* (New York: The Macmillan Company, 1952).
3. Flavius Josephus, *Antiquities of the Jews* trans. William Whiston, (Grand Rapids: Kregel Publications,1960).
4. Simon Greenleaf, *Testimony of the Evangelists* (Grand Rapids: Baker House, 1956).
5. William Ramsay, *The Bearing of Recent Discovery on the Trustworthiness of the New Testament* (Grand Rapids: Baker Book House, 1953) 80.
6. Lionel Luckhoo, *Evidence Irrefutable Which Can Change Your Lives*. Dallas: Luckhoo Ministries).
7. Otto Betz, *What Do We Know About Jesus?* (Westminster Press, Philadelphia, 1968).
8. Solomon Zeitlin, "The Halaka in the Gospels and its Relation to the Jewish Law at the time of Jesus" (*Hebrew Union College Annual*) Vol. I p 372-373.
9. Solomon Zeitlin, "The Halaka in the Gospels and its Relation to the Jewish Law at the time of Jesus" (*Hebrew Union College Annual*) Vol. I p 372-373.
10. Frederick F. Bruce, *The New Testament Documents: Are They Reliable?* (Downers Grove, IL: Inter Varsity Press, 1967).
11. William Albright, *Recent Discoveries in Bible Lands* (New York: Funk and Wagnalls, 1955).
12. Internet site: http://www.geocities.com/Athens/Parthenon/2104/biblioNT.html.
13. Frederic G. Kenyon, *The Story of the Bible*, Special U.S. Edition (Grand Rapids: Eerdmans Co. 1967) 133.
14. Merrill F. Unger, *Archeology and the New Testament* (Grand Rapids: Zondervan Publishing House, 1962).
15. Bernard Ramm, *Protestant Christian Evidences* (Chicago: Moody Press, 1957), 239.
16. Bernard Ramm, *Protestant Christian Evidences* (Chicago: Moody Press, 1957), 239.
17. Tacitus, *Annals*, XV 44. A.D. 112.
18. Suetonius, *Life of Claudius*, 25.4, A.D. 125.

19. Pliny the Younger, *Epistle* X. 96. A.D. 112.
20. Pliny the Younger, *Epistle* X. 96. A.D. 112.
21. Lucian of Samosata, *The Passing Peregrinus.*
22. Flavius Josephus, *Antiquities of the Jews* trans. William Whiston (Grand Rapids: Kregel Publications,1960. Bk. XVIII, Chap. III, Section 3).
23. Phillip Schaff, *History of the Christian Church* (Oak Harbor, WA: Logos Research Systems, Inc.) 1997.
24. Craig Blomberg, *The Historical Reliability of the Gospels.* (Intervasity Press,1987).
25. Arnold Toynbee, ZPEG (vol. 3:697).
26. Flavius Josephus, *Antiquities of the Jews* trans. William Whiston (Grand Rapids: Kregel Publications,1960.Book. XX, Chap. IX, sect. 1).
27. Flavius Josephus, *Antiquities of the Jews* trans. William Whiston (Grand Rapids: Kregel Publications,1960. Book. XVIII, Chap. V, sect. 2).
28. Julius Africanus, *Post Nicene Fathers*, Edinborough,
29. Charles R. Condor, *Palestine Exploration Fund Report*, Quarterly Report, April,1875.
30. Charles R. Condor, *Palestine Exploration Fund*, Quarterly Report, January 187, p. 98.
31. Philip Schaff, *The Person of Christ* American Tract Society, 1913.
32. Robert Eisenman, *The Dead Sea Scrolls Uncovered* New York: Penguin USA, 1993.
33. Geza Vermes, *The Dead Sea Scrolls in English* London: Penguin Books, 1987.
34. Jose O'Callaghan, *Bible Review*, December, 1995.

5

Scientific Evidence that the Bible is Accurate

The greatest evidence that the Scriptures are truly inspired by God is that they reveal an astonishing amount of advanced scientific knowledge that cannot be explained unless a supernatural source inspired the Scriptures. The Bible is not a scientific book; however, when it does make scientific statements, they are stunning in their accuracy. These biblical statements were thousands of years in advance of the scientific knowledge present in the day when the writers penned the words of the Holy Scriptures. The psalmist David wrote, "That I may publish with the voice of thanksgiving, and tell of all thy wondrous works" (Psalm 26:7). As you consider God's "wondrous works" and the astonishing level of scientific knowledge from the Bible presented in this chapter, ask yourself a question: How could the writers of the Scriptures possibly know these facts unless they were supernaturally inspired by God?

Throughout the Word of God are statements that can now be tested as to their accuracy due to the incredible advances in

The Signature of God

scientific knowledge in the last few decades. The Book of Genesis describes the supernatural creation of man in these words, "And the Lord God formed man of the dust of the ground, and breathed into his nostrils the breath of life; and man became a living being" (Genesis 2:7). For many years scientists laughed at the apparent simplicity of the scriptural account that God used "the dust of the ground" to construct the complex elements and molecules that make up a human being. However, after a century of scientific examination of the elements within the human body, scientists have been startled to discover that clay and earth contain every single element found in the human body. A *Reader's Digest* article in November 1982, described a fascinating discovery by the researchers at NASA's Ames Research Center which confirmed the Bible's account that every single element found in the human body exists within the soil. The scientists concluded, "We are just beginning to learn. The biblical scenario for the creation of life turns out to be not far off the mark."[1]

It might surprise you to know that many of the greatest scientific minds of the last several centuries were Bible-believing Christians who totally accepted the scientific accuracy of the Word of God. For example, Isaac Newton, perhaps the greatest scientific mind in history, firmly accepted the Word of God and creation. Other strong believers in God who changed the face of scientific knowledge included: Lord Kelvin, the creator of the science of thermodynamics; Louis Pasteur, the discover of penicillin; Johann Kepler, the brilliant astronomer who created modern astronomy; and Robert Boyle, the greatest chemist of his age. With every new scientific discovery we find additional proof of the complexity of the great design that God used to create our universe.

The Creation of The Universe

The Book of Genesis begins with the words, "God created the heaven and the earth." Until 1950, most scientists believed in some variation of the "steady state theory," which suggested that the universe had eternally existed as we observe it today. This theory was in total contradiction to the Word of God which, as recorded in its opening pages, affirms that

God had created the entire universe at a definite point of time in the past. New discoveries in astronomy and astrophysics then forced the scientific world to change their theory. Today, virtually all scientists accept some variation of the "Big Bang Theory" that suggests the whole universe came into existence at a particular point of time, when an incredibly dense mass of matter exploded, forming all of the stars, galaxies, and planets we witness today.

Dr. P. Dirac, a Nobel Prize winner from Cambridge University, wrote: "It seems certain that there was a definite time of creation." Until quite recently, the word creation was never written or spoken by scientists with approval. Then, a scientific article in the 1982 issue of *Physics Letters*, an international journal of physics, contained an article by Dr. A. Vilenkin which was entitled, *Creation of the Universe From Nothing*, that noted scientists claim the creation of the universe is "outside the scope of presently known laws of physics."[2]

The Word of God clearly tells us that "God created the heaven and the earth." (Genesis 1:1). However, in opposition to the theoretical explosion of the Big Bang Theory, the Bible affirms that God created everything in the universe with absolute purpose and intelligence. The evidence from nature and the incredible scientific discoveries pointed out in this book reveal the meticulous design of the supernatural intelligence and power of God in that initial moment of creation when "God created the heaven and the earth."

The Lord challenged Abraham to count the stars to demonstrate the awesome number that He had created by His supernatural power. "Then He brought him outside and said, 'Look now toward heaven, and count the stars if you are able to number them.' And He said to him, 'So shall your descendants be' " (Genesis 15:5). The unaided human eye can see and count about 1,029 stars. With a pair of binoculars or an inexpensive telescope you can see over 3,300 stars. In the last few years modern telescopes have allowed us to view over two hundred million stars in our own galaxy called the Milky Way.

As late as 1915 astronomers believed that our galaxy composed the entire universe. Then in 1925, the great astronomer

Edwin Hubble used his new one-hundred-inch mirror telescope on Mount Wilson, the largest in the world at that time, to view whole new galaxies of stars that were more than six million trillion miles away from earth. Professor Hubble proved that the universe contained as many galaxies outside our galaxy as there were stars inside our home galaxy, the Milky Way. During the last century very powerful telescopes of astronomers revealed the known universe contains over ten billion galaxies like our Milky Way. However, in the last few months, scientists have used the Hubble Telescope to focus on a tiny point in space so small that it is equal to focusing your eye on an area the size of a grain of sand held at arm's length.

After intensely examining this very small area of space the astronomers determined that it contained an additional fifteen hundred galaxies, each the size of our Milky Way. They were astonished to discover that the universe is more than five times larger than we previously believed. They now know that the known universe contains more than fifty billion galaxies with each galaxy containing more than two hundred million stars. The mind of man can scarcely conceive of such a vast universe in which stars extend out from our solar system for millions of trillions of miles in every direction. To obtain a sense of the vastness of our universe, try this exercise.

Take a piece of paper and draw two circles with one small circle representing our sun at the top of the page. Using the scale of one inch to represent ten million miles, draw a much smaller circle nine inches lower at the bottom of the page to represent our earth. Now let's draw another small circle to represent our nearest neighboring star, Alpha Centauri. You would need to draw the circle representing the star Alpha Centauri over forty miles away from your piece of paper to correctly represent the vast distance between the earth and the closest star. Light travels through space at an amazing speed of 187,000 miles every second or six trillion miles every year. A ray of light leaving our closest neighbor, Alpha Centauri, would take four years to reach our planet as it crosses an astonishing twenty-four trillion miles of empty space.

The psalmist David wrote, "By the word of the Lord the

heavens were made, And all the host of them by the breath of His mouth. . . . For He spoke, and it was done; He commanded, and it stood fast" (Psalm 33:6,9). Despite all of the billions spent on astronomy, scientists have failed to come up with a credible theory to account for the existence of either the universe or even our own earth. In 1980, the astronomer Professor Herman Bondi declared the total failure of modern science to account for the universe: "As an erstwhile cosmologist, I speak with feeling of the fact that theories of the origin of the universe have been disproved by present day empirical evidence as have various theories of the origin of the solar system."[3] Another great astronomer, Sir Harold Jeffreys, wrote, "To sum up, I think that all suggested accounts of the origin of the solar system are subject to serious objections. The conclusion in the present state of the subject would be that the system cannot exist."[4] In other words, Professor Jeffreys admitted that none of the atheistic theories can account for the universe as it exists. Perhaps they should return to the first words in Genesis as recorded by Moses, "In the beginning God created the heaven and the earth" (Genesis 1:1).

The Bible declares that God separated the waters below from the waters that were above (in the heavens): "And God said, Let there be a firmament in the midst of the waters, and let it divide the waters from the waters. And God made the firmament, and divided the waters which were under the firmament from the waters which were above the firmament: and it was so" (Genesis 1:6,7). This biblical statement declares that God created a large amount of water which He placed in the heavens or outer space. Does any evidence exist to prove the accuracy of this statement from the Bible? The existence of water in space seemed improbable, to say the least, to scientists until quite recently. However, further astronomical discoveries have proven conclusively that massive amounts of water do exist in space, just as the Bible claimed. Naturally, because of extreme temperatures, the waters in space are frozen into permanent ice. Recently our satellites discovered large quantities of ice in the ice caps of Mars as well as in the rings of Saturn. In addition, we now know that the huge comets that travel through our solar system are composed of massive amounts of ice. NASA announced on March 5, 1998, that the Lunar Prospector spacecraft had detected evidence of massive amounts of ice beneath the surface of the moon (estimated at 6.6 billion tons). (Internet: http://nssdc.gsfc.nasa.gov/planetary/ice/inc_moon.html)

A massive block of ice from space collided with the earth at the beginning of this century at a point in northern Russia: "In the morning of 30 June 1908, a fantastic explosion occurred in central Siberia. . . . Witnesses described an enormous meteoric bolide visible in the sky for a few seconds. Other witnesses from a distance of 60 kilometers (36 miles) from the point of impact were knocked over. . . . Seismic shocks were registered over the whole world . . . this event was due to the collision with the earth of a block of ice weighing 30,000 tons which . . . released energy equivalent to that of a thermonuclear bomb of 12 megatons."[5] Researchers found that this Siberian explosion was caused by a small fragment of the comet Encke that broke away during its passage through our solar system. The latest scientific research has revealed that massive amounts of ice also exist at the outer edge of our solar system. The Ort Cloud at the edge of our solar system is a vast region of space that is estimated to hold as many as a trillion large comets composed of ice and rock. Each large comet is calculated to contain as much as one trillion tons of ice. The vast amount of water in our oceans is less than a fraction of the quantities of water that exist in the "firmament above" in the heavens as reported in the Book of Genesis. A passage in Job also refers to the ice and frost in the heavens: "Hath the rain a father? or who hath begotten the drops of dew? Out of whose womb came the ice? and the hoary frost of heaven, who hath gendered it? The waters are hid as with a stone, and the face of the deep is frozen. Canst thou bind the sweet influences of Pleiades, or loose the bands of Orion?" (Job 38:28-31).

The Law of Conservation of Energy

After exhaustive experiments, modern scientists have developed two fundamental laws of the science of thermodynamics that describe the nature of our known universe. The first law is the Law of Conservation of Energy which reveals that "energy can be neither created nor destroyed." The Law of Conservation of Energy was explained by the science writer Isaac Asimov as follows: "Energy can be transferred from one place to another, or transformed from one form to another, but it can be neither created nor destroyed." In other words, this law states that the whole amount of energy that exists throughout our universe remains constant and can never change. For example, when they explode a nuclear device, the uranium 235 and plutonium within the warhead are not annihilated. The matter is simply transformed into a staggering release of heat and light energy. Every experiment has confirmed this Law of Conservation of Energy as the most basic fundamental understanding of the way the universe works. This law describes the present state of the universe after its initial creation by God.

Although this fundamental law of the universe was only discovered and proven scientifically during the last century, the Word of God recorded this principle thousands of years ago. Moses wrote in Genesis: "And on the seventh day God ended his work which he had made; and he rested on the seventh day from all his work which he had made. And God blessed the seventh day, and sanctified it: because that in it he had rested from all his work which God created and made" (Genesis 2:2,3). This inspired passage clearly declares that when God completed the creation of man on the sixth day, "He rested from all His work which He had made." After He created man on the sixth day, His work was complete: this accounts for the First Law of Conservation of Energy. In addition, the Scriptures reveal why nothing can now be either totally destroyed or annihilated because Jesus Christ, who created all things, is "upholding all things by the word of His power" (Hebrews 1:3). In another passage the writer of the Book of Hebrews declared that Jesus, the Creator of the universe, had finished His acts of creation: "For he that is entered into his rest, he also hath ceased from his own works, as God did from his" (Hebrews 4:10).

The Law of Entropy

The second law of science is the Law of Entropy. This second Law of Thermodynamics describes the fact that all systems and elements of the universe tend to disintegrate to a lower order of available energy or organization. Another way of expressing this universal fact of entropy is to note that, over time, all things, whether a house or a sword, will tend to disintegrate to dust or rust, a lower order of organization than the original house or sword. Throughout history mankind has observed that everything, from a human body to a castle, begins to decay from the moment of maximum amount of order or organized information at the beginning until, years later, the object ceases to function. When you think seriously about this universal principle you can immediately see that this principle proves that it is absolutely impossible for the theory of evolution to be true. Evolution suggests that all simple systems and elements become increasingly more organized and complicated by random chance. However, common sense and scientific observation have proven that all systems and elements over time tend to disintegrate to something less organized and less useful. In fact, the second Law of Thermodynamics, the Law of Entropy, absolutely proves the theory of evolution is nonsense.

Consider the implications. The Law of Conservation of Energy proves that the universe could not have created itself. It had to be created by a supernatural force outside the universe. "In the beginning God created the heaven and the earth" (Genesis 1:1). However, the Law of Entropy shows that the whole universe is running down as it decays to a lower order of available energy. This fact reveals that the universe must have been created at some point in the past and has been running down like a clock ever since that initial moment of creation. The current evolutionary theory that postulates a universe that was created from nothing by itself is totally contradicted by all the known laws of science. In addition, the Law of Entropy reveals that the universe must have been created at some definite point in the past to account for the fact that all scientific observation confirms that everything continues to decay. As an example, the fact that the sun burns up its nuclear fuel, at the rate of 200,000 nuclear explosions every second, provides the enormous radiation that floods our solar system. However, since it is burning up its store of fuel, logic declares that there must have been a point in time somewhere in the distant past when the sun was created and began this process.

The Gospel writer Luke described the coming of Christ in the daytime as follows: "Even thus shall it be in the day when the Son of man is revealed." However, several verses later, Luke described the same event by declaring that Christ will come in the night: "I tell you, in that night there shall be two men in one bed; the one shall be taken, and the other shall be left" (Luke 17:34). To the natural mind of his day, Luke's words must have sounded like a contradiction. How could a single event, the coming of the Messiah, occur simultaneously "in the day" and "in the night"? This statement by Luke must have appeared impossible and contradictory at any time from the first century until recently. However, we can now understand that, on whatever day Christ returns, it will be a daytime event for those on one side of the globe while the event will occur during the night for those living on the other side of the planet. How could Luke have known this scientific fact two thousand years ago?

The psalmist David wrote a wonderful song of praise to God in recognition of the awesome glory of the heavens that he could witness from the roof of his palace in Jerusalem: "Their line has gone out through all the earth, And their words to the end of the world. In them He has set a tabernacle for the sun, Which is like a bridegroom coming out of his chamber, And rejoices like a strong man to run its race. Its rising is from one end of heaven, And its circuit to the other end; And there is nothing hidden from its heat" (Psalm 19:4-6). In his song of praise King David declared that the sun traveled in "his circuit unto the ends of it [the heavens]." During the last few centuries many Bible critics denounced this statement as inaccurate because they falsely claimed the Bible's statement declared that the sun moved in an orbit around the earth. However, the Bible never made that claim. The Scriptures declare that the sun moved "in his circuit unto the ends of it [the heavens]." Recent discoveries by the Hubble Telescope confirmed the accuracy of the Scriptures when they proved that the sun actually moves through space in a circuit covering an enormous orbit that lasts over two hundred and sixty million years.

The Earth – Created by God For Humans

Critics of the Bible have often falsely suggested that the Bible stated the earth was flat because of the biblical expression, "the four corners of the earth" (Isaiah 11:12; Revelation 7:1), as if the writers actually believed in a flat earth. However, this phrase was simply a colloquial expression. It is still used by educated individuals to indicate either the whole earth or the four extremities of the globe from a central position. God inspired the prophet Isaiah to reveal that our planet was a globe, knowledge that was far in advance of what the men in that day knew. "It is he that sitteth upon the circle of the earth, and the inhabitants thereof are as grasshoppers; that stretcheth out the heavens as a curtain, and spreadeth them out as a tent to dwell in" (Isaiah 40:22). This expression "the circle of the earth" clearly describes the earth as a sphere or globe.

The Book of Job tells us that, "He stretcheth out the north over empty space; he hangs the earth on nothing" (Job 26:7). This was an astonishingly advanced and accurate scientific statement. The ancient pagans, who were contemporary with Job, believed that the earth was balanced on the back of an elephant that rested on the back of a turtle. Other pagans believed that the mythological hero Atlas carried the earth on his shoulders. However, four thousand years ago, Job was inspired by God to correctly declare that God "hangs the earth on nothing." Only a century ago scientists believed that the earth and stars were supported by some kind of ether. Yet Job accurately stated that our planet moves in its orbit through empty outer space. An astonishing discovery by astronomers recently revealed that the area to the north of the axis of our earth toward the polar star is almost empty of stars in contrast to the other directions. There are far more distant stars in every other direction from our earth than in the area to the far north of our planet. As Job reported, "He stretches out the north over empty space" (Job 26:

7). Mitchell Waldrop wrote the following statement in an article in *Science* magazine. "The recently announced 'hole in space,' a 300 million-light-year gap in the distribution of galaxies, has taken cosmologists by surprise. . . . But three very deep core samples in the Northern Hemisphere, lying in the general direction of the constellation Bootes, showed striking gaps in the red shift distribution."[6] This relative emptiness in the direction to the North of our solar system is not visible by the naked eye. It is only as the result of very careful observation by telescopes that scientists have recently proven that Job was correct.

Jewish scholars in Israel have calculated that the Torah describes the exact duration of the time that passes between the appearance of new moons as precisely 29 days, 12 hours, 44 minutes and 5 seconds or 29.53059 days. With billions of dollars of research and sophisticated observation through telescopes NASA has only recently calculated that a new moon appears every 29.530588 days! The Scriptures declare, "In the beginning God created the heaven and the earth" (Genesis 1:1). This statement revealed that God created our earth and the universe in a single moment of time. However, Genesis also reveals God's purpose: "Then God blessed them, and God said to them, 'Be fruitful and multiply; fill the earth and subdue it; have dominion over the fish of the sea, over the birds of the air, and over every living thing that moves on the earth' " (Genesis 1:28).

After examining the complexity of the variables that govern this solar system and our planet earth many scientists have declared that this solar system is "anthropic." This word simply means that this earth bears evidence that it was designed by a superior intelligence to allow human life to exist. The scientists use this word "anthropic" to indicate that they have discovered an astonishing number of scientific variables that fit within a very narrow range that allows human life to exist on this planet. Let me explain. If our earth was located much farther away from our sun we would freeze like the planet Mars. If it was much closer to the sun then we would be burned up like the hot surface of Mercury or the 860-degree temperature on Venus. If the magnetic forces within our planet were stronger or weaker, life could not exist. If our earth did not revolve every twenty-four hours then one-half of the planet would be in permanent darkness without vegetation. Meanwhile, if the earth did not revolve, the other side of the planet would be an uninhabitable desert as it suffered from the overwhelming heat of permanent exposure to the sun.

If our earth was not tilted at twenty-three degrees, we would not have the seasonal variation that produces the incredible abundance of crops that feed our planet's huge population. Without the twenty-three degree tilt, less than half of the present land used for cultivation of crops would grow vegetables. The moon produces the tides that continually replenish the oceans with oxygen allowing the fish to breathe. If the earth were significantly smaller, the lessened gravity would be incapable of holding the atmosphere that is essential for breathing. A much thinner atmosphere would provide no protection from the 25,000 meteors that burn up in the atmosphere over the earth every day. In addition, a thinner atmosphere would be incapable of retaining the higher temperatures required for human and animal life to exist. If our planet earth was twice as large, the effect of increased gravity would make everything on the planet's surface weigh eight times what it weighs today. This increased weight would destroy many forms of animal and human life.

Professor Robert Jastrow has stated that "the smallest change in any of the circumstances of the natural world, such as the relative strengths of the forces of nature, or the properties of the elementary particles, would have led to a universe in which there could be no life and no man. For example, if nuclear forces were decreased by a few percent, the particles of the universe would not have come together in nuclear reactions to make the ingredients, such as carbon atoms, of which life must be constructed."[7] The professor noted, the same argument can be made about the strength of the electromagnetic force and the strength of the gravitational force. In other words, if the universe was changed in the slightest way, no human life could exist. The ultimate conclusion of these scientists is that our universe, solar system and, especially, our earth was purposely constructed by a very powerful intelligence within very narrow scientific parameters to allow human life to flourish. The prophet Nehemiah wrote the following declaration centuries before the birth of Jesus Christ: "You alone are the Lord; you have made heaven, the heaven of heavens, with all their host, The earth and everything on it, The Seas and all that is in them. And You preserve them all. The host of heaven worships You" (Nehemiah 9:6).

The Hydrological Cycle of Weather

People living in past centuries did not have a clear understanding about the weather and climatic patterns that controlled our planet's environment. However, the books of Job, Ecclesiastes, Isaiah and Jeremiah all describe details about the complexity of the weather system far beyond the knowledge of the inhabitants living at that time. The complete hydrological cycle governing evaporation, cloud formation, thunder, lightning and rain is explained in surprising detail in the words of the Old Testament. For example, Ecclesiastes states, "If the clouds be full of rain, they empty themselves upon the earth" (Ecclesiastes 11:3). Ecclesiastes confirms that most clouds are formed by evaporation from the oceans: "All the rivers run into the sea, yet the sea is not full; to the place from which the rivers come, there they return again" (Ecclesiastes 1:7). Interestingly, a recent study by the United States Department of Agriculture proved that most of the water that forms into the clouds worldwide comes from the evaporation of the waters found in the oceans that cover over seventy percent of the planet's surface.

The Book of Job asked the question, "Do you know how the clouds are balanced, Those wondrous works of Him who is perfect in knowledge?" (Job 37:16). When you consider the weight of water compared to air it is astonishing that enormous quantities of water are raised from the oceans and lakes every hour by evaporation and lifted thousands of feet in the air where they remain suspended for long periods. Air rises upward as it cools supporting the water vapor in the clouds until the drops become large and heavy enough to fall to earth as rain. The answer is also found in Job, "For He draws up drops of water, which distil as rain from the mist, Which the clouds drop down and pour abundantly on man. Indeed, can anyone understand the spreading of clouds, the thunders from His canopy?" (Job 36:27-29). This incredible biblical passage reveals the complete hydrological cycle of evaporation, cloud formation, and precipitation.

The Complexity of Weather Patterns

King Solomon described the complex climatic circular wind patterns that determine the weather throughout the globe. "The wind goes toward the south, and turns around to the north; the wind whirls about continually, and comes again on its circuit" (Ecclesiastes 1:6). How could Solomon have known three thousand years ago that the planetary winds followed a circular pattern from south to north and south again? Job speaks of God controlling the weather: "For He looketh to the ends of the earth, and seeth under the whole heaven; To establish a weight for the wind, and apportion the waters by measure. When He made a law for the rain and a path for the thunderbolt" (Job 28:24-26). In this intriguing statement the Bible reveals that the winds are governed by their weight, a fact that scientists have only determined in the last century. How could Job have known that the air and the wind patterns are governed by their actual weight? Meteorologists have found that the relative weights of the wind and water greatly determine the weather patterns.

This passage also reveals a profound appreciation of the fact that there is a scientific connection between lightning, thunder, and the triggering of rainfall. Apparently, a slight change in the electrical charge within a cloud is one of the key factors that causes microscopic water droplets in the clouds to join with other droplets until they are heavy enough to fall to earth. In addition, we now know that a powerful electrical charge as high as 300 million volts in a cloud sends a leader stroke down through the air to the ground. Instantaneously, only one-fiftieth of a second later, a second more powerful return stroke travels back up to the cloud following the path through the air opened by the leader stroke. The thunder occurs because the air within this channel or path has been vaporized by superheating it to fifty thousand degrees by the lightning. The superheated air expands outward at supersonic speed creating the noise of thunder. Job's description, "He made a law for the rain and a path for the thunderbolt" (Job 28:26) is startling in its accuracy. No human could have known this in ancient times without the divine revelation of God.

King David, the writer of Psalms, refers mysteriously to "the paths of the seas." He wrote, "The fowl of the air, and the fish of the sea, and whatsoever passeth through the paths of the seas" (Psalm 8:8). It wasn't till 1786 that Benjamin Franklin published the information he gleaned from conversations with ocean-going captains that huge currents such as the Gulf Stream ran like deep rivers far beneath the surface of the Atlantic Ocean. The massive Gulf Stream carries more than five thousand times as much water as the great Mississippi River. This awesome current that warms the climate of the U.K. and Western Europe, carries more than twenty-five times as much water as all the rivers on the planet. Scientists have discovered that the Gulf Stream is only a small part of an enormous "gyre," a huge thirteen-thousand-mile current of water circling the Atlantic Ocean. They have recently discovered that the Pacific Ocean has its own "Black Current" gyre as well.

CNN ran a news report in May 1996, of marine scientists' discovery of a massive river of water flowing north beneath the Pacific Ocean, parallel to the coast of the western United States. However, they also found that another huge current ran under the surface of the ocean above the first current, only this higher current flowed south at a very fast flow rate. The turbulence produced by these opposing currents passing each other at different depths in the Pacific produced massive storms beneath the surface of the ocean. These massive currents not only warm the north of the planet but they are also essential to refreshing the otherwise stagnant waters of the ocean and constitute an essential part of the life system of the planet. How could King David have known thousands of years ago that there were huge currents or rivers that existed in the depths of the boundless oceans?

In another passage Job referred to deep springs of water at the bottom of the ocean. "Have you entered the springs of the sea? Or have you walked in search of the depths?" (Job 38:16). In this verse the Bible refers to the existence of springs of water flowing beneath the depths of the sea. It is only in the last thirty years that underwater exploration of the ocean depths has revealed a remarkable phenomenon of numerous huge springs of fresh water pouring out of the ocean floor. The Book of Job also contains questions that suggest a level of knowledge that would be impossible for a human writer living in the Middle East during ancient times. For example, Job refers to deep oceans whose surface waters are frozen hard like a stone: "From whose womb comes the ice? And the frost of heaven, who gives it birth? The waters harden like a stone, And the surface of the deep is frozen" (Job 38:29,30). How could someone like Job, living in the area of Saudi Arabia in ancient times, have known about Arctic ice caps?

Evolution or Creation?

Billions of people have been taught throughout their life that science has proved that evolution is true and that the Bible is scientifically wrong about creation. As a result of this virtually universal acceptance, evolution has destroyed the faith of countless people during the past one hundred and fifty years. This false theory of evolution has caused untold numbers of people to refuse to seriously consider the claims of the Bible regarding personal salvation because they wrongly believed the Bible was full of errors. The theory of evolution holds that there is no God and that everything in the whole universe, including the complexities of biological life, has developed by random chance over billions of years.

However, the theory of evolution is falling apart today in the face of the total lack of evidence to support its hypothesis. Very few scientists still subscribe to the original theory of evolution as proposed by Charles Darwin over a century ago. Many of them accept that the mathematical odds against life forming by random chance is impossible. As one example, Dr. Harold Urey, a Nobel Prize winner for his research in chemistry wrote about the impossibility of evolution, but still admitted he believed in the theory! "All of us who study the origin of life find that the more we look into it, the more we feel that it is too complex to have evolved anywhere." Incredibly, Dr. Urey then added these words, "*We believe as an article of faith that life evolved from dead matter on this planet. It is just that its complexity is so great, it is hard for us to imagine that it did.*" (Italics added). His admission proved that his acceptance of evolution was not based on logic or evidence, but on blind faith. He found the alternative to evolution, a divine Creator, totally unacceptable. At the Alpach Symposium conference which dealt with the growing problems with the theory of evolution, one of the speakers admitted that the reason evolution was still supported by intellectuals, the education establishment, and the media had nothing to do with whether it was true or false. "I think that the fact that a theory so vague, so insufficiently verifiable and so far from the criteria otherwise applied in 'hard' science has become a dogma can be explained only on sociological grounds."[8] In other words, evolution survived despite the lack of evidence because they wanted to believe it was true.

Darwin admitted that millions of "missing links," transitional life forms, would have to be discovered in the fossil record to prove the accuracy of his theory that all species had gradually evolved by chance mutation into new species. Unfortunately for his theory, despite hundreds of millions spent on searching for fossils worldwide for more than a century, the scientists have failed to locate a single missing link out of the millions that must exist if their theory of evolution is to be vindicated. It is significant that the various educational groups supporting evolutionary teaching have encouraged their members to refuse to enter debates about evolution with creation science supporters at high schools and colleges. The evolution supporters found to their dismay that the audiences almost always believed in evolution before the debate began but that they accepted the evidence for divine creation by the end of the debate.

It is not my purpose to fully explore the errors of evolution, nor to fully present the overwhelming evidence for the creation of the universe by God. Many excellent scholars have written books that demolish the theory of evolution in defense of the Bible's account of creation. In the Appendix at the end of this book I list several excellent books that I strongly recommend to anyone who wishes to study this subject in depth. However, I will outline in this chapter some of the compelling evidence that proves that evolution is simply impossible and supports creation as outlined in the Bible. As we explore this topic we will also encounter overwhelming evidence proving the inspiration of the Scriptures.

When you understand the incredible number of problems with the theory of evolution you are immediately struck with the thought that there is something very strange about the continuing universal acceptance of this theory. However, the answer is clear. If the theory of evolution is rejected, then people have no other credible alternative than the Bible's account of creation by a personal God. This alternative is unacceptable to many people in modern society because they dread the thought of facing their God. They would like to evade this issue by firmly avoiding examining the overwhelming evidence against evolution through the use of ridicule and rejection. In the final analysis the greatest obstacle to seeing the truth about God's role in creation is often our own attitudes and prejudices. If we will lay aside our former attitudes and carefully examine the evidence, the truth about creation as well as our need for a relationship with God will become evident through the Scriptures.

The odds against life evolving by chance on earth are absolutely staggering. It is impossible to believe that the awesome complexity involved in the simplest living cell could have occurred as a result of chance even if this process had occurred over billions of years. Scientists found that over twenty different amino acids are required to produce the proteins that exist in the smallest living cell. Despite scientific experiments where they tried to create these twenty amino acids in the laboratory, they failed every time. The proteins that make up living cells are composed of long thin lines of amino acids only one-millionth the size of a human hair. The smallest living thing contains more than five hundred amino acids. All amino acids have side groups of atoms. Scientists found that 50 percent of the side groups of atoms that are attached to non-living amino acids are on the left side and another 50 percent are on the right side.

When biologists examined proteins within living cells they discovered that all proteins are "left handed." In other words, all living cells contain amino acids with their side group of atoms on the left side only. Amino acids produced in a laboratory are exactly like those found in non-living matter with 50 percent "left-handed" and 50 percent "right-handed." Yet, living cells can only exist when the atoms are solely "left-handed." To calculate the likelihood of life occurring by chance, the scientists calculated the probability that amino acids would form chains of atoms solely on the "left-hand." The odds against this happening by chance are one chance in 10^{123}. In other words, it is absolutely impossible that even a single protein could have been formed by chance alone, let alone the staggering number of awesomely complex proteins that make up the multitude of living creatures in our world. The only logical explanation for this situation is the instantaneous creation by God.

The proteins in living creatures are composed of long chains of different amino acids that must be linked together in a precise sequence to allow the protein to live. The evolutionary scientist believes that these complex amino acids simply came together by chance in the exact necessary sequence to allow life to exist. This is mathematically impossible. Mathematicians have calculated that the odds against these five hundred amino acids lining up in the correct order to produce one single living cell is equal to one chance in 10^{200} which is ten followed by two hundred zeros. To put these numbers in perspective, remember that one trillion is 10^{12}, which is ten followed by twelve zeros. Even if the amino acids and chemicals could combine together a trillion times faster than they do in the laboratory, and the experiment used every single atom on the planet, the odds against a single living protein forming by chance would be less than one chance in ten followed by one hundred and sixty-six zeros. This incredible number vastly exceeds the total number of atoms within the known universe. The odds against a single living protein being formed by chance alone is equal to the chance that a blind-folded man could locate a single grain of sand painted gold within a universe composed of fifty billion galaxies of two hundred million stars apiece composed of nothing but sand.

However, the formation of life requires far more complex structures than simple amino acids and proteins. DNA (DeoxyriboNucleic Acid) creates the genetic code that commands the various elements in the cell to form the building blocks of life itself. Mathematicians have calculated that the odds against a single DNA gene forming by chance is equal to one chance in ten followed by one hundred and fifty-five zeros, a number that staggers the mind. Anyone who can believe that life on earth evolved by random chance without the presence of a supernatural intelligence designer must do so on absolute blind faith. Their decision to accept evolution reflects a deep need to evade the overwhelming evidence and logic that proves the universe was created by a divine intelligent being — God.

The Genetic DNA Code Governing Life

The incredibly intricate genetic DNA code controls every element and cell in the body of any biological creature. The genetic code contains a staggering amount of information. Professor Leslie Orgel, a scientist working in this area wrote: "The origin of the genetic code is the most baffling aspect of the origins of life."[9] Scientists who study genetics realize that the amount of genetic information encoded in the DNA of the most simple form of life, contains an almost inconceivable amount of information that is far more complicated than the computer software that runs the complete accounting program controlling the inventory, costs, sales and financial records of hundreds of General Motors plants throughout the world. Sir Fred Hoyle, one of the greatest biologists in the last century wrote: "Precious little in the way of biochemical evolution could have happened on the earth. If one counts the number of trial assemblies of amino acids that are needed to give rise to the enzymes, the probability of their discovery by random shufflings turn out to be less than one in 10,400,000.[10]

As a result of his findings, Hoyle eventually abandoned his agnosticism and became a believer in a special creation of life. Several top scientists have concluded that life must have been brought from outer space to the earth due to the impossible mathematical odds against the spontaneous development of life on earth. Some of these scientists, such as Sir Fred Hoyle and Dr. Frances Crick arrived at the theory that life originated in some far part of the universe and was later imported to earth by some extraterrestrial intelligence. However, this novel solution does not solve their problem at all. This solution only pushes the problem away from the earth to some unknown place in space. How could life have been created by random chance in some far part of the universe? Obviously, only God could have created life with all of its incredible complexity and order.

The Book of Proverbs declares that, "A merry heart does good, like medicine, but a broken spirit dries the bones" (Proverbs 17:22). While many Bible readers accepted this advice from Proverbs as a general statement, they would be surprised to learn that modern psychiatry has discovered that good humor and laughter truly improves our overall health. An article in the *Birmingham News* entitled "Laughter: Prescription for Health," confirms the statement found in Proverbs. "At some point during laughter, your body issues a prescription from the pharmacy in your brain." The article revealed that scientists discovered that the emotion of humor triggers the release of certain hormones and endorphins that greatly improve our overall sense of well-being.

Moses, in Leviticus 17:11, declared, "For the life of the flesh is in the blood." This statement revealed advanced scientific knowledge at a time when the level of pagan medical knowledge was abysmal. This statement by Moses was exceptionally astute because doctors have discovered that our blood is essential to all of our body's life processes. The blood carries nutrients and material that produce growth, healing, store energy as fat, and support every organ in our body. When the blood supply is restricted to any part of the body, that part begins immediately to die. Blood is essential to fighting disease, clotting wounds and growing new skin and cells. For centuries ignorant doctors used to "bleed" their patients by draining large amounts of blood from their bodies in a vain attempt to defeat disease. They did not realize that our blood is the key to our life. Truly, as the Bible declares, "the life of the flesh is in the blood."

The Population of the Earth

Those who reject the Bible's account of divine creation believe the evolutionary argument that mankind evolved by chance from lower life forms over billions of years. One of their conclusions is that mankind has existed on this earth for more than a million years. In contradiction to this evolutionary position, the Bible declares that mankind was created approximately six thousand years ago according to the chronological data presented in the Old Testament. While the Scriptures do not tell us when God originally created "the heaven and the earth," the Bible clearly declares, through a detailed list of the generations from Adam to Christ, that mankind was created on the earth approximately four thousand years before the birth of Jesus Christ. Obviously, a huge discrepancy exists between the evolutionists' suggestion of man's origin approximately one million years ago compared to the Bible's declaration of man's creation by God approximately six thousand years ago.

Let us consider the growth rate of our human population to determine whether the Bible's account of man's creation only six thousand years ago, or the evolutionary scientists' account of man's evolution over one million years is consistent with known scientific data. According to the Scriptures, eight people comprising four couples survived the great Flood approximately forty-three hundred years ago as described in biblical chronology (estimated date: 2300 B.C.). To be conservative, we will make these calculations assuming that mankind started forty-three hundred years ago with only one surviving couple and that all families produced only 2.5 children on average over the following centuries. This rate of population growth is much slower than we are experiencing in this century. If families produce only two children on average then the population would remain static without any growth. This conservative assumption of an average of 2.5 children per family will allow for the natural depletion caused by war, famine and disease.

Throughout history the average lifespan has lasted

approximately forty-three years per generation. Using these assumptions, during the last forty-three hundred years, there would have been one hundred generations lasting forty-three years each. The calculations reveal that our population should have grown from the time of the Flood till today to reach approximately six billion people. It is fascinating to note that the earth's population today (6.25 billion worldwide) is almost identical with what we would expect if mankind began repopulating the earth after the Flood forty-three hundred years ago. I am indebted to Professor Henry M. Morris for his brilliant study on this topic in his excellent book, *The Biblical Basis For Modern Science*, which I highly recommend for any reader who wishes to explore this topic in greater depth.[11] In this chapter I am simplifying the calculations but the results are consistent.

Now let us consider what the earth's population would be if the evolutionary theory were correct. The evolutionary scientists who believe that man has existed for over a million years have an almost insurmountable problem. Using the same assumption of forty-three years for an average human generation, the population growth over a million years would produce 23,256 consecutive generations. We calculate the expected population by starting with one couple one million years ago and use the same assumptions of a forty-three year generation and 2.5 children per family. The calculations reveal that we should have a total human population on earth today of 10^{2700} people. The evolutionary theory of a million years of growth would produce trillions × trillions × trillions × trillions of people that should be alive today on our planet. To put this in perspective, this number is vastly greater than the total number of atoms in our vast universe. If mankind had lived on earth for a million years we would all be standing on very high mountains of bones from the trillions of skeletons of those who had died in past generations. However, despite the tremendous archeological and scientific investigation in the last two centuries, the scientists have not found a fraction of the trillions of skeletons predicted by the theory of the evolutionary scientists. The conclusion is obvious. The Bible's account of Noah's family repopulating the earth following the Flood approximately forty-three hundred years ago is consistent with the current population of the earth.

The Wonders of Creation

The Bible claims that God created all of the living creatures on earth. When we examine these creatures we discover an awesome degree of complexity that simply defies the evolutionary theory that claims these animals and their behavior have occurred by chance alone. One of the most intriguing examples of God's design is found in the fact that birds have hollow bones. This makes them much lighter than they would be with normal solid bones and facilitates aerial flight. As an example of God's providential design, consider the woodpecker that is so familiar to North Americans.

As I write this chapter, a beautiful woodpecker is standing on a branch of the tree only five feet beyond my library window, pecking away in diligent search for an insect beneath the bark of the tree. The woodpecker has two toes in front and two toes in the rear allowing it to grip the trunk of a tree firmly while pecking for insects. While all other birds have their bill connected directly to their skull, only the woodpecker has an unusual spongy tissue between its bill and skull that acts as a shock absorber while it pecks forcefully at the trunk of a tree for hours at a time seeking to locate insects. Some woodpeckers have actually pecked through solid concrete in their quest for insects or to bury seeds for future food. The woodpecker's short tail feathers act as support to brace its body against the trunk of the tree while it pecks searching for food. When it locates a tunnel bored through the tree by an insect the woodpecker inserts its extremely long tongue into the narrow tunnel until it reaches its prey. Unlike other birds, the tongue of a woodpecker is not attached to the rear of its mouth. Remarkably, the woodpecker's tongue is five inches long coiled within its skull, allowing the bird to locate its insect prey deep within the tree trunk.

Those who reject divine creation believe that the awesome complexities of biological life have occurred by simple chance through evolution without intelligent design. This argument appears ridiculous to people who examine the awesome complexity of animal and human life. Those who honestly and carefully consider the evidence must conclude that God has created this marvellous design. As an example of this design we should consider the migratory pattern of birds.

The Manx shearwater birds that live in Wales migrate from South America to home every year flying approximately 250 miles every day. A Manx shearwater captured in Wales was transferred by plane in a crate to America. Then scientists released the bird in Boston. Surprisingly, the bird flew home across the trackless expanse of the Atlantic Ocean to its home in Wales, more than 3,100 miles away, in only twelve days despite the fact that the bird had never flown over the ocean before. How could this occur unless God planted within the bird the knowledge of where its home was located thousands of miles away? Another example of God's creative design is found in the ability of the rattlesnake to detect its prey. This ability depends on a small sense organ found between the nostril and the eyes of the snake, that is so sensitive it can detect a difference of temperature of only one thirty-third of a degree. This ability to detect the precise temperature of an object in front of the snake enables it to precisely measure the distance and direction to its prey. This ability to detect such a small temperature variation is so difficult that only a computerized thermometer device can detect so small a difference. How could such a sensitive awareness of temperatures have evolved in the rattlesnake by chance?

Evolutionists believe that the complex systems found in living creatures have been formed as a result of random chance. However, King David declared: "You [God] formed my inward parts; You covered me in my mother's womb. I will praise You, for I am fearfully and wonderfully made" (Psalm 139:13,14). Consider the case of the human eye and ask yourself whether or not such an astonishingly intricate system could have occurred by chance alone. When a baby is conceived in its mother's womb the genetic code governing the eye programs the baby's body to begin growing optic nerves from both the brain as well as the eye. Each eye will have a million nerve endings that begin growing through the flesh toward the baby's brain. Simultaneously, a million optic nerves will begin growing through the flesh towards the baby's eye. Each of the million optic nerves must find and match up to its exact mate to enable sight to exist. We are impressed when highway engineers are able to correctly align two thirty-foot wide tunnels dug from opposite sides of the mountain to meet somewhere precisely in the middle of the mountain. However, every day hundreds of thousands of children are born with the ability to see, whose bodies have precisely aligned a million separate optic nerves from each eye to meet its matching optic nerve ending that is growing out from the baby's brain. If you think this miracle of design has happened by random chance, you probably still believe in the Tooth Fairy.

The human eye has the ability to transmit to the brain over one and a half million messages simultaneously. The retina at the back of the eye contains a dense area of rods and cones that gather and interpret information presented to the eye. The retina contains over one hundred and thirty-seven million nerve connections which the brain uses to evaluate data in its attempt to interpret the scene in front of your eyes. One hundred and thirty million of these special cells are rods that enable us to have black and white vision. However, about seven million eye cells are cone-shaped cells that allow us to see color. Each of these one hundred and thirty-seven million cells communicates directly with the brain, allowing us to interpret the visual image in front of us. Amazingly, scientists have discovered that while the image we receive in our eye is "upside-down" the cellular structure in our eye actually reverses the image to "right-side up" within the eye before sending it to the mind. The eye then transmits the corrected image at three hundred miles an hour to the brain where we "see" the image that is before us.

The human brain is the most complex organ in the known universe. While it weighs less than three pounds, it contains an amazingly intricate connection of nerves with more than thirty billion special cells known as neurons. In addition, there are another two hundred and fifty billion glial cells that facilitate communication between neurons. Incredibly, every one of the thirty billion neurons are connected to other neurons in a staggering pattern of complicated connections. Every neuron is connected directly to more than fifty thousand other neurons allowing instantaneous transfers of messages across your brain. In less than a second your brain can calculate the trajectory of a football thrown at thirty miles an hour toward you without warning. In a moment your brain calculates your position, the ball's ultimate trajectory, and sends detailed electronic messages to the muscles in your arms and legs at more than three hundred miles a second to move you into position to catch the ball. Despite hundreds of billions of dollars and fifty years of advanced research by computer scientists, there are no computer systems on the planet that can equal this marvelous instantaneous computing system that is required to allow a ten-year-old boy to catch a football! When we carefully consider the evidence, I believe that any fair-minded observer will conclude that our universe and all of life was designed by God exactly as revealed in the Bible.

The Bible reveals that a supernatural God designed and created our extremely complicated universe. Any person with an unbiased mind who examines the evidence must consider the possibility that only a designer with miraculous powers could possibly account for the marvelously designed universe. The many scientific statements found throughout the Bible are one of the greatest evidences of God's inspiration. There are no scientific errors or mistakes found in its thousands of passages. These accurate scientific statements provide overwhelming evidence that God exists, and that He inspired the writers of Scripture to record His message to all of mankind. The remarkable scientific insights and revelations found throughout the Bible from Genesis to Revelation, are God's genuine signature on the pages of the Scriptures authenticating the Word of God.

Notes

1. *Reader's Digest*, November, 1982.
2. S. Hawking and G. Ellis, *The Large Scale Structure of Space-Time*, Cambridge: The University Press, 1973, p. 364.
3. Herman Bondi, *New Scientist*, Nov. 21, 1980, (Letters Section: Reference to quote by Karl Popperp) 611.
4. Harold Jeffreys, *The Earth: Its Origin, History, and Physical Constitution* (Cambridge: England: University Press, 1970) 359.
5. J. Audouzze, *The Cambridge Atlas of Astronomy* (Cambridge: The University Press, 1985) 219.
6. Mitchell Waldrop, "Delving the Hole in Space," (*Science*, Nov. 27, 1981).
7. Robert Jastrow, *The Intellectuals Speak Out About God* (Chicago: Regnery Gateway, 1984) 21.
8. Gershon Robinson, Mordechai Steinman, *The Obvious Proof* (New York: CIS Publishers, 1993) 87.
9. Leslie Orgel, "Darwinism at the Very Beginning of Life," (*New Scientist*, April, 1982)151.
10. Fred Hoyle, "Where Microbes Boldly Went," (*New Scientist*) 412-415).
11. Henry M. Morris, *The Biblical Basis For Modern Science* (Grand Rapids: Baker House, 1984) 414-426.

6

Advanced Medical Knowledge in the Bible

Most readers are blissfully unaware of the fact that the level of medical knowledge and sanitation practices in the western world until A.D. 1880 was virtually as pathetic in its ignorance as the situation found throughout the globe throughout the medieval period or in the Third World before western medicine arrived in the 1900s. Man's medical knowledge was abysmal until the beginning of the twentieth century as even the existence of germs was unknown until around A.D. 1890.

Yet, the first five books of the Bible, known as the Torah, or the Law, recorded by Moses approximately 1491-1451 B.C., reveal surprising advanced scientific principles. In addition, the Bible contains advanced medical and scientific knowledge about hygiene and sanitation. As you will discover, the Scriptures contain God's medical instructions for Israel that far exceeded the level of knowledge possessed by the Egyptians and other ancient societies of that day. This advanced information in the Bible, written over three and a half millennia ago, provides strong evidence that a divine Creator inspired it. What other rational explanation is there for this precise medical knowledge in the five books of the Law recorded while Moses led the Israelites through the wilderness of Sinai? God inspired Moses to record these medical commandments to protect the health of His Chosen People. The Book of Exodus reveals one of the most extraordinary promises that God ever made to mankind.

God's Promise:
"the Lord will take away from you all sickness"

God promised that, if they obeyed all of His commandments and statutes which He gave to Moses, the Lord would protect them from the plagues and sicknesses that afflicted the ancient Egyptians. This remarkable promise is found in Exodus 15:26, "If you diligently heed the voice of the Lord your God and do what is right in His sight, give ear to His commandments and keep all His statutes, I will put none of the diseases on you which I have brought on the Egyptians. For I am the Lord who heals you." Throughout the Bible, especially the first five books of Moses from Genesis to Deuteronomy, we discover exceptionally advanced medical laws and principles that are designed to protect us from the devastating diseases that have afflicted mankind throughout history.

For centuries the Jews had lived as slaves among the pagan Egyptians. Obviously they learned and adopted the traditional folk medicine and remedies of their Egyptian masters. As a result the Israelites would have been afflicted during their long captivity by the same terrible diseases and plagues that repeatedly devastated the people of ancient Egypt. The Book of Deuteronomy 28:27,28 records a number of these terrible diseases of the Egyptians. "The Lord will strike you with the boils of Egypt, with tumors, with the scab, and with the itch, from which you cannot be healed. The Lord will strike you with madness and blindness and confusion of heart."

However, if the Israelites would turn from their sins and follow the commandments of God, the Lord promised that "none of the terrible diseases of Egypt which you have known" would afflict the Jews from that moment on. "And the Lord will take away from you all sickness, and will afflict you with none of the terrible diseases of Egypt which you have known, but will lay them on all those who hate you" (Deuteronomy 7:15).

When the children of Israel left Egypt through the miraculous intervention of God, the Lord demanded that they obey His commandments against evil. God's specific medical laws and sanitation commandments that were given to Moses, would protect the Jews from the most terrible diseases of the Egyptians and their attendant high mortality rates. An examination of the medical remedies of the ancient Egyptians and other pagan cultures of the Middle East reveals an appalling ignorance of even the most rudimentary medical knowledge as we know it today. However, the laws of Moses contained specific laws and sanitation procedures that, if faithfully followed, would eliminate the dreadful diseases that afflicted the Egyptians of that day and still afflict most of mankind in the Third World today.

The Medical Knowledge of Ancient Egypt

It is fascinating to study the several hundred prescriptions in the *Papyrus Ebers* to gain an understanding of the level of medical and sanitary knowledge possessed by the Egyptians, the most advanced society on earth, in the days of Moses. Despite their advanced astronomical and engineering knowledge, as evidenced by their great temples at Karnak and the three great pyramids at Giza, the Egyptian's level of medical knowledge was extremely primitive and dangerous. Yet, they prided themselves on their great medical knowledge as revealed in various medical manuscripts that have survived the ravages of time, including the *Papyrus Ebers*, written about the time of Moses.

As an example of the medical ignorance and primitive state of their knowledge of infection, consider the Egyptian doctor's suggestion for healing an infected splinter wound as documented in the ancient *Papyrus Ebers*.[1] The prescription involves the application of an ointment mixture composed of the blood of worms mixed with the dung of a donkey. The various germs, including tetanus, contained in donkey's dung must have assured that the patient would rapidly forget the pain of his splinter as he died from an assortment of other diseases produced by his doctor's contaminated medicine. The medical solution for a patient's hair loss involved the application to his scalp of a solution composed of various fats from a horse, a crocodile, a cat, a snake, and a donkey's tooth crushed in honey. The Egyptian doctors had an equally wondrous cure for a poisonous snake bite. They poured "magical water" over a pagan idol and then gave it to the victim for what probably turned out to be his last drink on earth.

According to these ancient documents, the pharmacies of ancient Egypt provided popular prescriptions including "lizards' blood, swines' teeth, putrid meat, stinking fat, moisture from pigs' ears, milk, goose grease, asses' hoofs, animal fats from various sources, excreta from animals, including human beings, donkeys, antelopes, dogs, cats, and even flies." Believe it or not, this list is actually quoted from the pages of the *Papyrus Ebers* manuscript as translated in S. E. Massengill's *A Sketch of Medicine and Pharmacy*.[2] During my last research trip to the Middle East I located another fascinating book about ancient Egyptian medical knowledge. This book, *An Ancient Egyptian Herbal,* by Lise Manniche describes a number of Egyptian cures that use ingredients such as "cat's dung," "hippopotamus dung," "donkey's hoof," "gazelle dung," "snakeskins" and of course, the ever popular "fly dung" that appears in numerous prescriptions.[3]

The Egyptian's remedy for "constipation: zizyphus bread, gurma, cat's dung, sweet beer, wine." In another passage we read, "a painful tumour was treated with fly dung mixed with sycamore juice applied to the tumour so that it goes down by itself." Among these amazingly dangerous medicines we find an appalling suggestion for curing a baby of excessive crying: "A remedy for too much crying in a child: spn-seeds; fly dung from the wall; is made to a paste, strained and drunk for four days. The crying will cease instantly." No doubt the crying would cease with the death of the poor child receiving this deadly potion. As the author dryly noted, "In general, Coptic medicine is not held in very high esteem."

A majority of the medicines described in documents from ancient Egypt included dung from either humans or animals.

The mortality rate from infection must have been dreadful with such ignorant and deadly advice from doctors. Due to the total lack of knowledge of germs and infection, almost any serious illness or injury treated by the medical system of pagan Egypt would result in a painful and virtually certain death.

The Bible records that Moses was adopted and grew up as the son of "Pharaoh's daughter." Moses would have had access to the knowledge of the royal and priestly colleges of Egypt. The Jewish historian Flavius Josephus tells us in his *Antiquities of the Jews*, that Moses, as a prince of Egypt, became a great general in his successful war against the Ethiopian Empire. As a royal prince he was taught all that Egypt, as the most advanced culture of the day, could transmit to his genius. The Book of Acts (7:22) tells us: "And Moses was learned in all the wisdom of the Egyptians, and was mighty in words and deeds." Therefore, as a royal heir, he would have been educated in all of these "deadly" medical cures. Both the writer of the Torah and the millions of ancient Israelite slaves would have absorbed the medical knowledge and traditional treatments of the Egyptians during the centuries of Israel's captivity.

However, a close examination of the first five books of the Bible written by Moses does not include a single reference to these "deadly" medical practices of the pagan Egyptian society in which Moses and the Israelites were raised. Rather, we discover in the pages of ancient Scriptures the most advanced sanitation instructions and the most sophisticated medical knowledge that the world has ever known, until the explosion of medical research in the last century following World War I. Despite the natural human tendency to supplement our own natural education and knowledge to what God tells us, Moses resisted such temptations in writing exactly what God inspired him to write as he composed the Torah. There are no references to the disgusting and dangerous ancient Egyptian medical practices in the five books of Moses.

An intelligent reader must ask this question: Where did Moses obtain his incredibly advanced medical knowledge? Obviously he did not receive this accurate medical knowledge from the Egyptians or any other pagan culture of that time. This advanced and accurate knowledge in the Bible reveals a profound understanding of germs, infectious transmission routes, human sanitation needs and many other medical advances unknown outside the Bible during the last thirty-five centuries. Moses abandoned the medical ignorance of the Egyptians when he left the palace in Egypt and spent the next eighty years of his life in the wilderness. The first five books of the Bible contain detailed medical laws regarding the careful kosher inspection of meat and exacting sanitation regulations regarding the burial of bodies. How could Moses have acquired such a profound and medically advanced knowledge without help from some outside force?

The only answer that makes sense is that found in the first five of the books of the Bible. Moses declared that he received this knowledge from God by direct and supernatural inspiration. A careful examination of the medical treatises from the Egyptians and the comprehensive Babylonian Code of Hammurabi reveals absolutely nothing about preventative medicine to enable people to avoid these deadly diseases that devastated ancient societies. However, the presence of unparalleled advanced and accurate knowledge of diseases, sanitation and preventative medicine in the ancient Scriptures is one more incontrovertible proof that the Bible is truly the inspired Word of God. It is fascinating to note that a total of two hundred and thirteen out of the six hundred and thirteen biblical commandments found in the Torah (one third of God's commandments to Israel) were detailed medical regulations that insured the good health of the children of Israel if they would obediently follow the laws of God.

God's Ancient Laws of Hygiene and Sanitation

Medical science did not know of the existence of germs and their methods of transmission of infection until the 1890s. Doctors until then believed that the presence and transmission of disease was entirely haphazard and governed by simple chance or bad luck. Those who were sick with deadly diseases were cared for in the home without any awareness of the contagious transmission of disease from one sick individual to others around them.

People had no idea that invisible and deadly microscopic germs could exist on eating and cooking utensils. However, Leviticus 6:28, written over thirty-five hundred years ago, reveals a clear commandment to discard broken pottery (because the cracks could contain harmful germs): "But the earthen vessel in which it is boiled shall be broken. And if it is boiled in a bronze pot, it shall be both scoured and rinsed in water."

In other words, a cracked vessel should not be used for cooking or eating but should be discarded. The Bible tells us further that "if it be sodden in a brazen pot, it shall be both scoured, and rinsed in water" indicating that a metal pot should be disinfected by scouring and rinsing in water. These instructions certainly saved hundreds of thousands of Jews from infections over the centuries at a time when the rest of the world didn't even know that germs existed. How could Moses have known of the dangers of infectious germs in cooking and eating utensils thousands of years ago unless God actually inspired him to write these words?

Moses' writing also reveals a remarkable knowledge of deadly germs associated with dead animal bodies and anything they touch. Throughout history people stored and cooked their meat with ample spices to delay the rotting and to disguise the smell of decay. Without refrigeration, the eating of meat was often hazardous because of the great danger of infection. In Leviticus 11:35, Moses revealed his knowledge of the danger of germs from animal carcasses when he wrote, "And everything on which a part of any such carcass falls shall be unclean; whether it is an oven or cooking stove, it shall be broken down; for they are unclean, and shall be unclean to you." God inspired Moses to record these medical and sanitation instructions in the Bible to protect the Israelites from invisible, but deadly infectious germs, found in dead animal bodies that would sicken or kill them. It is important to remember that, until this past century began, even medical researchers and doctors strongly denied that disease could be transmitted by invisible germs or viruses.

The Book of Leviticus 7:24 forbids the people to eat of the flesh of any animal that has died naturally of disease or by wild animals: "And the fat of a beast that dies naturally, and the fat of what is torn by wild animals, may be used in any other way; but you shall by no means eat it." Any animal carcass found after natural death would be dangerous to eat because it would likely contain the germs that caused its premature death by diease or the infectious germs that would develop within hours of an animal's violent death following an attack by another animal. The children of Israel were saved from countless invisible germs and diseases by following these religious laws and prohibitions given by their God through their prophet Moses.

Laws Designed to Prevent Infectious Disease

God provided the Israelites with wise and beneficial laws to protect their health including advanced sanitation laws to prevent the spread of infections.

> This is the law when a man dies in a tent: All who come into the tent and all who are in the tent shall be unclean seven days; and every open vessel, which has no cover fastened on it, is unclean. Whoever in the open field touches one who is slain by a sword or who has died, or a bone of a man, or a grave, shall be unclean seven days. And for an unclean person they shall take some of the ashes of the heifer burnt for purification from sin, and running water shall be put on them in a vessel. (Numbers 19:14-17).

Throughout history mankind has suffered billions of untold deaths due to infections from microscopic germs. Germs from a dead human body are more dangerous to another human than germs from an animal's body because of the greater likelihood of transmission of infection. These deadly germs are everywhere, but especially within the bodies of those who are already sick or those who have died due to some disease. Mankind's ignorance of these deadly microscopic germs has exposed countless humans to premature death. However, thirty-five centuries ago the Bible clearly gave instructions that would protect us from many of these infectious diseases.

A brilliant Hungarian doctor in the late 1800s, Dr. Ignaz

Semmelweis, created a tremendous improvement in practical medical treatment and the control of deadly infectious diseases. I am indebted to the thought-provoking book, *None Of These Diseases*[4] by S. I. McMillen, M.D., for making me aware of the importance of the medical contributions of Dr. Semmelweis. An article in the *Encyclopædia Britannica* documents that, as a young doctor in Vienna in 1845, Semmelweis was appalled by the staggering rate of death by infection of women who gave birth in hospitals. While most children were born at home at that time, a number of women, usually the homeless or sick, gave birth to their children in the local hospitals. The level of infectious puerperal (child-bed) fever was horrendous with between 15 and 30 percent of such mothers dying in hospital. This tragic situation was considered normal at that time. Dr. Semmelweis noted that every morning the young interns examined the bodies of the mothers who had died and then immediately, without washing their hands, went to the next ward where they would examine the expectant mothers. This appalling behavior was considered normal medical practice in the late 1800s because the existence of microscopic infectious germs was unknown and unsuspected.[5]

However, the young doctor insisted that the doctors under his supervision follow his new orders to wash their hands vigorously in water with chlorinated lime prior to examining living patients. Immediately, the mortality rate from infection among the expectant mothers fell to less than 2 percent dying due to these infections. Despite these fantastic improvements the senior hospital staff despised Dr. Semmelweis's medical innovations and eventually fired him. Most of his medical colleagues rejected his new techniques and ridiculed his demands that they wash their hands because they could not believe infections could be caused by something invisible to the naked eye. Later he took a position with another hospital in Pest, Hungary [Budapest], the St. Rochus Hospital, which was experiencing an epidemic of puerperal fever in the ward where mothers were giving birth. Immediately, his new sanitary procedures had a positive effect, with the mortality rate dropping to less than

1 percent instead of the 15 percent that was normal in other hospitals in the area.

During the following six years, he received the approval of the Hungarian government which sent medical advisory letters to all district authorities demanding that all medical staff follow Dr. Semmelweis's instructions for washing hands and general hospital sanitation. Although the beneficial results of washing hands were obvious, the medical establishments of Europe and North America continued to ignore his techniques. Patients continued to die needlessly of infectious diseases while they were in the hospital. Decades of rejection by his colleagues finally drove Dr. Semmelweis to a nervous breakdown that placed him in a mental institution. Tragically, due to an infection he received through a cut on his hand during an operation in 1865, Dr. Semmelweis succumbed to the same infectious disease he spent his life trying to alleviate. Dr. Joseph Lister, the father of modern antisepsis (the science of fighting infection), said of him, "I think with the greatest admiration of him and his achievement."

Thousands of years ago, God commanded the Israelites to wash their hands in "running water" when dealing with those afflicted with infectious diseases. "And when he who has a discharge is cleansed of his discharge, then he shall count for himself seven days for his cleansing, wash his clothes, and bathe his body in running water; then he shall be clean" (Leviticus 15: 13). Until this last century most doctors who did choose to wash their hands, did so in a bowl of water which obviously would allow the germs to remain on their hands. However, Moses instructed the Israelites to wash in "running water" which is the only way to effectively remove these infectious germs.

Quarantine Laws to Prevent Plague and Leprosy

Throughout history the scourge of leprosy has killed untold millions of people and afflicted many more with misery. There is some debate among medical scholars about whether the Hebrew word translated "leprosy" in the Bible is exactly the same disease as the modern variant. It may have been another deadly infectious disease that differs from modern forms of leprosy. Amazingly, an examination of the detailed laws of Numbers and Leviticus reveals an advanced quarantine system for the control of infectious diseases at a time when ancient pagan nations did not understand the dangers of infections.

For example, the Bible commands that the priests act as medical control officers, examining all sick individuals and taking action to protect them and the community. "Then the priest shall look at it; and indeed if the swelling of the sore is reddish-white on his bald head or on his bald forehead, as the appearance of leprosy on the skin of the body, he is a leprous man. He is unclean. The priest shall surely pronounce him unclean; his sore is on his head" (Leviticus 13:43,44). In addition to identifying the diseased individual the priest was responsible for the quarantine of those afflicted with leprosy. "He shall be unclean. All the days he has the sore he shall be unclean. He is unclean, and he shall dwell alone; his habitation shall be outside the camp" (Leviticus 13:46).

The Lord's concern to protect His children from infectious disease was manifested in His command to forbid those who were still infected with disease from participating in the three great annual festivals of the Jews, lest they infect others. "But the man who is unclean and does not purify himself, that person shall be cut off from among the congregation, because he has defiled the sanctuary of the Lord. The water of purification has not been sprinkled on him; he is unclean" (Numbers 19: 20). Even after a man recovered from his disease and returned from medical isolation, the individual was subject to strict medical supervision for seven days under the medical orders of the priest to ascertain that he was truly healed. "He who is to be cleansed shall wash his clothes, shave off all his hair, and wash himself in water, that he may be clean. After that he shall come into the camp, and shall stay outside his tent seven days" (Leviticus 14:8).

After this period of quarantine the individual must submit to a careful medical exam by the priests to ascertain that he was truly free of disease and able to resume his position in society. "But on the seventh day he shall shave all the hair off his head and his beard and his eyebrows; all his hair he shall shave off.

He shall wash his clothes and wash his body in water, and he shall be clean" (Leviticus 14:9). When you consider these ancient medical instructions, you can see that they are remarkably similar to the medical quarantine orders a modern public health official would follow to absolutely determine that someone was cured of his disease and able to safely reenter society.

The continents of Europe and Asia have been periodically engulfed by epidemics of leprosy and plague, such as those in the medieval period, especially A.D. 1200 to A.D. 1400. These dreaded epidemics terrified the populations of Europe. Over sixty million people, almost one-third of the population of Europe in the fourteenth century are estimated to have died by the Black Death (bubonic plague). Entire counties and towns were devastated with no known survivors. Those who survived portray scenes that sounded like the haunting visions of Dante's descriptions of hell. Renowned doctors of the time were unable to respond adequately because of their lack of knowledge. They were reduced to offering medical advice to prevent the plague such as, "Stop eating pepper or garlic." Some suggested the plague was caused by the position of the planets and stars. Mostly, the doctors helplessly comforted their dying patients and finally succumbed to the disease themselves.

How was this dreaded plague finally stopped before it killed everyone in Europe? As ministers prayed for the sick and held their Bibles in their hands, little did they realize that God had already provided the divine solution to plague in the pages of Holy Scripture. While doctors failed the people totally, some church leaders wisely looked to God and the Bible for a divine medical solution to the apparently hopeless situation. During a trip to Vienna, I examined a strange-looking plague statue in the center of the city dedicated to the Black Death's countless victims and the actions of the church fathers, in accordance with Scripture, to abolish the curse of that plague. The history of that time reveals that the doctors could do nothing. It was only after the people began to follow the ancient biblical laws of sanitation and disease control that the epidemic was broken.

In the midst of fear and panic, several church leaders in Vienna began to search the Bible to discover whether or not there was a practical biblical solution to this plague. They discovered in Leviticus 13:46 that Moses laid down strict regulations from God regarding the medical treatment of those afflicted with leprosy or plague: "He shall be unclean. All the days he has the sore he shall be unclean. He is unclean, and he shall dwell alone; his habitation shall be outside the camp." God answered their prayers for deliverance when they finally began to obey His scriptural commands. The scourge of the Black Death plague was eliminated by following God's inspired commands given to Moses in the ancient past.

The Divine Laws of Quarantine

This divine medical rule demanded that a person who contracted leprosy or the plague must be isolated and segregated from the general population during his infectious period, until he was either healed or died. God's commands included detailed instructions regarding protection from infection for those priests who treated the segregated patient. After feeding and caring for the plague sufferer, the care givers must change their clothes, wash in running water, and expose both themselves and their clothing to sunlight. Doctors today know that sunlight and vigorous washing in running water are among the most effective preventative steps to minimize infectious transmission between patients. Moses' instruction to segregate infected patients from their families and other people was one of the most important medical advances in human history. Yet no other ancient nation followed these effective medical regulations. The only reasonable explanation is that Moses received this advanced medical knowledge from God's inspiration.

The biblical instructions reveal a profoundly advanced scientific understanding that invisible germs can be transmitted to others unless preventative sanitary steps are taken. Until the 1900s, all previous societies, except for the Israelites who followed God's medical laws regarding quarantine, kept infected patients in their homes—even after death, unknowingly exposing family members and others to deadly disease. During the devastating Black Death of the fourteenth century, patients who were sick or dead were kept in the same rooms as the rest of the family. People often wondered why the disease was affecting so many people at one time. They attributed these epidemics to "bad air" or "evil spirits." However, careful attention to the medical commands of God as revealed in Leviticus would have saved untold millions of lives. Arturo Castiglione wrote about the overwhelming importance of this biblical medical law, "The laws against leprosy in Leviticus 13 may be regarded as the first model of a sanitary legislation."[6]

Fortunately, the church fathers of Vienna finally took the biblical injunctions to heart and commanded that those infected with the plague must be placed outside the city in special medical quarantine compounds. Care givers fed them there until they either died or survived the passage of the disease. Those who died in homes or streets were instantly removed and buried outside the city limits. These biblical sanitary measures quickly brought the dreaded epidemic under control for the first time. Other cities and countries rapidly followed the medical practices of Vienna until the Black Death was finally halted.

Laws of Cleanliness – Next to Godliness

While people repeat the phrase, "Cleanliness is next to godliness" they often forget that God has actually provided stringent laws of cleanliness that, if followed, would immeasurably prevent disease and premature death. Throughout the Scriptures we find God commanding His people to follow laws of hygiene and cleanliness. To put these laws and instructions in perspective, we need to understand that cleanliness and bathing were almost unknown through much of human history. Most people lived from the cradle to grave in past centuries without ever having a bath. In fact, most Europeans until the 1840s believed that taking a bath was the most dangerous thing you could do to your health.

Most Europeans, until the end of the 1800s, experienced a bath less than once a year. King James I of England, who ordered the translation of the Bible, known as the King James Bible in 1611, never bathed once. He kept a bowl of talc beside him that he applied to his fingers and hands to keep them soft. When Kaye and I visited the thousand-room Hampton Palace several years ago, the guide pointed out that King James' numerous guests did not have access to a single bathtub in the whole castle. One of the reasons they loved snuff and perfume so much in those days was to mask dreadful body odors.

However, thousands of years ago God commanded the Israelites to deal with their uncleanliness by following His specific instructions to avoid infection and death. For example, even before God gave Moses the Ten Commandments at Mount Sinai, He told the Israelites to sanctify themselves by washing their clothes: "And the Lord said unto Moses, Go unto the people, and sanctify them to day and to morrow, and let them wash their clothes" (Exodus 19:10). Preparations for ministering in the Tabernacle required that Aaron and his sons wash their bodies before putting on their priestly garments: "And Aaron and his sons thou shalt bring unto the door of the tabernacle of the congregation, and shalt wash them with water" (Exodus 29: 4) prior to giving them their priestly garments. "Moses, Aaron, and Aaron's sons would wash their hands and their feet with water whenever they entered the tabernacle of meeting, and approached the altar, just as the Lord had commanded Moses" (Exodus 40:31,32). This rule still applied years later when the priests ministered in the Temple.

When you consider that the priests were responsible for preparing and sacrificing animals on the altar, the need for strict rules of washing are obvious in light of our present knowledge of the dangers from infectious germs. The Bible also contains detailed sanitation instructions concerning the purification following the birth of a child, and very detailed instructions were laid out regarding hygiene for women.

Incineration of Animal Waste to Prevent Disease

One of the most intriguing of the sanitation commandments found in the Bible is the demand that the internal organs and waste of the animals to be sacrificed were to be carefully burned "without the camp" to prevent the possibility of transmitting infection to the Israelites from the germ-filled waste of the sacrificed animals. It is noteworthy that the Israelites were commanded to create, in effect, an incinerator "outside the camp" to safely dispose of the dangerous infectious materials produced by their numerous sacrifices. "But the bull's hide and all its flesh, with its head and legs, its entrails and offal; the whole bull he shall carry outside the camp to a clean place, where the ashes are poured out, and burn it on wood with fire; where the ashes are poured out it shall be burned" (Leviticus 4:11,12). At a time when no one knew that animal waste and decaying organs would be dangerous because of the microscopic germs, the Bible commands the Israelites to destroy these infectious agents in the most sanitary method available to an ancient culture-burning outside the camp.

The Medical Importance of the Red Heifer Sacrifice

In Numbers 19, Moses wrote these inspired instructions regarding the mysterious sacrifice of the Red Heifer:

> Then the heifer shall be burned in his sight: its hide, its flesh, its blood, and its offal shall be burned. And the priest shall take cedar wood and hyssop and scarlet, and cast them into the midst of the fire burning the heifer. Then the priest shall wash his clothes, he shall bathe in water, and afterward he shall come into the camp; the priest shall be unclean until evening. And the one who burns it shall wash his clothes in water, bathe in water, and shall be unclean until evening. Then a man who is clean shall gather up the ashes of the heifer, and store them outside the camp in a clean place; and they shall be kept for the congregation of the children of Israel for the water of purification; it is for purifying from sin. And the one who gathers the ashes of the heifer shall wash his clothes, and be unclean until evening. It shall be a statute forever to the children of Israel and to the stranger who sojourns among them. He who touches the dead body of anyone shall be unclean seven days. He shall purify himself with the water on the third day and on the seventh day; then he will be clean. But if he does not purify himself on the third day and on the seventh day, he will not be clean. Whoever touches

the body of anyone who has died, and does not purify himself, defiles the tabernacle of the Lord. That person shall be cut off from Israel. He shall be unclean, because the water of purification was not sprinkled on him; his uncleanness is still on him. (Numbers 19:5-13).

The primary spiritual significance of the Sacrifice of the Red Heifer is the fact that it symbolically points to the ultimate sacrifice of Jesus Christ as our only hope of being cleansed from the uncleanliness of our sins. The *Talmud* claims that the Red Heifer sacrifice was the only one of God's commands that King Solomon, the wisest man who ever lived, claimed he did not understand. Although the priest obediently offered the sacrifice as demanded by God, Solomon apparently did not understand why Numbers 19 declared that the priest would be "unclean until evening." This unusual sacrifice symbolically pointed to Jesus Christ and His sacrifice because our Lord, who was perfectly sinless, judicially took upon Himself the sins of humans so that we who are sinful could become righteous before God. Christ paid the spiritual and physical price for our sins. Just as the Red Heifer was sacrificed "outside the camp" in contrast to all other sacrifices that took place in the Tabernacle or Temple, Jesus was sacrificed outside the city walls of Jerusalem. In contrast to the normal male animals sacrificed, the Red Heifer was one of the few female animals the Law commanded to be sacrificed. Significantly, our Lord was betrayed for thirty pieces of silver, the price of a female slave.

In addition to the obvious spiritual significance of the law of the Sacrifice of the Red Heifer we now understand that the water of purification described in Numbers 19 actually had the ability to destroy germs and infection. The resulting water of purification solution contained ashes from the Red Heifer sacrifice combined with cedar, hyssop and scarlet thread. This water of purification contained "cedar" oil that came from a species of juniper tree that grew in both Israel and the Sinai. This cedar oil would irritate the skin, encouraging the person to vigorously rub the solution into their hands. Most importantly, the hyssop tree-associated with mint, possibly marjoram-would produce hyssop oil. This hyssop oil is actually a very effective antiseptic and antibacterial agent. Hyssop oil contains 50 percent carvacrol which is an antifungal and antibacterial agent still used in medicine, according to the book *None Of These Diseases*.[7]

When we note that the waters of purification from the Red Heifer Sacrifice were to be used to cleanse someone who had become defiled and unclean due to touching a dead body, we begin to understand that this law was an incredibly effective medical law as well as a spiritual law. The Book of Hebrews reveals that Paul, an educated rabbi, understood that the Red Heifer sacrifice had a practical medical effect as well as its more obvious spiritual element. Paul declared that "the blood of bulls and goats and the ashes of a heifer, sprinkling the unclean, sanctifies for the purifying of the flesh" (Hebrews 9:13). The Jews stood apart from the pagan nations in their attention to sanitation and personal cleanliness as a result of the commands of God revealed in the Old Testament.

Another of the medical commands that is unprecedented in its understanding of the need for disinfecting items is found in the command of God regarding all captured material from an enemy's camp. This command of the Lord stated that, "whoever has killed any person, and whoever has touched any slain, purify yourselves and your captives on the third day and on the seventh day. Purify every garment, everything made of leather, everything woven of goats' hair, and everything made of wood" (Numbers 31:19,20). The clear instructions for disinfecting these items was as follows: "Everything that can endure fire, you shall put through the fire, and it shall be clean; and it shall be purified with the water of purification. But all that cannot endure fire you shall put through water. And you shall wash your clothes on the seventh day and be clean, and afterward you may come into the camp" (Numbers 31:23,24). These instructions would purify any contaminated materials captured from pagans that might carry dangerous germs.

Life Is in The Blood

Moses makes an intriguing statement in the Book of Leviticus about the importance of blood. "For the life of the flesh is in the blood" (Leviticus 17:11). Incredibly, Moses reveals that our blood is the essence of life. Our blood is one of the most amazing features in our wonderful body. We have over seventy-five thousand miles of blood vessels in our body, enough to circle the world three times! These incredibly tiny veins, arteries, and capillary vessels carry blood cells with nutrients to feed every one of the sixty trillion cells in our bodies. The sixty trillion amazingly complex cells that make up a human body are produced from a single microscopic cell formed when a father's sperm is joined to a mother's egg. This complex system of interconnected blood vessels must bring the needed nutrients to the particular cells that require these chemicals.

This is the equivalent of a courier company delivering trillions of packages daily to sixty trillion business customers over a route covering seventy-five thousand miles of territory. Each of our cells requires a number of different nutrients and chemicals. Special chemical sensors detect the nutrient needed as the blood passes through the bloodstream and allow that cell to connect with the necessary substance. In addition, we have over a million special types of white cells, antibodies specially designed to fight one particular disease. As soon as the body detects that it has been invaded by a particular germ or virus the whole blood system goes on special alert to produce an explosive increase in whatever antibody is required to fight the disease.

The Hebrew word for the heart is *lev*. This word heart and variations of it appear at least eight hundred and twenty-five times in the Old Testament and another one hundrd and sixty times in Greek in the New Testament. Our enormously complex blood system that allows life to exist is pumped by our heart, the most powerful muscle in our body. Though it is only the size of your clenched fist it is far stronger than our legs or arms. However, while the heart works non-stop for eighty years or more, the muscles of our legs or arms are exhausted after only a short time of exertion. Weighing less than a pound, this fantastically reliable organ pumps over one and a half million gallons of blood every year of our life. In the course of a normal lifespan the average human heart will pump forty million times pushing almost one million pounds of blood through the seventy-five thousand miles of blood vessels that make up our body. How could Moses have understood thirty-five centuries ago, that "the life of the flesh is in the blood" unless God revealed it to him by inspiration?

God's Command Concerning Circumcision

One of the most interesting of the medical details in the Bible is found in the specific instructions regarding the process of circumcising every Hebrew male child at the age of eight days as a sign of their obedience to the Covenant of God. Abraham was commanded specifically that, "He who is eight days old among you shall be circumcised, every male child in your generations" (Genesis 17:12). For thousands of years righteous Jews have faithfully obeyed this commandment as a sign of their acceptance of their covenant with God. Why would God demand that Moses command the Israelites to circumcise their male children on the eighth day of life rather than any other particular day? The Arabs and other Muslims, for example, may choose to circumsise their male children at any point from age three until their thirteenth birthday.[8] Medical scientists have been examining the biological processes that lead to blood clotting. The rapid healing of a wound begins with clotting of the blood. Any wound that fails to clot and continues to bleed, especially in a primitive environment, will provide a tremendous likelihood of infection.

Recently researchers discovered that two specific factors in our blood are closely related to the ability of our blood to quickly and safely clot to facilitate healing and resistance to infection. When a baby is born they have no bacteria in their intestines for the first few days. By day seven the bacteria multiply and produce vitamin K that is absorbed by the liver. The liver uses vitamin K to produce four significant proteins, including prothrombin, that are essential to allow the blood to clot properly. Without vitamin K and prothrombin protein the blood will not clot properly and the possibility of severe bleeding as well as infection would make circumcision dangerous in a primitive medical situation.

Medical researchers found that these two blood clotting factors, Vitamin K and prothrombin, rise to the highest level of your life (110 percent of normal) on the eighth day following birth.[7] Therefore, of all the days of the baby's life, the eighth day of life is the optimum day for an operation because of the high level of Vitamin K and the prothrombin which will clot the blood and facilitate wound healing. How would Moses have known that the eighth day of life was the ideal time to circumcise the Israelite male children unless God inspired him to write this command?

The Bible's Laws on Sanitation

Since the beginning of human civilization mankind has suffered from numerous diseases that are carried in human waste. When men lived primarily in widely distributed rural areas there was little danger of infection. However, as men began to move into villages, towns and cities, the danger of contamination grew geometrically. Throughout the Medieval and Renaissance periods, and in many societies of the Third World today, human waste is thrown into the gutter in the street and allowed to be flushed through the drains by occasional rains or floods. The stench from such a primitive system is beyond imagination.

During the days of Shakespeare, the River Thames in London was an open sewer containing untreated human waste. Even then, four hundred years ago, salmon could not survive in the river because of toxic poisons. People could not bear to walk near the River Thames because of the stench from the open cesspool. It is interesting to note that modern pollution treatment has now succeeded in reclaiming the Thames to the point where fishermen are actually catching edible salmon from the bridges of London. According to an article in the *Encyclopædia Britannica*, the foul smells arising from the River Thames in London in past centuries was so terrible that they hung burlap sacks saturated in chloride of lime in the windows of Parliament in an ineffective attempt to minimize the odors.

The smells in cities and towns were as indescribable and as deadly as the comparable odors in Calcutta today. The result of this deplorable unsanitary condition is that humans died in huge numbers every year as they succumbed to a variety of germ-related diseases including typhoid, dysentery and cholera. As difficult as it might be to believe, even the educated people of the day ignored the appalling threat to their health represented by the lack of any sanitation whatsoever. It is not an exaggeration to claim that hundreds of millions of people have died throughout history due to infectious disease produced by the absence of even the most elementary sanitation treatment of human waste. Yet obedience to God's inspired law of sanitation, proclaimed thousands of years ago in the pages of Scripture, would have saved countless millions of lives from needless death caused by germs spread through untreated and unburied sewage.

My reason for dwelling on this unpleasant subject is an attempt to emphasize the extraordinary nature and consequences of the advanced sanitation commands issued by God over three and a half thousand years ago. At a time when no one humanly understood anything about the true deadly nature of microscopic germs and infections, God instructed Moses about how he could insure adequate sanitation for his huge Jewish refugee population. As the tragic history of refugee situations reveals, they almost inevitably lead to terrible infections, such as cholera and typhoid, due to the lack of adequate sanitation facilities. The germs from untreated human waste, produced in such unorganized refugee groups, contaminate the ground water and lead to horrendous and deadly epidemics.

God's basic sanitation order regarding human waste for the Children of Israel was recorded in the Book of Deuteronomy: "Thou shalt have a place also without the camp, whither thou shalt go forth abroad: And thou shalt have a paddle upon thy weapons; and it shall be, when thou wilt ease thyself abroad, thou shalt turn back and cover that which cometh from thee" (Deuteronomy 12:12-13). While such a basic sanitation law concerning latrines may seen very normal and obvious to us today, it is an extraordinary instruction when you consider that it was made thirty-five centuries before the existence of invisible germs was discovered.

As a student of biblical and military history I have long

noted the historical truth that the vast majority of soldiers who have been killed during the countless wars have succumbed to infectious disease rather than bullets or other weapons of war. The history of war until A.D. 1900, reveals that five times as many soldiers usually died due to disease than to wounds inflicted by enemy weapons. Sickness and plague often determined the outcome of a battle. Often the army that suffered the greatest diseases lost the war. A huge percentage of the diseases of mankind, especially in war or refugee situations, developed due to the lack of sanitation regarding waste disposal. Even as late as the Boer War in South Africa (1899-1902), an analysis of military casualties indicates that five times as many soldiers died or were incapacitated due to infections, caused by exposure to germs generated from waste, than those wounded or killed by weapons. When armies marched across a country and besieged a city, tens of thousands of soldiers were forced to encamp in the open for months. Without obedience to the strict sanitation rules found in the Bible, the unburied waste from these soldiers inevitably ended up in the ground water system and ultimately infected the rest of the army.

It is certain that the strict obedience to the Law of God by the soldiers of Israel allowed them to escape many of the terrible diseases that afflicted their pagan enemies. It is likely that Israel was assisted in winning many of its ancient battles against the pagan troops of Syria and Moab because Jewish soldiers were not exposed to the tremendous infections that would afflict their enemies who did not know God's laws of sanitation. Consider the logistic problems of trying to meet the human needs of hundreds of thousands of Jews during the forty years in the wilderness. Most Israelites would have died due to infectious diseases during those years if God had not instructed Moses to teach His Chosen People these advanced laws of sanitation. In his book, *A History of Medicine*, the medical historian Arturo Castiglione declared that Moses' sanitation commands to his army were, "certainly a primitive measure, but an effective one, which indicates advanced ideas of sanitation."[9]

These simple but profoundly important instructions from God told the Israelites that each soldier must carry a shovel and bury his waste. Such instructions would assure that there would be no risk of infection to himself and his fellow soldiers from the waste. This command on building latrines is so obvious to us today that it is easy to overlook its importance as a proof of the divine inspiration of the Scriptures. Before the recent medical advances during the last one hundred and thirty years, doctors did not know that microscopic infections from human and animal waste were among the deadliest dangers to mankind. Yet, here we find this advanced sanitation and medical knowledge clearly expressed in the Bible written thousands of years ago.

Where could Moses have learned this incredibly important and life saving medical knowledge about the dangers of human waste unless he received a divine revelation as he recorded? Moses could not possibly have learned this knowledge from his schooling in the medicine of Egypt. Remember that one of the favorite ingredients found in the traditional medicines of ancient Egypt, as described in the Egyptian *Ebers Papyrus*, was manure from insects, animals, and humans. How could Moses have written these incredibly accurate and advanced medical instructions unless God inspired him? A careful analysis of the material in this chapter provides compelling evidence that the Scriptures contain medical information that cannot have been known by natural means. Therefore the Bible contains evidence that God has inspired the human writer, Moses.

Notes

1. S. E. Massengill, *A Sketch of Medicine and Pharmacy* (Bristol, Tenn.: S. E. Massengill Co. 1943).
2. S. E. Massengill, *A Sketch of Medicine and Pharmacy* (Bristol, Tenn.: S. E. Massengill Co. 1943).
3. Lise Manniche, *An Ancient Egyptian Herbal* (London: British Museum, Press,1989).
4. S. I. McMillen, *None Of These Diseases* (Minnianapolis: Successful Living, 1972).
5. S. I. McMillen, *None Of These Diseases* (Minnianapolis: Successful Living, 1972)
6. S. I. McMillen, *None Of These Diseases* (Minnianapolis: Successful Living, 1972).
7. S. I. McMillen, *None Of These Diseases* (Minnianapolis: Successful Living, 1972).
8. S. I. McMillen, *None Of These Diseases* (Minnianapolis: Successful Living, 1972).
9. Arturo Castiglione, *A History of Medicine* (New York: Alfred A. Knopt, Inc. , 1941, P. 71).

7

Precise Fulfillment of Bible Prophecy – The Signature of God

"From all the angelic ranks goes forth a groan,
'How long, O Lord, how long?'
The still small voice makes answer 'Wait and see,
O sons of glory, what the end shall be.'"

Thomas Macaulay, *Marriage of Tirzah and Ahirad.*

This study of the fulfillment of biblical prophecy provides overwhelming proof that God is controlling human history. Despite the apparent anarchy of daily events, the hand of God is still moving behind the scenes of current history to bring about His divine will. The details in the history of God's Chosen People was precisely prophesied throughout the Bible. Each of the three long captivities of Israel were prophesied: their first exile in Egypt, which lasted four hundred and thirty years; the seventy years of captivity in Babylon; the final worldwide dispersion of the Jewish people for the last two thousand years. Every time Israel was out of the Promised Land, the duration of the captivity was foretold regarding how long God would keep the Jews in exile. The actual time of the miraculous rebirth of Israel on May 15, 1948, apparently was foretold by the prophet Ezekiel over twenty-five centuries before it occurred. It is obvious to any who will examine this evidence that history is following a purposeful pattern, a design laid down centuries ago in the Word of God. The question we must ask is this, "Who is the designer?" And, "What is His purpose in history and in our own lives?"

The Bible itself declares that the evidence of fulfilled prophecy is the unmistakable proof of God's inspiration of Scripture. It is clear from the words of the prophet Isaiah that God Himself declared that correctly and precisely prophesying future events is the absolute proof that the Lord inspired biblical writers to write the Scriptures. The prophet Isaiah recorded God's declaration: "Behold, the former things have come to pass, and new things I declare; before they spring forth I tell you of them" (Isaiah 42:9).

No one except God can accurately predict future events in detail. Neither Satan nor his demons can predict the future. Twenty-five centuries ago the prophet Isaiah recorded these powerful words directly from God Almighty. "Remember the former things of old, for I am God, and there is none else; I am God, and there is none like Me, Declaring the end from the beginning, and from ancient times the things that are not yet done, saying, 'My counsel shall stand, and I will do all My pleasure'" (Isaiah 46:9,10). The Bible contains 1,817 individual predictions concerning 737 separate subjects found in 8,352 verses. These numerous predictions comprise 27 percent of the 31,124 verses in the whole of the Scriptures. Multitudes of biblical scholars over the last two thousand years have explored many of these prophecies and their detailed fulfillments as proven by ample historical evidence.

Only God Can Correctly Prophesy the Future

Despite the fact that the world is full of spiritual texts written by multitudes of religious writers, a close examination of this literature reveals that not one of these texts contains detailed prophecies that have been fulfilled. The reason is quite simple: Since no one but God can know the future accurately, religious philosophers who wrote other texts were wise enough to refrain from attempting detailed prophecies which would quickly prove their authors to be in error. "Thus says the Lord, the King of Israel, and his Redeemer, the Lord of hosts: 'I am the First and I am the Last; besides Me there is no God. And who can proclaim as I do? Then let him declare it and set it in order for Me, since I appointed the ancient people. And the things that are coming and shall come, let them show these to them' " (Isaiah 44:6-7). The classical and religious literature of the Greeks, Romans, and other Middle Eastern cultures contains no specific, detailed prophecies regarding future events, people, or trends. There were no prophecies concerning the coming of Buddha, Moham-med, or any other religious leader. However, the Old Testament prophecies predicted numerous precise details about the life, death, and resurrection of Jesus of Nazareth.

Despite the impossible odds against correctly guessing future events, multitudes of false prophets have attempted to make predictions in the past and continue to do so in our generation. However, these human predictions are almost always wrong with the exception of a very few lucky guesses. As I noted in my first book, *Armageddon – Appointment With Destiny*,[1] a fascinating study of the predictive claims of New Age psychics called "The Shattered Crystal Ball" appeared in the *Readers Digest* magazine. The study proved that these modern psychics are hopelessly wrong in their predictions. "The study analyzed the accuracy of the ten top psychics whose prophecies were published over a three-year period, 1976 to 1979. The study compared all of the published predictions with their subsequent success or failure rate. The results are certainly intriguing: 98 percent of their predictions were totally incorrect!

Only 2 percent of their predictions were fulfilled . . . six out of the ten psychics were wrong 100 percent of the time."

Some New Age writers have claimed that several non-biblical prophets such as Nostradamus (A.D. 1555) were able to correctly predict the future. Many modern New Age writers have claimed that Nostradamus predicted that Adolph Hitler would be the future leader of Germany in one of his hundreds of predictions called "Centuries." This claim is totally false! In fact, Nostradamus never mentioned Adolph Hitler by name in any of his predictions. The closest he came to "Hitler" was his mention of the word "Ister" in several predictions that the majority of interpreters admit refers clearly to a European river called the Ister River, a tributary of the River Danube. However, some writers who wrote their analysis after World War II have falsely claimed that Nostradamus actually predicted the history of Hitler, the German dictator. Incredibly, they claim that the name "Hitler" is quite close to the word "Histler" which is not all that different than the actual word "Ister" that appeared in Nostradamus's prediction!

The New Age writer Erika Cheetham, who wrote *The Final Prophecies of Nostradamus*[2] in 1989, admitted in her book that, "until 1936, approximately, all commentators on the Centuries thought that the word referred to the River Danube, the Ister." Even strong supporters of Nostradamus, such as Henry C. Roberts, the editor of *The Complete Prophecies of Nostradamus*, admitted in his Introduction that these prophetic writings of Nostradamus are "unintelligible."[3] He wrote that these predictions are "unintelligible and garbled to the uninitiate. The strange, broken, and often incoherent nature of the quatrains, both in French and English, is the hallmark of prophetic media."

Other New Age writers have made great claims for the accuracy of the predictions of Edgar Cayce, the so-called American "sleeping prophet" who lived in the early part of the last century. I had the experience of interviewing both Hugh Lynn Cayce, the son of Edgar Cayce, and his grandson in the early 1970s at their research center in Virginia Beach, Virginia. It was fascinating to listen to them describe the research they had completed for a manuscript that would reveal numerous mistaken predictions Edgar Cayce made during his career. Some of these false predictions were prophecies Cayce made about where they could locate oil wells or mineral deposits. Not surprisingly, they indicated that they did not intend to publish the manuscript.

No One But God Knows the Future

The ability of humans to correctly predict future events or trends is virtually non-existent outside of lucky guesses. Despite the great knowledge and genius of mankind we are unable to correctly predict future events and trends. As examples of this blindness as to the future, consider the following statements. The director of the U.S. Patent Office resigned his high position in 1875. He complained in his letter to the government that there was no point in continuing the Patent Office because "there's nothing left to invent." Since his resignation we have witnessed an astonishing number of brilliant inventions and developments every year in all areas of knowledge and science.

Only a few years later, in 1887, the brilliant French chemist Marcellin Berthelot wrote, "From now on there is no mystery about the universe." In the years that followed we have seen the mysteries of the atomic structure of matter unfold, the creation of a hundred new sciences including biophysics, astrophysics and molecular biology. Another great scientist at that time, Professor Simon Newcomb, wrote a highly acclaimed manuscript that proved that it was mathematically impossible for any machine that was heavier than a balloon to fly in the air. Every day thousands of large airplanes take off from thousands of airports carrying an enormous number of passengers throughout the world. An equally brilliant French philosopher by the name of Poincare ridiculed a scientist's speculations about unleashing the power of the atom through chain reactions in uranium. "Common sense alone is enough to tell us that the destruction of a town by a pound of metal is an evident impossibility." Tragically, the discoveries of awesome nuclear energies locked within the element known as uranium allowed scientists to create atomic weapons of staggering power that annihilated two Japanese cities, Hiroshima and Nagasaki, in only seconds with only a few pounds of metal. A fascinating book by Louis Pauwels and Jacques Bergier entitled *Morning of the Magicians* wrote about the massive changes in technology that challenged all of the assumptions of modern civilization.[4]

More recently, in 1943, Thomas Watson, the chairman of IBM, declared, "I think there is a world market for maybe five computers." Today, the world contains well over a billion computer devices. In the 1940s the first generation of computers were so large that they filled a whole room and weighed several tons. The magazine *Popular Mechanics* examined the state of scientific knowledge in 1949 and made this forecast about the future of computer development. "Computers in the future may weigh no more than 1.5 tons." Today we have sophisticated computers capable of billions of calculations per second that weigh less than five pounds and are much smaller than a notebook. In 1981, Bill Gates, the brilliant creator of Microsoft, the largest computer software company in history, declared, "640K (640,000 bytes of memory) should be enough for anybody." Little did he realize that in two decades the average personal desktop computer, such as the Macintosh G4 computer I am using to write this book, would contain as much as 256MB (256 million bytes) of RAM (Random Access Memory) and 200 gigabytes of memory on its hard drive. These inaccurate predictions by noted experts and leaders in their field reveal the profound limitations of human intelligence and our inability to correctly forecast future events.

However, when we turn to the pages of the Holy Scriptures we discover a staggering number of precise predictions that were made thousands of years ago concerning the future of nations and individuals. A careful analysis of these predictions reveals that every one has been fulfilled with an awesome precision that can only be explained by divine knowledge predicting the event, and the hand of God bringing the event to pass. Let's examine one of the most incredible of the thousands of Old Testament prophecies that actually predicted that rebirth of Israel in the spring of 1948.

Ezekiel Prophesied Israel's 1948 Rebirth

Several years ago I discovered that God had hidden in the pages of Scripture a precise prophecy about the exact time when He would miraculously restore His chosen people to their ancient Holy Land. While everyone knew that the Scriptures contained numerous prophecies that the Jews would return to Israel in the last days, God's prediction about the exact time of Israel's return to the Promised Land was not revealed until after the fulfillment of the prophecy. In God's divine purpose, many details about the prophecies concerning the last days were sealed in biblical visions in such a way that they could not be clearly discerned prior to their accomplishment. Then, when the prophecy was fulfilled, this confirmed the inspiration of the Scriptures and glorified God.

A careful examination of the prophecies reveals that God often specified in great detail the exact duration of time involved in various predictions concerning Israel. However, times were never given in prophecies that deal with the Church. There are no prophecies that reveal the time of the Rapture. The Lord has specifically hidden the time of the future resurrection of the saints from all but Himself. The Lord Himself told us, "But of that day and hour knoweth no man, no, not the angels of heaven, but My Father only" (Matthew 24:36). The failure to appreciate this fact has led to many errors in prophetic interpretation.

The interpretation of Ezekiel's prediction about the time of Israel's rebirth first appeared in my book *Armageddon – Appointment With Destiny*[5] in 1988. Despite the fact that over five hundred thousand people have read this material in various editions and languages of *Armageddon*, no one has been able to refute the accuracy of this incredible biblical prophecy that was given to the prophet Ezekiel when he was taken captive to Babylon twenty-five centuries ago.

Israel's Return to the Land in May 15, 1948

Israel's relationship to the Holy Land is a major focus of biblical prophecy, both fulfilled and unfulfilled. God prophesied precisely when Israel would return to the Promised Land after her citizens went into exile in the first two captivities, the Egyptian Bondage and the Babylonian Captivity.

Israel's First Captivity and Return from Egypt

On the 14th day of Nisan, the exact day that would later become the date of Passover, the Lord appeared to Abraham to proclaim the Covenant for the Promised Land. God also prophesied that Abraham's descendants would be in affliction and bondage for a period of 400 years. "And he said unto Abraham, Know of a surety that thy seed shall be a stranger in a land that is not their's, and shall serve them, and they shall afflict them four hundred years" (Genesis 15:13). The affliction of the seed of Abraham (his descendants) began just thirty years after God gave Abraham the promise of the land. "And the child [Ishmael] grew, and was weaned: and Abraham made a great feast the same day that Isaac was weaned. And Sarah saw the son of Hagar the Egyptian, which she had born unto Abraham, mocking. Wherefore she said unto Abraham, Cast out this bond woman and her son: for the son of this bond woman shall not be heir with my son, even with Isaac" (Genesis 21:8-10).

This jealous mocking of Isaac by his older brother, Ishmael, began the affliction of Abraham's seed in Canaan and eventually ended four centuries later in bondage in Egypt and in the killing of male infants (Abraham's descendants) by the Egyptians. "Now the sojourning of the children of Israel, who dwelt in Egypt, was four hundred and thirty years. And it came to pass at the end of the four hundred and thirty years, even the selfsame day it came to pass, that all the hosts of the Lord went out from the land of Egypt" (Exodus 12:40-41).

On Passover, on the exact day that the 430 years ended, God fulfilled His promise and brought Israel out of the bondage of Egypt to become a mighty nation. The apostle Paul, in his letter to the Galatians, confirmed that God fulfilled His promise to end the captivity precisely 430 years after the promise was given to Abraham (Galatians 3:17).

Israel's time of affliction was prophesied to last exactly 400 years. It began 30 years after God gave His Covenant promise to Abraham. Significantly the 400 year period prophesied in Genesis

15:13 ended precisely to the day when the Jewish captivity ended. "And it came to pass at the end of the four hundred and thirty years; even the self-same day; it came to pass, that all the hosts of the Lord went out from the land of Egypt" (Exodus 12:41).

Israel's Second Captivity and Return from Babylon

The prophet Jeremiah predicted the exact duration of the captivity of the Jewish exiles in Babylon would be 70 years. "And this whole land shall be a desolation and an astonishment, and these nations shall serve the king of Babylon seventy years" (Jeremiah 25:11). The Babylonian army conquered Israel in the spring of 606 B.C. Both secular history and the Bible reveal that, as predicted, the Babylonian Captivity ended exactly 70 years later in the spring of 536 B.C., in the Jewish month Nisan, when the Persian King Cyrus freed the Jews to return to their land (Ezra 1:3).

Israel's Third Captivity and Return in 1948

The three major Jewish prophets, Daniel, Jeremiah and Ezekiel, were all alive at this time. Naturally, the prophet Ezekiel (590 B.C.) was aware of the prophet Jeremiah's prophecy that the Jews would be able to return from Babylon after 70 years in 536 B.C. However, God gave him a new revelation that looked much farther into the future revealing how long it would be until the Jewish people would finally re-establish their nation in the last days. The prediction began with God's declaration that "this shall be a sign to the house of Israel" (Ezekiel 4:3). The full prediction is found in Ezekiel 4:3-6:

> This will be a sign to the house of Israel. Lie also on your left side, and lay the iniquity of the house of Israel upon it. According to the number of the days that you lie on it, you shall bear their iniquity. For I have laid on you the years of their iniquity, according to the number of the days, three hundred and ninety days; so you shall bear the iniquity of the house of Israel. And when you have completed them, lie again on your right side; then you

shall bear the iniquity of the house of Judah forty days. I
have laid on you a day for each year. (Ezekiel 4:3-6)

In this passage the prophet Ezekiel clearly declares that this
prophecy would be "a sign to the house of Israel" and that each
day represents one biblical year. The prediction revealed that
Israel would be punished for a combined period of 430 years
(390 years plus another 40 years). The beginning point for this
further period of captivity occurred in the spring of 536 B.C.,
at the end of the first seventy years of predicted captivity in
Babylon (Jeremiah 25:11). However, in the month Nisan, 536
B.C., only a small remnant of the Jews from the nation of Judah
chose to leave their homes in Babylon and return to Jerusalem.
The Jewish exiles who remembered their former homes in Israel
were now over 70 years old. Their children who had been born
in Babylon naturally had little connection or attachment to the
former home of their parents. The vast majority were quite
happy to remain in the pagan Persian Empire as colonists rather
than immigrate six hundred miles to rebuild the devastated
colony of Israel.

God decreed to Ezekiel a period of punishment of 430 years
for Israel's and Judah's sin (390 years + 40 years = 430 years).
However, when we deduct the 70 years of punishment the Jews
had already endured during the 70-year Babylonian captivity,
which ended in 536 B.C., *there still remained a total of 360 years of
further punishment beyond the year 536 B.C.* When we examine the
history of that period we note that the Jews did not return to
establish an independent country at the end of either 360 or of
430 years of additional punishment from 536 B.C. In light of the
precision of Ezekiel's prophecy, it was difficult to understand
why nothing occurred at that time to fulfill the detailed prediction.

Both the Bible and history reveal that Israel did not repent
of its sins at the end of the seventy-year captivity in Babylon. In
fact, the Scriptures record in the books of Ezra and Nehemiah
that the minority of fifty thousand who chose to return with
Ezra to the Promised Land did so with little faith. The vast
majority of the Jews willingly remained in pagan Babylon. They

failed to repent of their disobedience, which was the reason God sent them into captivity in the first place. This majority who refused to immigrate home to Israel, composing over 95 percent of the Jewish captives, simply settled down as colonists in what is now Iraq-Iran. Over the centuries that followed, travelers such as Benjamin of Tuldela reported that thousands of Jews still lived in several of the cities of present-day Iraq, Iran, and Afghanistan.

I discovered the solution to the mystery of the duration of Israel's worldwide dispersion and return in a divine principle that God revealed to Moses in Leviticus 26. In this chapter the Lord established promises and punishments for Israel based on her obedience and her disobedience to His commands. God declared to Israel four times in this passage that if, after being punished for her sins, she still did not repent, the punishments previously specified would be multiplied by seven (the number of completion). "And after all this, if you do not obey Me, then I will punish you seven times more for your sins" (Leviticus 26:18; see also Leviticus 26:21, 23-24, 27-28). In other words, if Israel failed to repent of her disobedience, the punishments already decreed by God would be multiplied or extended seven times. Since the majority of Israel refused to repent of her sin after the Babylonian Captivity ended, the period of 360 years of further punishment declared by Ezekiel 4:3-6 was multiplied by seven times. This meant that the Jews would remain without an independent nation for another 2,520 biblical years from 536 B.C., the beginning point of the prediction (360 years × 7 = 2,520 years biblical years).

The Biblical Year of 360 Days

The period of punishment was to last 2,520 biblical years rather than 2,520 calendar years. The reason is that the Bible always used the ancient Jewish calendar composed of 360 days, making up a biblical year, in both the historical and prophetic passages. The true length of the Jewish, biblical prophetic year was only 360 days because it was a lunar-solar year composed of twelve months of 30 days each. The modern solar year of 365.25 days was unknown to the ancient nations in the Old Testament.

According to articles on Chronology in the *Encyclopædia Britannica* (6th Edition) and *Smith's Bible Dictionary*, Abraham used a 360-day year. The Genesis' record (7:11-8:4) of Noah's flood confirms that the ancient year consisted of twelve months of thirty days each. Moses declared in Genesis that the period of 150 days when the flood waters were at their height lasted precisely five months from the seventeenth day of the second month to the seventeenth day of the seventh month, proving that each month consisted of thirty days. Sir Isaac Newton relates that "all nations, before the just length of the solar year was known, reckoned months by the course of the moon, and years by the return of winter and summer, spring and autumn; and in making calendars for their festivals, they reckoned thirty days to a lunar month, and twelve lunar months to a year, taking the nearest round numbers, whence came the division of the ecliptic into 360 degrees."

Therefore, if we wish to understand the precise times involved in the fulfillment of prophecy, we need to calculate using the same biblical lunar-solar year of 360 days which the prophets used. Both the prophet Daniel and John, in the Book of Revelation, clearly used a year of 360 days. The failure to understand the true length of the biblical year as 360 days has prevented some prophecy students from clearly understanding many prophecies which contain a precise time element. This 360-day prophetic year is also borne out in the Book of Revelation where John's vision refers to the future Great Tribulation period. He describes the Great Tribulation of three and one-half years as lasting precisely 1,260 days (Revelation 12:6), "a time, times and half a time" where a "time" in Hebrew stands for a year of 360 days (verse 14), and "forty-two months" of thirty days each (13:5). All of these biblical references confirm that the 360-day biblical year is the one we must use to correctly understand biblical prophecy and chronology.

It is worthwhile to note that the dates normally used in biblical chronology such as 606 B.C. and 536 B.C. in connection with the Babylonian Captivity are usually calculated based on biblical data such as the statement in Jeremiah 29:10: "For thus saith the Lord, That after seventy years be accomplished at Babylon I will visit you, and perform my good word toward you, in causing you to return to this place." In other words, the duration of time between the beginning and end of the Babylonian Captivity was seventy biblical years (of 360 days) although the scholars naturally calculate the dates for biblical chronology as if our regular solar year (365.25 days) was used.

Therefore, Ezekiel's prophecy of the 430 years declared that the end of Israel's punishment and her final restoration to the land would be accomplished in 2,520 biblical years of 360 days each which totals precisely 907,200 days. To convert this period into our calendar year of 365.25 days we simply divide the period of 907,200 days by 365.25 days to reach a total of 2,483.8 of our modern calendar years. Therefore, Ezekiel prophesied that the end of Israel's worldwide captivity would occur precisely 2,483.8 years after the end of the Babylonian Captivity which occurred in the spring of 536 B.C. In these calculations we must keep in mind that there was only one year between 1 B.C. and A.D. 1. There was no year Zero. As an illustration, there were only twelve months between the Feast of Passover on 14th of Nisan in the spring of 1 B.C. and the next annual Feast of Passover in the spring of A.D. 1.

To Calculate When Ezekiel Prophesied the Jews Would Become a Nation Again

The Babylonian captivity ended in the Spring of 536 B.C.	536.4 B.C.
	MINUS
The duration of Israel's captivity (from Ezekiel 4:3-6)	2,483.8 calendar years
	1947.4 A.D.
To adjust for the fact there was no year zero between 1 B.C. and A.D. 1, we adjust one year	Plus 1 year
Therefore; the end of Israel's captivity would occur: The Rebirth of Israel	1948.4 1948 – May 15

On the afternoon of May 14, 1948, the Jews proclaimed the independence of the reborn state of Israel. As an old rabbi blew on the traditional shofar, a ram's horn, the Jewish people celebrated the end of their tragic worldwide dispersion and captivity in precise fulfillment of the prophecy made thousands of years earlier by the prophet Ezekiel. At midnight, as May 15, 1948, began, the British Mandate officially ended and Israel became an independent nation. This great day marked the first time since the days of Solomon that a united Israel took its place as a sovereign, independent state among the nations of the world.

In Ezekiel's peculiar prophecy we witness a fulfillment of prophecy in our generation of such remarkable precision, that one is forced to marvel at the power of God to foresee and control all of man's plans and their outcomes. Despite the apparent anarchy of the events of our time, God is still on the throne of this universe and remains in full control of events. The universe is unfolding precisely as our Lord ordained and foresaw millenniums ago. In addition, this amazingly accurate fulfillment of prophecy in our lifetime should focus our attention on the prophecy of Jesus Christ about the budding of the fig tree.

The Bible used the symbol of the fig tree or figs in six different passages as an exclusive symbol of the nation Israel (Judges 9:8-15; Hosea 9:10; Jeremiah 24:1-10; Matthew 21:18-20, etc.). "Now learn this parable from the fig tree: When its branch has already become tender and puts forth leaves, you know that summer is near. So you also, when you see all these things, know that it is near, at the very doors. Assuredly, I say to you, this generation will by no means pass away till all these things are fulfilled" (Matthew 24:32-34). In light of the startling precision of the fulfillment of Ezekiel's prophecy about Israel's rebirth and the prophecy of Jesus that the generation who witnessed this rebirth "will by no means pass away till all these things are fulfilled" every one of us should realize that we are living in the generation when Christ indicated He will return to judge mankind.

Predictions About Jesus Christ the Messiah

The Old Testament contains over three hundred passages that refer to the first coming of the Messiah. Within these hundreds of prophecies, Bible scholars have found forty-eight specific details about the life, death and resurrection of Jesus. These scriptural prophecies were published over five centuries before Christ was born in Bethlehem. In this chapter we will discuss seventeen of these prophecies, examine the evidence for their fulfillment, and prove that Jesus of Nazareth fulfilled them, showing that He is the promised Messiah, the Son of God.

The Laws of Probability

The study of statistics includes the theory and Laws of Mathematical Probability. The Laws of Probability are not abstract. They are so dependable that huge insurance companies write policies promising to pay a million dollars to the family of a thirty-year-old male in return for a small premium of only $30 per month. How can they take on such a huge risk in return for only $30 in monthly premiums? The answer is found in the Laws of Probability. After careful analysis of the mortality tables, insurance companies know that only a tiny fraction of the thirty-year-old clients they insure will actually die within the next year. Every day insurance companies risk billions of dollars on similar well established calculations of mathematical probability.

The Laws of Probability reveal that if the probability of a single event occurring randomly is one chance in five, and the probability of another event occurring is one chance in ten, then the combined probability that both events will occur together in sequence is five multiplied by ten. Thus, the combined chance of both events occurring in sequence is one chance in fifty.

To put this in a perspective we can appreciate, consider the odds when we toss a coin in the air. Since a coin has two sides, the odds are 50 percent or one chance in two that you will get "heads" when you toss a dime. However, suppose that you toss two dimes in a row. What are the odds against getting "heads" twice in a row? The answer is one in four. The combined odds are $2 \times 2 = 4$. The odds of tossing ten coins in a row and getting ten "heads" one after another are quite staggering. According to the laws of probability, the odds against getting ten "heads" are one chance in 1,024. Don't bet your salary that you can beat such odds. However, when you consider the odds against these seventeen prophecies about the life and death of Jesus Christ happening by chance, you will realize that the evidence is compelling that Jesus was the promised Messiah and the Savior of all who will believe in Him.

To further prove the inspiration and authority of the Bible, let us examine only one area of specific prophecy, out of literally hundreds, that has to do with the life and death of the coming Messiah who will save humanity from their sins. In this chapter we will examine a series of specific predictions that were made by different Jewish prophets who lived in widely separated communities over a period of a thousand years. These predictions were fulfilled over five hundred years after they were recorded. We will also examine the possibility that these individual predictions could have occurred by random chance alone. After considering the evidence presented in this chapter, you will understand that the precise fulfillment of these different predictions in the life of one man was so improbable, that any unbiased observer must accept that the Bible was truly inspired by God and that Jesus Christ is the promised Messiah.

Seventeen Incredible Prophecies about the Messiah

In this chapter we will examine seventeen specific prophecies in this analysis of Old Testament predictions that were fulfilled in the life of Jesus of Nazareth. As you consider the likelihood that any one of these particular prophecies could have occurred by chance, ask yourself if it was possible that all seventeen of these predictions could have been fulfilled by random chance in the life of one man, Jesus Christ.

The Old Testament Predictions
About the Coming Messiah

The odds against these
events occurring by chance

The First Prediction
His birth in Bethlehem from the tribe of Judah

Probability: 1 chance in 2,400

The Old Testament Prediction:

"But you, Bethlehem Ephrathah, though you are little among the thousands of Judah, yet out of you shall come forth to Me the One to be ruler in Israel, Whose goings forth have been from of old, from everlasting" (Micah 5:2).

"The scepter shall not depart from Judah, nor a lawgiver from between his feet, until Shiloh comes; and to Him shall be the obedience of the people" (Genesis 49:10).

The New Testament Fulfillment:

"Now after Jesus was born in Bethlehem of Judea in the days of Herod the king, behold, wise men from the East came to Jerusalem" (Matthew 2:1).

There were twelve tribes in ancient Israel from which the Messiah could have been born. Yet He was born from the tribe of Judah as Moses predicted fifteen hundred years earlier. Since there were twelve tribes, the odds were 12 to 1 against Moses guessing correctly the tribe of Christ's birth. In addition, there were over two thousand villages and towns in the densely populated area allotted to the tribe of Judah during the first century of this era. However, to be conservative I used the figure of 1 chance in 2,400 to estimate the odds against anyone guessing that He would be born in Bethlehem and that He would descend from the tribe Judah centuries before Jesus was born.

The Second Prediction
He would be preceded by a messenger

Probability: 1 chance in 20

The Old Testament Prediction:

"The voice of one crying in the wilderness: 'Prepare the way of the Lord; make straight in the desert a highway for our God'" (Isaiah 40:3).

The New Testament Fulfillment:

"In those days John the Baptist came preaching in the wilderness of Judea, and saying, 'Repent, for the kingdom of heaven is at hand!' " (Matthew 3:1,2).

I estimated the odds as 1 in 20, but historical records do not reveal any other king to my knowledge who was preceded by a messenger such as John the Baptist. To calculate the combined probability of these two predictions we must multiply 2,400 times 20 which equals only one chance in 48,000 that Jesus would fulfill both predictions by chance.

The Third Prediction
He would enter Jerusalem on a colt

Probability: 1 chance in 50

The Old Testament Prediction:

"Rejoice greatly, O daughter of Zion! Shout, O daughter of Jerusalem! Behold, your King is coming to you; He is just and having salvation, lowly and riding on a donkey, a colt, the foal of a donkey" (Zechariah 9:9).

The New Testament Fulfillment:

"Then they brought him to Jesus. And they threw their own garments on the colt, and they set Jesus on him. And as He went, they spread their clothes on the road. Then, as He was now drawing near the descent of the Mount of Olives, the whole multitude of the disciples began to rejoice and praise God with a loud voice for all the mighty works they had seen" (Luke 19:35-37).

Of all the kings of history I do not know of a single king who ever entered his capital on a colt, as Jesus did on Palm Sunday, A.D. 32, in fulfillment of this prophecy. The combined odds of the three predictions occurring by chance are 50 x 48,000 which equals one chance in 2,400,000. With the addition of every subsequent prediction the laws of probability reveal that the combined odds against anyone fulfilling these multiple prophecies are simply astronomical.

The Fourth Prediction
He would be betrayed by a friend

Probability: 1 chance in 10

The Old Testament Prediction:

"Even my own familiar friend in whom I trusted, Who ate my bread, Has lifted up his heel against me" (Psalm 41:9).

The New Testament Fulfillment:

"And while He was still speaking, behold, Judas, one of the twelve, with a great multitude with swords and clubs, came from the chief priests and elders of the people. Now His betrayer had given them a sign, saying, 'Whomever I kiss, He is the One; seize Him'" (Matthew 26:47,48).

Although it is not that unusual for a secular king to be betrayed by a close associate the betrayal of a religious leader is quite unusual historically. However, to be conservative, I have assigned the odds of this occurring by chance as only one chance in ten. The combined probability for these four predictions (10 × 2,400,000) is now only one chance in 24 million.

The Fifth Prediction
His hands and feet would be pierced

Probability: 1 chance in 100

The Old Testament Prediction:

"For dogs have surrounded Me; The assembly of the wicked has enclosed Me. They pierced My hands and My feet" (Psalm 22:16).

The New Testament Fulfillment:

"And when they had come to the place called Calvary, there they crucified Him, and the criminals, one on the right hand and the other on the left" (Luke 23:33).

The combined probability of these five predictions (10 × 24 million) has now reached an astonishing one chance in 2.4 billion.

The Sixth Prediction
He would be wounded by His enemies

Probability: 1 chance in 10

The Old Testament Prediction:

"But he was wounded for our transgressions, he was bruised

for our iniquities: the chastisement of our peace was upon him; and with his stripes we are healed" (Isaiah 53:5).

The New Testament Fulfillment:

"Then he released Barabbas to them; and when he had scourged Jesus, he delivered [Him] to be crucified" (Matthew 27:26).

Throughout history most kings who were killed were murdered suddenly. Very few were ever subjected to torture as was inflicted on our Lord Jesus Christ. The odds against this occurring by chance were less than one chance in ten. The combined odds for the six predictions (10 × 2.4 billion) now rises to one chance in 24 billion.

<h3 style="text-align:center">The Seventh Prediction
His betrayal for 30 pieces of silver</h3>

Probability: 1 chance in 50

The Old Testament Prediction:

"Then I said to them, 'If it is agreeable to you, give me my wages; and if not, refrain. 'So they weighed out for my wages thirty pieces of silver'" (Zechariah 11:12).

The New Testament Fulfillment:

"What are you willing to give me if I deliver Him to you? And they counted out to him thirty pieces of silver" (Matthew 26:15).

Consider how impossible it would be to correctly predict five hundred years in advance the exact price of betrayal that would be paid for the death of a future king. The odds (50 × 24 billion) now rise to one chance in one trillion, two hundred billion.

<h3 style="text-align:center">The Eight Prediction
He will be spit upon and beaten</h3>

Probability: 1 chance in 10

The Old Testament Prediction:

"I gave My back to those who struck Me, and My cheeks to those who plucked out the beard; I did not hide My face from shame and spitting" (Isaiah 50:6).

The New Testament Fulfillment:

"Then they spat in His face and beat Him; and others struck Him with the palms of their hands" (Matthew 26:67).

Although many kings throughout history were killed, very few were tormented, beaten and ridiculed. However, Jesus Christ bore those stripes for our healing and salvation. The odds of these eight predictions (10 × one trillion, two hundred billion) occurring by chance are now one chance in 12 trillion.

The Ninth Prediction
His betrayal money would be thrown in the Temple and then given to buy a potter's field

Probability: 1 chance in 200

The Old Testament Prediction:

"And the Lord said to me, 'Throw it to the potter'; that princely price they set on me. So I took the thirty pieces of silver and threw them into the house of the Lord for the potter" (Zechariah 11:13).

The New Testament Fulfillment:

"Then he threw down the pieces of silver in the temple and departed, and went and hanged himself. But the chief priests took the silver pieces and said, 'It is not lawful to put them into the treasury, because they are the price of blood.' And they took counsel and bought with them the potter's field, to bury strangers in" (Matthew 27:5-7).

This complicated prophecy actually seems contradictory on its surface. However, despite its apparent impossibility every detail of this prophecy was fulfilled in precise detail. Judas threw the thirty pieces of betrayal money into the Temple. Later the priests used this money to purchase a potter's field to bury strangers including Judas who, overcome with guilt, hanged himself. I calculated the odds extremely conservatively as one chance in 200. However, the combined odds (200 × 12 trillion) against these nine predictions occurring have risen to one chance in 2,400 trillion.

The Tenth Prediction
He would be silent before His accusers

Probability: 1 chance in 100

The Old Testament Prediction:

"He was oppressed and He was afflicted, yet He opened not His mouth; He was led as a lamb to the slaughter, and as a sheep before its shearers is silent, so He opened not his mouth" (Isaiah 53:7).

The New Testament Fulfillment:

"And while He was being accused by the chief priests and elders, He answered nothing. Then Pilate said to Him, 'Do You not hear how many things they testify against You?' And He answered him not one word, so that the governor marveled greatly" (Matthew 27:12-14).

When we are accused of a crime we naturally defend ourselves, even when we are guilty. Consider how unlikely this prediction was that a totally innocent man would stand before His accusers in absolute silence without speaking to defend himself. While I assigned the odds as one chance in one hundred the realistic chances against this event occurring are much higher. The odds against these ten predictions occurring (100 × 2,400 trillion) is now one chance in 24,000 trillion.

The Eleventh Prediction
He would be crucified with thieves

Probability: 1 chance in 100

The Old Testament Prediction:

"Therefore I will divide Him a portion with the great, and He shall divide the spoil with the strong, because He poured out His soul unto death, and He was numbered with the transgressors, and He bore the sin of many, and made intercession for the transgressors" (Isaiah 53:12).

The New Testament Fulfillment:

"Then two robbers were crucified with Him, one on the right and another on the left" (Matthew 27:38).

The continued multiplication of these odds reaches a truly staggering number when we examine the chances that all seventeen prophecies occurred by chance. At the end of this analysis I will give the final calculation of these incredible odds.

The Twelfth Prediction
People would gamble for His garments
Probability: 1 chance in 100

The Old Testament Prediction:
"They divide My garments among them, And for My clothing they cast lots" (Psalm 22:18).

The New Testament Fulfillment:
"Then the soldiers, when they had crucified Jesus, took His garments and made four parts, to each soldier a part, and also the tunic. Now the tunic was without seam, woven from the top in one piece. They said therefore among themselves, 'Let us not tear it, but cast lots for it, whose it shall be,' that the Scripture might be fulfilled which says: 'They divided My garments among them, and for My clothing they cast lots.'" (John 19: 23,24).

Think of how unlikely it was that Roman soldiers would bother to gamble to see who would win the right to claim the garments of a crucified prisoner. Yet, the prophecy was fulfilled precisely.

The Thirteenth Prediction
His side would be pierced
Probability: 1 chance in 100

The Old Testament Prediction:
"And I will pour on the house of David and on the inhabitants of Jerusalem the Spirit of grace and supplication; then they will look on Me whom they have pierced; they will mourn for Him as one mourns for his only son, and grieve for Him as one grieves for a firstborn" (Zechariah 12:10).

The New Testament Fulfillment:
"But one of the soldiers pierced His side with a spear, and immediately blood and water came out" (John 19:34).

The cruelty of the Romans was expressed in the unspeakable pain inflicted on prisoners in their lengthy death on the cross. However, despite their orders to produce a drawn-out death, the Roman centurion was motivated by God to pierce

Christ's side with his spear. The blood and water flowing out of Christ's side proved that He had already died before the spear entered His side. The odds against anyone plunging a spear into the side of a man being crucified on a cross is estimated conservatively as one chance in 100.

The Fourteenth Prediction
None of His bones would be broken

Probability: 1 chance in 20

The Old Testament Prediction:

"He guards all his bones; Not one of them is broken" (Psalm 34:20).

The New Testament Fulfillment:

"But when they came to Jesus and saw that He was already dead, they did not break His legs" (John 19:33).

When a prisoner of Rome was crucified, his body was placed on the cross in such a manner that the only way he could breathe was by painfully lifting his upper body, using the strength of his legs, to expand his diaphragm. When the Roman soldiers wished to speed up the death of the condemned prisoner they would break his legs with a club and thus prevent him from lifting himself up to breathe. Within minutes the prisoner would die due to oxygen deprivation and fluid accumulating in his lungs. To avoid desecrating the Sabbath, which was about to begin, the soldiers broke the legs of the prisoners on either side of Jesus to assure their quick death. However, in fulfillment of the ancient prophecy, Jesus had already "given up the ghost" and died by His own will. Therefore, they did not break Christ's legs and thus fulfilled the prophecy.

The Fifteenth Prediction
His body would not decay

Probability: 1 chance in 10,000

The Old Testament Prediction:

"For You will not leave my soul in Sheol, Nor will You allow Your Holy One to see corruption" (Psalm 16:10).

The New Testament Fulfillment:

"He, foreseeing this, spoke concerning the resurrection of

186

the Christ, that His soul was not left in Hades, nor did His flesh see corruption" (Acts 2:31).

Obviously, the odds against anyone dying and their body not decaying, but later rising from the dead, are obviously astronomical. However, I have estimated the odds as only one chance in 10,000 because several other individuals were resurrected in the Old Testament, such as the Shunammite widow's son who was raised from the dead by Elisha (2 Kings 4:28-37) and Lazarus who was resurrected by Jesus (John 11:43,44).

The Sixteenth Prediction
His burial in a rich man's tomb
Probability: 1 chance in 100

The Old Testament Prediction:

"And they made His grave with the wicked; but with the rich at His death, because He had done no violence, nor was any deceit in His mouth" (Isaiah 53:9).

The New Testament Fulfillment:

"Now when evening had come, there came a rich man from Arimathaea, named Joseph, who himself had also become a disciple of Jesus. This man went to Pilate and asked for the body of Jesus. Then Pilate commanded the body to be given to him. And when Joseph had taken the body, he wrapped it in a clean linen cloth, and laid it in his new tomb which he had hewn out of the rock; and he rolled a large stone against the door of the tomb, and departed" (Matthew 27:57-60).

The probable site of the tomb of Christ, the Garden Tomb, is located just north of the Damascus Gate of the old walled city of Jerusalem, only a few hundred yards from the probable site of Golgotha. When the tomb was discovered in the last century, archeologists found that only one body depression was ever used. The owner did not complete the stone carving work to bury a second body. In addition, they found a huge cistern capable of holding 200,000 gallons of water beneath the garden, indicating that it was a rich man's garden tomb. Furthermore, they found the remains of an ancient wine press in the garden.

The Seventeenth Prediction
The darkness covering the earth
Probability: 1 chance in 1,000

The Old Testament Prediction:

"'And it shall come to pass in that day,' says the Lord God, 'That I will make the sun go down at noon, and I will darken the earth in broad daylight'" (Amos 8:9).

The New Testament Fulfillment:

"Now from the sixth hour until the ninth hour there was darkness over all the land" (Matthew 27:45).

Although this prophecy is one of the most incredible of the seventeen, the *Third History of Thallus*, a pagan Greek historian of the third century, reported that there was an unusual darkness that blotted out the sun for a number of hours at the time of Passover in the year A.D. 32, the year of Christ's crucifixion. Although Thallus speculated that this darkness was the result of an eclipse, any astronomer can tell you that it is absolutely impossible that an eclipse could have occurred at that time, because Passover was carefully calculated to occur at the time of the full moon. The position of the sun, moon, and earth at the time of the full moon makes it impossible that this darkness recorded by the historian Thallus could have been the result of a natural eclipse. However, his report about the darkness does confirm that the Bible's prophecy and the New Testament record of its fulfillment is accurate.

This analysis has shown that seventeen detailed prophecies, made five centuries before the birth of Jesus of Nazareth, were fulfilled with absolute precision in the life, death, and resurrection of Jesus Christ. The question to consider is this: What are the chances that all seventeen of these predictions occurred by chance rather than by the divine plan of God? Either these seventeen predictions are simply the result of chance or this evidence provides overwhelming proof that God inspired the Bible and is in control of history.

The combined probability against these 17 predictions occurring is equal to:

1 chance in 480,000,000,000,000,000,000,000,000,000,000

or

1 chance in 480 Billion × 1 Billion × 1 Trillion

In other words, there is only one chance in 480 billion × 1 Billion × 1 Trillion that these Old Testament prophets could have accurately predicted these seventeen specific prophecies about the life, death, and resurrection of Jesus Christ by chance alone. The odds are equally impossible that any man could have fulfilled these detailed prophecies by chance alone. Let any reader assign any other estimates (lower or higher) they might choose for these probabilities that these predictions occurred. Regardless of the size of the estimates for probability you assign to these individual predictions, you will still be confronted with a combined probability so staggering in its magnitude that it will be impossible to honestly convince yourself that these events occurred by chance. In the unlikely event that you still are not convinced, consider the fact that we have examined only seventeen of the forty-eight major prophecies given in the Old Testament about the promised Messiah. If we were to calculate the odds against all forty-eight predictions occurring by chance we would arrive at a number so large that it would exceed our capacity to comprehend it.

Some Bible critics have suggested that Jesus of Nazareth, as a rabbi, knew about these predictions and simply arranged the events of His life to fulfill these specific predictions. However, consider the impossibility of any normal human arranging the fulfillment of these specific predictions. How would you arrange to be born in Bethlehem and manage to be descended from the tribe of Judah? How would you arrange the price of your betrayal to be precisely thirty pieces of silver? How would you arrange to be crucified with thieves and then, to be buried in a rich man's grave? If you could arrange to have these remarkable events fulfilled you are the Son of God. Obviously, only God could either foresee these events in advance or arrange to fulfill these precise predictions in the life of Jesus Christ.

These Prophecies Prove the Bible Is Inspired By God

When we consider these seventeen specific Messianic prophecies, the odds against any one person fulfilling these predictions by random chance alone, or that any prophet would correctly guess these details, is absolutely astronomical. To fully grasp the reality that these fulfilled prophecies prove that Jesus Christ is the promised Messiah and Son of God, consider the following illustration:

First, the odds against the prophets correctly guessing all seventeen prophecies are:

1 chance in 480 Billion × 1 Billion × 1 Trillion!

To understand these incredible odds we must try to get a picture of these odds in our minds. Imagine that every one of these chances was represented by a small grain of sand. Furthermore, imagine that one single grain of sand is painted gold and represents the one chance out of this astronomical number that Christ fulfilled these predictions by chance. We are going to blindfold you and ask you to search for the single gold-painted grain of sand. Imagine that the entire galaxy known as the Milky Way, encompassing two hundred million stars like our sun plus millions of planets, moons, and asteroids is composed only of some of these 480 Billion × 1 Billion × 1 Trillion grains of sand. In our galaxy filled with this incredible number of grains of sand, your target is the only grain of sand that is painted gold. Remember that our galaxy is so vast that if you could travel in the Star Trek Enterprise space craft at the speed of light, 187,000 miles per second, it would still take you a hundred thousand years to cross the galaxy. If we were to blindfold you and send you blindly searching through our entire galaxy to find a single gold-painted grain of sand, you would face the same impossible odds in finding the gold grain of sand as the probability against these seventeen prophecies occurring by chance alone.

With such odds against you, would you bet a thousand dollars that you would find a single gold grain in a whole galaxy filled with sand? I doubt that you would risk your money on such impossible odds. Yet, tragically, every year millions will die who have bet their lives and their eternal souls on the "chance" that these fulfilled prophecies about Jesus Christ are not reliable. They believe they can safely ignore the claims of Christ upon their lives. However, in light of the overwhelming evidence for the authority of the Bible and the reality of Jesus Christ as God's Messiah, each of us needs to personally consider the decision we must make about our response to Christ's life, death and resurrection.

A few weeks ago I found a web site on the Internet that dealt with answering the questions of Islamic people searching for information about Jesus Christ. This site contained a letter from a former Palestinian named Walid who had lived his life as a Muslim militant filled with hatred for the Jews. However, one day he happened to find my book *Armageddon – Appointment With Destiny* that included this analysis of several of the key prophecies about Jesus of Nazareth. To demonstrate the power of fulfilled prophecy to reach the mind and soul I will share a portion of this man's *Story of Walid* that appears on this web site.[6]

A Portion of *The Story of Walid*

Internet site: http://wri.leaderu.com/pages/walid.html

Sometime in 1992 I was fascinated when I read a book titled *Armageddon, Appointment With Destiny*, by Grant Jeffrey. Some of the things explained in this book had many detailed prophecies about Jesus: his birth, life, death and resurrection; and the re-creation of the state of Israel. Many of these prophecies came to pass just as God put them down in the Bible! What also amazed me, is to find out that the chances for a man to predict hundreds of historic events written hundreds and thousands of years before their occurrences are one in zillions . . . what is more fascinating is that the margin of error had to be zero, especially when the fulfillment of many of these prophecies are happening in my generation. This kind of evidence had to come from a divine origin, that origin had to be God Almighty.

Walid communicated with me last week and confirmed that he accepted Jesus Christ as his Savior after becoming motivated to read the Gospels after becoming convinced that the fulfilled prophecies proved that Jesus was truly the promised Messiah and Son of God. He now loves the Jews as he loves his own Arab people and prays for their salvation.

In light of the Bible's own declaration that fulfilled prophecy is the absolute proof that it was written under the direct inspiration of God, I believe the material in this chapter provides compelling evidence of the authority and inspiration of the Scriptures.

Notes

1. Grant R. Jeffrey, *Armageddon – Appointment With Destiny* (Toronto: Frontier Research Publications, Inc. 1988) 14,15.
2. Erika Cheetham, *The Final Prophecies of Nostradamus* (New York: The Putnam Publishing Group, 1989).
3. Henry C. Roberts, *The Complete Prophecies of Nostradamus* (Jericho, N.Y.: Nostradamus, Inc. 1976).
2. Louis Pauwels and Jacques Bergier, *Morning of the Magicians* (New York: Stein and Day, 1964) 9,10,14.
5. Grant R. Jeffrey, *Armageddon – Appointment With Destiny* (Toronto: Frontier Research Publications, Inc., 1988).
6. Internet site: http://wri.leaderu.com/pages/walid.html.

8

Evidence From Prophecies Fulfilled in Our Generation

Now as He sat on the Mount of Olives, the disciples came to Him privately, saying, 'Tell us, when will these things be? And what will be the sign of Your coming, and of the end of the age?' (Matthew 24:3).

One of the greatest proofs that the Bible is inspired is the evidence of thousands of detailed prophecies that were fulfilled to the smallest particular throughout history. Centuries before the events occurred the ancient prophets foretold the rise and fall of empires and cities including Babylon, Tyre, and Nineveh. However, in the balance of this chapter I would like to examine several astonishing prophecies that were fulfilled in our lifetime that prove the Bible's inspiration and also point to the nearness of Christ's return.

For thousands of years Christians have studied the Bible's ancient prophecies and wondered if they would live to witness the return of Christ to redeem humanity. Many today are longing for the return of Jesus Christ. Naturally, sceptics remind us that past generations also looked for the Second Coming but never saw the promise fulfilled. Why should we believe our generation will witness the return of Christ when so many other generations were disappointed? Thirty-eight years of careful study of Bible prophecies have convinced me of the overwhelming evidence that Jesus Christ will likely return in our generation. Jesus and the other prophets described numerous prophecies that would occur in the lifetime of those who would see Him return with their own eyes. Is ours the generation that will see Christ coming for His Church? The answer to this question will have profound implications for our life, our witnessing, and our priorities in our living.

In this chapter we will examine numerous prophecies relating to the last days and the biblical passages where the original prophecies were announced over two thousand years ago. Each of these prophecies refers to a unique event that was never fulfilled in any past generation. By their unique nature many of these predictions could not be fulfilled again in another generation. Our Lord Jesus Christ warned, "Now when these things begin to happen, look up and lift up your heads, because your redemption draws near" (Luke 21:28). Let's examine in detail several of these fascinating predictions to illustrate the tremendous precision of biblical prophecies as proof that God inspired the writers of the Bible.

The Rebirth of Israel

The rebirth of Israel is one of the most extraordinary and unlikely of all the prophecies in the Bible. In an earlier portion of this chapter we examined the marvelous precision of the prophecy in which Ezekiel predicted that Israel would be reborn in the spring of 1948.

Jesus Christ foretold the rebirth of Israel in his famous prophecy of the "fig tree" budding that was recorded in Matthew's Gospel. Our Lord declared in Matthew 24:32-35: "Now learn a parable of the fig tree; When his branch is yet tender, and putteth forth leaves, ye know that summer is nigh: So likewise ye, when ye shall see all these things, know that it is near, even at the doors. Verily I say unto you, This generation shall not pass, till all these things be fulfilled. Heaven and earth shall pass away, but my words shall not pass away." No other ancient nation ever ceased to exist for a period of centuries and then returned to take its place on the stage of world history. "Who hath heard such a thing? Who hath seen such things? Shall the earth be made to bring forth in one day? or shall a nation be born at once? For as soon as Zion travailed, she brought forth her children" (Isaiah 66:8).

Most nations evolved gradually over the centuries, such as Egypt or France. In the time of the ancient prophecies, no one had ever witnessed a nation being created "in one day." Yet, in his prediction, Isaiah prophesied that Israel would come into existence in "one day." The prophecies of Isaiah and Ezekiel were fulfilled precisely as predicted on May 15, 1948.

Predictions About the Present Arab-Israeli Conflict

However, the prophecies surrounding the rebirth of Israel did not stop with the declaration of Israel's independence in 1948. Three thousand years ago God inspired King David to predict that the reborn nation of Israel would be immediately surrounded by enemies, including the Arab nations of Jordan, Egypt, Saudi Arabia and Syria.

> For, lo, thine enemies make a tumult: and they that hate thee have lifted up the head. They have taken crafty counsel against thy people, and consulted against thy hidden ones. They have said, Come, and let us cut them off from being a nation; that the name of Israel may be no more in remembrance. For they have consulted together with one consent: they are confederate against thee: The tabernacles of Edom, and the Ishmaelites; of Moab, and the Hagarenes; Gebal, and Ammon, and Amalek; the Philistines with the inhabitants of Tyre; Assur also is joined with them: they have holpen the children of Lot. Selah. (Psalm 83:2-8)

In this incredible prophecy, David described the modern states of the Middle East by naming the ancient nations that have now joined with the Palestinians in their attempt to destroy the Jewish state in the last days.

The Miraculous Restoration of the Hebrew Language

The prophet Zephaniah had predicted something equally impossible as the rebirth of Israel. God predicted through His prophet Zephaniah that He would restore the ancient dead language of Hebrew as the living, spoken language of Israel. Hebrew ceased to be the common language of the Jews long before the life of Christ. "For then will I turn to the people a pure language, that they may all call upon the name of the Lord, to serve him with one consent" (Zephaniah 3:9).

No other nation has ever lost its language and later recovered it. No one is speaking ancient Egyptian or Chaldee today. A Jewish scholar by the name of Eliazar ben Yehuda began working early in the last century in Israel, in his attempt to revive the dead language of Hebrew with its original seven thousand words related to Temple worship as used by the priests.[1] He invented thousands of new words for fountain pen, airplane, etc. He created a fourteen volume dictionary for the new living language of Hebrew as detailed in the book *Tongue of the Prophets* by Robert St. John.

Ultimately, Eliazar re-created modern Hebrew as the living language of five million Israelis. As the Jews began to return from seventy different nations to their Promised Land in 1948 after two thousand years of exile, the government and army began to unify these widely divergent peoples into a united people through teaching them the revived Hebrew language. The Jews of Israel will someday fulfill the prophecy of Zephaniah by calling "upon the name of the Lord, to serve him with one consent" when they see their Messiah.

The Return of the Ethiopian Jews to Israel

The prophet Zephaniah predicted another seemingly impossible prophecy when he declared that God would return the Ethiopian Jews to the land of Israel after they were separated from their Jewish brethren for almost three thousand years. In the days of King Solomon a group of Jews from each of the twelve tribes immigrated to Ethiopia with Prince Menelik, the son of King Solomon and the Queen of Sheba, as detailed in my book *Armageddon*.[2] The prophet foretold their return to their homeland in the last days in these words, "From beyond the rivers of Ethiopia my suppliants, even the daughter of my dispersed, shall bring mine offering" (Zephaniah 3:10). Another prophet, Isaiah, also confirmed this prediction. "I will say to the north, Give up; and to the south, Keep not back: bring my sons from far, and my daughters from the ends of the earth" (Isaiah 43:6).

Isaiah predicted the miraculous return of the Jews from both Russia (the north) and from Ethiopia (the south). In the later part of the 1980s and especially in the spring of 1991 over twenty-five thousand black Jews returned home to Israel from Ethiopia in fulfillment of Zephaniah's ancient prophecy.[3] Numerous prophecies foretold of the final return of the exiles to the Holy Land. "Thus saith the Lord God; Behold, I will take the children of Israel from among the heathen, whither they be gone, and will gather them on every side, and bring them into their own land" (Ezekiel 37:21).

The Astonishing Fertility of Israel

In addition to recovering their homeland, their lost language and their exiles, the prophet Isaiah predicted that Israel would become fertile again. "He shall cause them that come of Jacob to take root: Israel shall blossom and bud, and fill the face of the world with fruit" (Isaiah 27:6). The returning Jews have transformed the previously deserted and desolate land into the most agriculturally efficient land on earth according to the United Nations. Some 90 percent of Israel's flower production is now exported, mostly to Europe. Israel now supplies over 90 percent of the citrus fruit consumed by hundreds of millions of Europeans. The kibbutz (collective settlement) and moshav (cooperative settlement) today account for 79 percent of Israel's agricultural produce.[4]

Another prophecy connected with Israel's return was made by the prophet Joel who declared that the desert nation of Israel would experience tremendous increases of rain in the last days.

"Be glad then, ye children of Zion, and rejoice in the Lord your God: for he hath given you the former rain moderately, and he will cause to come down for you the rain, the former rain, and the latter rain in the first month" (Joel 2:23). As the rainfall increased dramatically during the last century the returning Jewish exiles planted over two hundred million trees and transformed the complete environment of the Promised Land. "And the parched ground shall become a pool, and the thirsty land springs of water: in the habitation of dragons, where each lay, shall be grass with reeds and rushes" (Isaiah 35:7).

Another curious prediction was found in Ezekiel 38 which claimed that Israel would dwell "without walls or gates" in the last days. In the ancient past even small villages as well as cities depended on walls for defense against invading armies. Yet God inspired Ezekiel to record the following verse in his prophecy about the coming Russian-Arab invasion of Israel. "And thou shalt say, I will go up to the land of unwalled villages; I will go to them that are at rest, that dwell safely, all of them dwelling without walls, and having neither bars nor gates" (Ezekiel 38: 11). How could Ezekiel have known twenty-five centuries ago that the development of modern weapons such as bombs, airplanes and missiles, would have made walls and gates irrelevant for defensive purposes in the last days? Even army bases and Israel's settlements in the West Bank and Gaza have no walls today.

Israel's Plans to Rebuild the Temple

The Bible contains numerous prophecies that tell us that Israel will rebuild the Temple in the last days. The prophet Isaiah wrote, "And it shall come to pass in the last days, that the mountain of the Lord's house shall be established in the top of the mountains, and shall be exalted above the hills; and all nations shall flow unto it" (Isaiah 2:2). In the Book of Revelation (11:1,2) John tells us that the angel took him into the future to measure the Temple that will exist during the seven-year tribulation period.

The apostle Paul confirms this in his prophecy about the Antichrist occupying the future Temple. "Let no man deceive you by any means: for that day shall not come, except there come a falling away first, and that man of sin be revealed, the son of perdition; Who opposeth and exalteth himself above all that is called God, or that is worshiped; so that he as God sitteth in the temple of God, showing himself that he is God" (2 Thessalonians 2:3,4). The prophet Ezekiel described his vision of the future Temple with Levites and priests worshiping God: "And thou shalt give to the priests the Levites that be of the seed of Zadok, which approach unto me, to minister unto me, saith the Lord God, a young bullock for a sin offering" (Ezekiel 43:19).

The Oil of Anointing

One of the most unusual aspects of the ancient Tabernacle and Temple was the oil of anointing that was specially prepared with five specific ingredients to anoint the Temple and the High Priests. Moses described God's command to Israel: "And thou shalt make it an oil of holy ointment, an ointment compound after the art of the apothecary: it shall be an holy anointing oil. And thou shalt anoint the tabernacle of the congregation therewith, and the ark of the testimony" (Exodus 30:25,26). One of the five ingredients needed to make the oil was *afars'mon*. However, the oil and its ingredients were lost, seemingly forever, when the Romans destroyed the Temple in A.D. 70 and burned the only two groves where *afars'mon* trees grew. Without this special ingredient, they could never obey God's command to anoint the rebuilt Temple.

In addition, the prophet Daniel foretold that, when the Messiah returns, He will be anointed with this oil of anointing. "Seventy weeks are determined upon thy people and upon thy holy city, to finish the transgression, and to make an end of sins, and to make reconciliation for iniquity, and to bring in everlasting righteousness, and to seal up the vision and prophecy, and *to anoint the most Holy*" (Daniel 9:24). How could these prophecies be fulfilled when one of the key ingredients was lost forever. Incredibly, several years ago, archeologists in Israel led by Dr. Joseph Patrich of Hebrew University found a clay flask buried in a cave near the Dead Sea caves.[5] The flask was filled with the ancient oil of anointing and was located by the archeologists followed the ancient directions listed in the Copper Scroll that described where the priests had hidden various treasures of the Second Temple. Scientists from Hebrew University confirmed with Carbon 14 dating that the oil was two thousand years old and is composed of the five precise ingredients described in Exodus 30:25,26. The complete story of the Copper Scroll and the search for the lost treasures of the Temple, including the oil of anointing, is in my new book, *Unveiling Mysteries of the Bible.* (See Order Form, back page.)

This precious sacred oil of anointing is now in the possession of the two Chief Rabbis of Israel. Someday, when Israel's Messiah, Jesus Christ, returns to the rebuilt Temple I believe Daniel's prophecy will finally be fulfilled when Christ will be anointed with that ancient sacred oil as God's Anointed King.

Vessels For Future Temple Worship

Ezekiel foretold that the sacred vessels and linen robes will be prepared for use in the Temple in the Millennium. "They shall enter into my sanctuary, and they shall come near to my table, to minister unto me, and they shall keep my charge. And it shall come to pass, that when they enter in at the gates of the inner court, they shall be clothed with linen garments; and no wool shall come upon them, while they minister in the gates of the inner court, and within" (Ezekiel 44:16,17).

The Temple Institute in the Old City of Jerusalem is one Israeli group that is actively preparing for the rebuilding of the Temple in preparation for the Messiah's appearance. The Temple Institute has constructed over seventy-five objects and vessels as well as linen priestly garments required for future Temple services. To view some of the objects of worship that have already been constructed by the Temple Institute you can visit their intriguing web site.[6]

The yeshivas, or Jewish Bible colleges in Jerusalem have trained over five hundred young men from the tribe of Levi to correctly fulfill their future duties of Temple worship, music, and sacrifice. The prophecies describe the resumption of the sacrifice of the Ashes of the Red Heifer to produce the waters of purification (Numbers 19) needed to cleanse the defiled Temple objects, the priests, and the defiled stones on the Temple Mount. The prophet Ezekiel confirmed that the waters of purification will be used to cleanse the future Temple and the Jewish people. "Then will I sprinkle clean water upon you, and ye shall be clean: from all your filthiness, and from all your idols, will I cleanse you" (Ezekiel 36:25).

The Revival of the Roman Empire

The Bible foretold the revival of the Roman Empire in the final generation when the Messiah will return to establish His eternal kingdom:

> And the fourth kingdom [the revived Roman Empire] shall be strong as iron: forasmuch as iron breaketh in pieces and subdueth all things: and as iron that breaketh all these, shall it break in pieces and bruise. And whereas thou sawest the feet and toes, part of potter's clay, and part of iron, the kingdom shall be divided; but there shall be in it of the strength of the iron, forasmuch as thou sawest the iron mixed with miry clay. And as the toes of the feet were part of iron, and part of clay, so the kingdom shall be partly strong, and partly broken. And whereas thou sawest iron mixed with miry clay, they shall mingle themselves with the seed of men: but they shall not cleave one to another, even as iron is not mixed with clay. And in the days of these kings shall the God of heaven set up a kingdom [the Millenial Kingdom of Jesus Christ], which shall never be destroyed: and the kingdom shall not be left to other people, but it shall break in pieces and consume all these kingdoms, and it shall stand for ever. (Daniel 2:40-44).

Other prophecies in Daniel 7 and Revelation 13 and 17 confirm the revival of the Roman Empire in the last days in the unique form of a ten-nation superstate. Following the devastation of two world wars the leadership of Europe came together after World War II to plan the creation of a confederate form of superstate bringing the major nations of Europe together for the first time since the days of Rome. In 1957, six countries signed the Treaty of Rome laying the foundation for the future United States of Europe. Henri Spaak, the former secretary-general of NATO admitted in a BBC documentary on the European Union that "we felt like Romans on that day. . . . We were consciously re-creating the Roman Empire once more."[7] Since then, the Maastricht Treaty consolidated the fifteen nations of the European Union into the world's first superstate. It is now an economic, political, and potentially, a military colossus that will dominate world events in the near future.

The Rebuilding of Babylon

One of the most unusual of the Bible's prophecies reveals that the city of Babylon will be rebuilt and later destroyed by God at the time of Armageddon by supernatural fire from heaven like Sodom and Gomorrah. The prophet Isaiah foretold this destruction as follows: "Howl ye; for the day of the Lord is at hand; it shall come as a destruction from the Almighty. . . . And Babylon, the glory of kingdoms, the beauty of the Chaldees' excellency, shall be as when God overthrew Sodom and Gomorrah" (Isaiah 13:6,19). In this remarkable prediction the prophet declared that Babylon will not only exist again but it will be destroyed on the Great Day of the Lord. As unlikely as it seems, the Iraqi government of Saddam Hussein has spent over $2.5 billion dollars rebuilding the ancient city of Babylon. He intends that it will become the center of their future renewed Babylonian Empire that will rule the entire Middle East as a regional superpower armed with deadly nuclear, chemical, and biological weapons of mass destruction.

President Saddam Hussein of Iraq has spent decades rebuilding this ruined city and its magnificent palaces in all of its ancient glory. Many of the sixty million new clay bricks constructed to rebuild the walls that extend 56 miles in circumference contain the following inscription: "In the era of President Saddam Hussein all Babylon was constructed in three stages. From Nebuchadnezzar to Saddam Hussein, Babylon is rising again."[8]

Interestingly, the whole city of Babylon was built over an underground lake of asphalt and oil. God has already provided the fuel for its final destruction. In another prophecy, God foretold that the wicked city will burn forever. "For it is the day of the Lord's vengeance, and the year of recompenses for the controversy of Zion. And the streams thereof shall be turned into pitch, and the dust thereof into brimstone, and the land thereof shall become burning pitch. It shall not be quenched night nor day; the smoke thereof shall go up for ever: from generation to generation it shall lie waste; none shall pass through it for ever and ever" (Isaiah 34:8-10). Several years ago during the Gulf War we had a foretaste of this burning of Babylon when Saddam Hussein set hundreds of Kuwaiti oil wells on fire and covered the desert with smoke and fire.

One World Government

Over two thousand years ago the prophets Daniel and John described that there would be a global, world government led by the coming dictator, the Antichrist in the last days (Daniel 7: 14). "And it was given unto him to make war with the saints, and to overcome them: and power was given him over all kindreds, and tongues, and nations. And all that dwell upon the earth shall worship him" (Revelation 13:7,8).

There has never been a world government during thousands of years of human history. However, as I outlined in my book, *Final Warning*,[9] the elite are moving behind the scenes to produce a world government as quickly as possible. The rising power of the United Nations, the World Trade Organization, and World Court are moving us quickly beyond the days of national sovereignty and individual nations.

Deadly Pestilence

The Bible describes terrible plagues and horrible sores occurring throughout the world's population in the Great Tribulation. The plagues that will destroy hundreds of millions in the last days may include the effects of biological and chemical weapons. Zechariah also described the terrible plagues at the Battle of Armageddon: "And this shall be the plague wherewith the Lord will smite all the people that have fought against Jerusalem; Their flesh shall consume away while they stand upon their feet, and their eyes shall consume away in their holes, and their tongue shall consume away in their mouth" (Zechariah 14:12).

So I looked, and behold an ashy pale horse, . . . and its rider's name was Death, and Hades . . . followed him closely; and they were given authority and power over a fourth part of the earth, to kill with the sword and with famine and with plague (pestilence, disease) and with wild beasts of the earth. (Revelation 6:8, [Amplified Bible Version]).

The prophecy of the Four Horsemen of the Apocalypse warned that a fourth of humanity will be killed by plague and pestilence symbolized by the fourth horseman during the Tribulation. How could this prophecy be fulfilled literally? Tragically, the AIDS epidemic throughout Africa, South America, and Asia is demonstrating how this prophecy may be fulfilled in our generation. The December, 2001, AIDS figures from the UN and the World Health Organization indicate that 40 million people suffer from the deadly disease with three quarters of them in southern Africa.[10] The AIDS plague is now poised to destroy a large portion of mankind in the worst epidemic in history. Thus far it appears that no one has survived AIDS for much more than twelve years. Jesus warned His disciples about plagues in the last days, "For nation shall rise against nation, and kingdom against kingdom: and there shall be famines, and pestilences, and earthquakes, in divers places" (Matthew 24:7).

In North America and Europe the AIDS virus is still primarily infecting people within the homosexual community and drug users who share illegal drugs through needles. However, in the Third World huge numbers of heterosexuals in Africa, South America, and Asia are now infected with AIDS and are infecting others. Scientists have determined that widespread unprotected promiscuous sexual activity between males and females facilitates the rapid transmission of the AIDS virus throughout the sexually active population in the Third World (Africa, Asia, South America). The combination of high levels of promiscuity, a virtual absence of effective sanitation, minimal AIDS education, and a lack of antibiotics or condom protection has produced an epidemic of all sexually transmitted diseases, including the deadly AIDS virus throughout Africa and Asia. South America is beginning to follow the same deadly pattern.

In the Second World (the former U.S.S.R. and Eastern Europe) we are witnessing an astonishing and threatening explosion of AIDS that may become a deadly plague that could destroy their hopes to rebuild their society after seven decades of communist tyranny. The primary method of AIDS transmission in Russia (93 percent), the former U.S.S.R. and Eastern Europe is through the illegal misuse of injected drugs through shared use of needles.[11] The normal justice practice of arresting and imprisoning hard drug users unfortunately places them in a situation where they can only obtain illegal injected drugs by sharing used (often HIV infected) needles in the terrible conditions of unsanitary jails in Eastern Europe and the former U.S.S.R.

As an example of the desperate crisis, there were less than 100 AIDS cases registered with medical authorities in the Ukraine during the five years between 1989 till 1994. However, Ukrainian medical authorities now estimate that 300,000 of their citizens are now infected with AIDS only eight years later (a staggering increase in only eight years of 3000 percent).[12] The number of people infected with AIDS in Russia has increased more than fifteen times in the last few years. The economic collapse of Russia (with an Gross National Product reduced to the same size as Portugal) and the corruption of all government services suggests that this plague will only grow worse.

The only real and practical solution to the AIDS crisis is to return to God's laws regarding a monogamous marriage relationship between a faithful husband and wife. This is the only true "safe sex" that exists in a world of promiscuous behavior and sexually transmitted disease. In the early 1990s, the Central Intelligence Agency produced a report on the AIDS epidemic in Africa that was staggering in its conclusions. The evidence pointed to the greatest epidemic and loss of life in human history. The CIA report predicted that, at worst, as many as 75 percent of the population of sub-Sahara Africa might become infected with AIDS over the next twelve years. This would mean the ultimate infection and eventual death by AIDS of up to three hundred million people in Africa alone. We are now witnessing the greatest tragedy in history in the approaching partial extinction of the population of a whole continent. The mind can scarcely imagine death on this massive scale.

The *South African Medical Journal* in July 1991, reported that a staggering 47 percent of black male and female blood donors who were tested were found to test positive for AIDS during 1989. The latest reports from UNAIDS indicate that almost 30 million Africans have AIDSs, virtually three-quarters of the 40 million people throughout the globe that presently have AIDS.[13] The tragedy is that Africa, the poorest continent and the one least able to provide adequate medical care for those afflicted with this terrible plague of this generation, has suffered the worst exposure to this global AIDS epidemic. The latest studies on AIDS infection rates in southern Africa released recently at the 2002 annual AIDS conference in Spain revealed that the life expectancy for the citizens living in southern Africa has dropped from over age 60 to less than age 40 – a loss of twenty years of productive life that is unprecedented in human history. The prognosis for Asia and parts of South America is tragically similar. One study in the mid-1990s showed that almost every soldier in the army of several East African nations that agreed to be tested were found to be infected by the AIDS virus.

In a report by Charlene Laino of MSNBC from Durban, South Africa, July 10, 2002 she wrote about the greatest tragedy facing the world today.

> For the first time since the Black Plague of the 14th century, the population of some African countries is expected to drop as AIDS continues to sweep through rural and urban communities alike, experts reported here Monday at the 13th International AIDS Conference. And in regions hardest hit by the fatal scourge, life expectancy will plummet to age 30 by the end of the decade — the lowest level in 100 years.[14]

Worldwide Famine

The apostle John described his vision of the horrible famine in the last days. "And I looked, and behold, a black horse, and he who sat on it had a pair of scales in his hand" (Revelation 6: 5). The scales represent famine, and the prophet explains that a day's wages at that time will only buy enough wheat or barley to feed the workman, not his family.

The United Nations claims that millions in southern Africa are now at risk of dying from devastating famine. In February, 2002, the Rome-based UN Food and Agriculture Organisation said.

> The UN food agency has warned that more than four million people in southern Africa faced severe food shortages because of bad weather and a reduction in the areas planted with crops. The aggregate output of southern Africa's main staple, maize, is a quarter lower than 2000 levels at 13,4-million tons and 'well below the average of the past five years.' Serious food shortages were affecting rural and urban areas of Malawi, Zambia and Zimbabwe because maize stocks were at 'extremely low levels.'[15]

Despite the great advances in food production and food storage techniques more people are suffering from malnutritian today than at any other time in history. The UN estimates that hundreds of millions of people are in danger of starvation while another billion people lack proper nutrition and access to clean water. In light of the massive changes in world weather patterns we may witness terrible famine in the future in countries that felt themselves immune to hunger.

However, the Bible's prophesies devastating global famine affecting one quarter of the earth during the seven years of the coming Tribulation period. Famine conditions will be compounded by the use of weapons of mass destruction used in the horrific wars of the Antichrist together with the drop in world agricultural production in response to the cataclysmic divine judgments of great heat, frightening darkness, global plague, disruptive earthquakes, and poisoned waters.

Preparations for the Mark of the Beast

The Book of Revelation describes the end of cash and the creation of a cashless society in the last days where the possession of a certain number, "666," will be essential to enable you to "buy or sell." This was an astonishing prophecy when John proclaimed it in the first century:

> And he causeth all, both small and great, rich and poor, free and bond, to receive a mark in their right hand, or in their foreheads: And that no man might buy or sell, save he that had the mark, or the name of the beast, or the number of his name. Here is wisdom. Let him that hath understanding count the number of the beast: for it is the number of a man; and his number is Six hundred threescore and six. (Revelation 13:16-18)

However, we are already 95 percent cashless in America today. Studies reveal that less than 5 percent of the total money in our society exists as paper currency or coins. Revelation describes a time when the number 666 will be placed beneath the skin on the right hand or forehead to control people in the Antichrist's empire. For the first time in history we are developing technology which would allow tiny computer chips holding your complete medical and financial records to be placed beneath the skin of the right hand or forehead.

Recently, scientists developed a miniature computer chip so powerful that it will hold up to five gigabytes of information in a chip the size of a dime. This tiny chip will hold as much information as contained in thirty complete sets of the *Encyclopædia Britannica*. This chip could also be configured in a shape the size of two grains of rice that could be injected beneath the skin. Your complete financial life records could be held by such a chip which could be read from a distance by electronic scanners. *Business Week* magazine reported on June 3, 1996[16] that MasterCard International is testing a "smart card" computer chip that includes information about your fingerprint and identity that can be embedded in a credit/debit card. Card scanners in stores and banks will scan your fingerprint and compare it to the information on the card to verify your identity. How could the apostle John have known that the future would hold such incredible technology unless God inspired him to write the words recorded in Revelation 13:16-18?

Worldwide Television Communications

Another intriguing prophecy relating to our era is found in the Book of Revelation that describes worldwide television communications. The prophet John prophesied that in the future tribulation the Antichrist will kill two of God's witnesses who will stop the rain for three-and-a-half years. The prophet declared that the people living around the world will see their deaths and observe their bodies lying unburied for three-and-a-half days in Jerusalem. The whole world will hold a party, exchanging gifts in their relief that their tormentors are dead. Then these people will watch astonished as God resurrects His two witnesses to heaven (Revelation 11:9,10).

How could the news that these men were killed travel instantaneously around the world in only three-and-a-half days in any other generation than today? Only seventy years ago it would have taken a week for the news to travel from Israel to Japan or New York. However, today CNN instantly transmits pictures and sound about any important event worldwide. Over a billion people around the world can simultaneously watch the Olympic events every four years. For the first time in history, this prophecy about the whole world watching an event in Jerusalem can be literally fulfilled in this last decade.

The Gospel of the Kingdom Shall Be
Preached in all the World

One of the most wonderful of the prophecies concerns the prediction of Jesus Christ that: "And this gospel of the kingdom shall be preached in all the world for a witness unto all nations; and then shall the end come" (Matthew 24:14). The Bible has now been translated in more than 3,850 languages covering 98 percent of the world's population in every nation, tribe and dialect. Electronic communication transmits the message of hope in Jesus Christ worldwide.

According to the A.D. 2000, *World Christian Encyclopedia,* researchers on the growth of religions throughout the globe have determined through careful research that over *115,000 people every single day* accept Jesus Christ as their personal Savior.[17] Until recently Islamic authorities have confidently asserted that the Moslem faith would soon dominate the world because Islam was obviously the world's fastest growing religion. However, the detailed and meticuous research by the A.D. 2000 *World Christian Encyclopedia* reveals that almost 17 million people accept personal faith in Jesus Christ every year in addition to the 53 million who are born into Christian believers homes and are naturally raised as Christians. When we subtract that attrition rate from natural deaths (about 21 million annually) we are left with a minimum growth of 42 million new Christian believers every year (115,000 new believers every single day). Approximately two billion people throughout the world claim to be Christian with probably one-third of them (650 million) personally committed to Christ's Great Commission to reach the world's population with the offer of personal salvation. In addition it is fascinating to note that the growth of Christianity is now (4.7%) almost twice as great as the present growth of the Islamic faith (2.6%).[18]

We have never witnessed such a great explosion of those following the Christian faith from the first days of the Church until today. There were only one million Christians in China in 1949 after a century of faithful missionary work. However, the Church in China has grown astronomically despite tremendous persecution and the killing of untold millions of believers in concentration camps. Today, the lowest estimates calculate that there are more than one hundred million true followers of Christ in communist China.

Despite the pessimistic analysis of some writers that the population of the earth is growing faster than the growth of the Church, the truth is that the gospel is being preached in all the world with astonishing success during these last days. A 1991 study by the National Council of Churches concluded that church membership is growing at twice the rate of the overall population growth throughout the world. Their study noted that the greatest growth was in evangelical churches. Muslim authorities have often boasted that their religion is growing faster than any other. However, while Islam is rapidly expanding (primarily through biological growth) studies reveal that Christianity (especially evangelical Christianity) is growing even more rapidly. Evangelical Christianity is the only religious group in the world with significant growth through conversion, at a rate almost double that of Islam according to the most detailed study of world religious growth.[19]

A fascinating study by the Lausanne Statistics Task Force examined the progress of evangelism during the last five centuries. Their researchers concluded that the growth of the church throughout the globe is far greater than previously reported. The number of born again Christians has grown three times faster than the world's population in the seventeen years since 1980. The historically verifiable records of the Lausanne Statistics Task Force reveal an incredible growth in the number of Christians worldwide.

The Explosive Growth of Christian Faith in our Generation

In 1430 one in 99 of the world's population was Christian
In 1790 one in 49 of the world's population was Christian
In 1940 one in 32 of the world's population was Christian
In 1970 one in 19 of the world's population was Christian
In 1980 one in 16 of the world's population was Christian
In 1983 one in 13 of the world's population was Christian
In 1986 one in 11 of the world's population was Christian
In 1997 one in 10 of the world's population was Christian
Source: *Lausanne Statistics Task Force on Evangelism*[20]

In only sixty years the number of Christians throughout the world has grown by an astonishing 1300 percent. The evangelical Church is now growing almost three times faster than the expanding world population,[21] but it is important to note that this explosive growth is taking place almost entirely within the evangelical and charismatic part of the Christian Church. Evangelical Christianity has grown worldwide in only six decades from only forty million dedicated Christian evangelical believers in 1934 to more than 540 million born-again Christians today, while the world's population has grown by only 400 percent.

Christian radio broadcasts are now reaching almost half of the world's 360 "mega-languages," covering 78 percent of the earth's population, according to the broadcasting group World By 2000. Evangelical broadcasters are now preaching the Gospel to every language group throughout the globe. The combination of tremendous evangelism efforts by mission organizations, the dedication of more than one million national pastors, and the work of Christian broadcasters is rapidly fulfilling the Great Commission in our lifetime.

The Growth of Pentecostal and Charismatic Christianity

The remarkable growth of Pentecostal and Charismatic Christianity in the last century may be the single most significant spiritual development in 20th century Christianity.

The growth of Pentecostals and Charismatics among global Christianity has been truly extraordinary according to the A.D. 2000 *World Christian Encyclopedia.* In 1900, there were only approximately 900,000 Pentecostal and Charismatic Christians. By 1970 this number had grown to 72 million (6.4% of Christians globally). In one century, by 2000, the number of Pentecostal/ Charismatics had exploded to 523.7 million people (27.7% of all Christians). Today there are 141.43 million from Latin America, 134.9 million from Asia, 126 million from Africa and 37.6 million from Europe with another 83.8 million Pentecostals and Charismatics from North America, etc.[22]

Knowledge and Travel Shall Increase in the Last Days

Twenty-five centuries ago the Book of Daniel predicted that there would be an explosion of knowledge and a huge increase in travel in the last days. Daniel wrote these words: "But thou,

O Daniel, shut up the words, and seal the book, even to the time of the end: many shall run to and fro, and knowledge shall be increased" (Daniel 12:4). Throughout thousands of years of history the level of knowledge only increased incrementally. In some generations the level of general knowledge actually decreased. Yet, in the last century and a half, there has been an explosion of knowledge beyond anything ever experienced in human history. There are more scientists alive today than have lived in all of the rest of history.

Recently it was calculated that the total level of human knowledge is growing so quickly that it literally doubles every twenty-four months. This is staggering in light of Daniel's inspired prediction from the ancient past. In addition, Daniel stated that a characteristic of the last days would be an awesome increase in mobility as "many shall run to and fro." The speed of transportation has also exploded in the last century. Throughout history most people have never traveled faster than a galloping horse. Today men travel at over eighteen thousand miles an hour in the U.S. space shuttle Discovery. In addition, while most people in past centuries never traveled more than twenty miles from the place they were born, millions of people now travel the globe as part of their normal course of daily business or annual vacation.

Preparations for the Battle of Armageddon

Numerous prophecies deal with the climactic battle at the end of this age that will bring about the defeat of the Antichrist's armies and the ultimate victory of Jesus Christ to establish His kingdom on earth for a thousand years. The prophet John named the place of the final battle in this war between the Antichrist and the armies of the Kings of the East. "And he gathered them together into a place called in the Hebrew tongue Armageddon" (Revelation 16:16). John also stated that the army of the eastern nations from the "kings of the east" would consist of an astonishing two hundred million soldiers. This statement was almost impossible in light of the fact that the population of the entire Roman Empire in the days of John was only two hundred million people. "And the four angels were loosed, which were prepared for an hour, and a day, and a month, and a year, for to slay the third part of men. And the number of the army of the horsemen were two hundred thousand thousand: and I heard the number of them" (Revelation 9:15-16).

However, the population of the nations of Asia are growing so quickly that they could field an army in the next few years containing almost two hundred million soldiers. As a result of China's cruel and evil One Child Policy, Chinese couples often abort an unborn baby when tests indicate it will be female. They keep aborting fetuses until the tests reveal that the woman has a male fetus. Then they allow the male child to be born. Numerous reports by human rights organizations reveal that China, India, and North Korea are involved in the selective abortion of female unborn infants. In addition, many in these nations kill young girls who are not wanted by their parents.

As a result, the *Toronto Star* newspaper reported in 1995 that Chinese officials admitted that they have a staggering imbalance between boys and girls. This sexual imbalance resulted in an excess of over seventy million young men in China in the year 2000 with no women for them to marry. This growing imbalance of sexes throughout Asia will produce up to two hundred million excess young men of military age in the next decade. This situation could fulfill the prophecy of John about the two-hundred-million-man army from the East that will fight in the Battle of Armageddon.[23]

A Military Highway Across Asia and the Drying Up of the Euphrates River

Another prophecy in Revelation declares that the Euphrates River will be dried up to allow this enormous army of two hundred million soldiers to cross from Asia to invade Israel: "And the sixth angel poured out his vial upon the great river Euphrates; and the water thereof was dried up, that the way of the kings of the east might be prepared" (Revelation 16:12).

Throughout history the Euphrates River has been an impenetrable military barrier between East and West. However, the government of Turkey recently constructed the huge Ataturk Dam that can now dam up the waters of the Euphrates for the first time in history. The prophet John foretold a future military highway across Asia that would allow this huge army to march toward the final battle in Israel. John describes the building of this highway in these words: "The way of the kings of the east might be prepared" (Revelation 16:12).

The Chinese government has spent enormous sums and expended the lives of hundreds of thousands of construction workers building a military super-highway across Asia heading directly toward Israel. China sent its laborers to work side-by-side with Pakistan laborers in building this all-weather highway through the Karakorum mountains that paralleled the ancient Silk Road followed by Marco Polo.[24] This highway has no economic purpose and no foreigners are allowed anywhere near this road. The highway has been completed through the south of China, Tibet, and Pakistan. This curious prophecy about "the way of the kings of the east" is being fulfilled in the 1990s setting the stage for the final battle of this age.

The Odds Against These Prophecies Being Fulfilled in Our Generation

In this chapter we have examined a number of significant prophecies fulfilled in our lifetime that point to the Lord's return in this generation. Almost two thousand years have passed from the time of Christ until our generation. At its simplest level we can ask: What are the odds that even ten of these specific prophecies would be fulfilled by chance during our lifetime? If these prophecies could not have occurred by random chance, then their fulfillment is proof that God inspired the writers of the Bible to correctly predict these future events! In the Bible there are several types of generations. One generation is defined as the length of life of the average person-seventy or eighty years.

However, a generation of governing is usually defined as forty years, as indicated in the forty-year reigns of Gideon, King David, King Solomon, et cetera. During the last two thousand years since the days of Christ, there were fifty such forty-year generations. Therefore, the odds are one chance in fifty that any one of these specific prophecies happened by chance in our generation rather than some other generation. Examine the prediction about the rebirth of Israel, as prophesied by Matthew 24:32, as an example. There was only one chance in fifty that Israel would become a nation in our lifetime, rather than in some other generation such as A.D. 350, or A.D. 1600.

According to the laws of combined probability the chance that two or more events will occur in a given time period is equal to the chance that one event will occur multiplied by the chance that the second event would occur. If the odds are fifty to one against Israel being reborn in our lifetime by chance and the odds are also fifty to one against the revival of the Roman Empire in our generation; then the combined probability is fifty times fifty which equals one chance in twenty-five hundred. To calculate the probability of these prophecies occurring by chance:

What are the Odds That These Prophecies Were Fulfilled by Chance?

There are 40 years to a generation.
There are 50 generations from Christ till today.
Therefore:
The odds are 1 in 50 of any of these prophecies occurring in our lifetime
The odds are:
1 event = 1 × 50 1 in 50
2 events = 50 × 50 1 in 2,500
3 events = 50 × 50 (3 times) 1 in 125,000
4 events = 50 × 50 (4 times) 1 in 6.25 million
5 events = 50 × 50 (5 times) 1 in 312.5 million
6 events = 50 × 50 (6 times) 1 in 15.6 billion
7 events = 50 × 50 (7 times) 1 in 780 billion
8 events = 50 × 50 (8 times) 1 in 39 trillion
9 events = 50 × 50 (9 times) 1 in 1,950 trillion
10 events = 50 × 50 (10 times) 1 in 97,500 billion

Obviously, the odds against even ten prophecies occurring by random chance alone in one generation are simply staggering. The above calculation suggests that there is only one chance in 97,500 Trillion that these particular predictions from the Bible could be fulfilled by chance in our lifetime. Another way of looking at this is that the chance that the prophets of the Bible correctly guessed these prophecies is also one chance in 97,500 Trillion. If we calculated the odds against all twenty of these prophecies occurring by chance, the numbers would be beyond our ability to comprehend. In other words, it is simply impossible that men alone could have written the Bible without the supernatural assistance and inspiration of God.

This analysis demonstrates the truly incredible odds against even ten specific prophecies being fulfilled by chance in our generation. The odds against only ten prophecies occurring by random chance was $50 \times 50 \times 50 \times 50 \times 50 \times 50 \times 50 \times 50 \times 50 \times 50 =$ one chance in 97,500 Trillion!! This number is so large that it is hard to conceive of it. However, to illustrate these incredible odds; consider this. The odds of 97,500 Trillion to one are equal to the estimated number of grains of sand that would fill our entire planet. Imagine that we were to take a single grain of sand out of this staggering number of grains of sand and paint it blue. Then we blindfold you and let you search the planet for this buried grain of sand as long as you wish. Remember the entire globe consists of grains of sand and you would need to consider the possibility that the blue painted grain of sand was buried ten miles or, possibly, a thousand miles deep beneath the planet's surface. When you think you have found the right place, stop and pick up a random grain of sand. If you were lucky enough to pick up the only grain of sand painted blue by pure chance, you would have equalled the odds of one chance in 97,500 Trillion against even these ten prophecies being fulfilled by chance in our generation. Frankly, I don't think you would find that grain of sand. Likewise, it is simply impossible that these twenty prophecies were fulfilled by random chance.

The Scriptures teach that the final generation of this age will witness the fulfillment of a staggering number of prophecies pointing to the soon return of the promised Messiah. The evidence presented in this chapter also provides intriguing evidence that proves that only God could have inspired the writers of the Scriptures to accurately predict the startling number of predictions already fulfilled in our lifetime. The words of Jesus speak especially to our generation, "Now when these things begin to happen, look up and lift up your heads, because your redemption draws near" (Luke 21:28).

Notes

1. Robert St. John, *Tongue of the Prophets* (North Hollywood: Wilshire Book Company, 1952).
2. Grant R. Jeffrey, *Armageddon - Appointment With Destiny* (Toronto: Frontier Research Publications, Inc., 1988).
3. Internet site: http://www.us-israel.org/jsource/Judaism/ ejhist.html.
4. Internet site: http://www.agron.co.il/english/ agrocult.asp.
5. *Associated Press*, 16 February, 1989.
6. Internet site: http://www.templeinstitute.org/vessels/ altar.html.
7. Internet site: http://europa.eu.int/abc/obj/chrono/ 40years/3testim/coll-en.htm.
8. Internet site: http://www.zionministry.com/index.html.
9. Grant R. Jeffrey, *Final Warning* (Toronto: Frontier Research Publications, Inc., 1995).
10. United Nations, UNAIDS/WHO (Geneva: United Nations, 2001.
11. Rosie DiManno, "HIV engulfs former Soviet Union with a fury" *Toronto Star*, July 10, 2002.
12. Rosie DiManno, "HIV engulfs former Soviet Union with a fury," *Toronto Star*, 10 July, 2002.
13. Internet site: http://www.unaids.org/worldaidsday/ 2001/EPIgraphics2001/EPIgraphic4_en.gif.
14. Internet site: http://www.msnbc.com/news/ 430295.asp?cp1=1.
15. "Poor Harvests Raise Fears of African Famine," *Agence France Press* 20 February, 2002.
16. *Business Week*, 3 June 1996, p.123.
17. David B. Barrett, *World Christian Encyclopedia*, 2nd Ed. (Oxford: Oxford University Press, 2001).
18. David B. Barrett, *World Christian Encyclopedia*, 2nd Ed. (Oxford: Oxford University Press, 2001).
19. David B. Barrett, *World Christian Encyclopedia*, 2nd Ed. (Oxford: Oxford University Press, 2001).

20. Lausanne Statistics Task Force on Evangelism. Internet site: http://www.adherents.com/Na_170.html
21. David B. Barrett, *World Christian Encyclopedia*, 2nd Ed. (Oxford: Oxford University Press, 2001).
22. David B. Barrett, *World Christian Encyclopedia*, 2nd Ed. (Oxford: Oxford University Press, 2001).
23. David Rennie, "Girls Lost as Chinese Reach 1.2 Billion," London: *Daily Telegraph*, 29 March, 2001.
24. Internet site: http.www.atimes.com/ind-pak/DE25Df02.html.

9

The Mysterious
Bible Codes

"It is the glory of God to conceal a matter, but the glory of kings is to search out a matter." (Proverbs 25:2)

Several years ago researchers in Israel discovered a staggering phenomenon of hidden codes within the Hebrew text of the Old Testament that reveal a remarkable knowledge about future events and personalities that cannot be explained unless God supernaturally inspired the writers to record His precise words. The material in this chapter is possibly the most intriguing evidence presented in this book that will point to the truth that the Scriptures are truly inspired by God.

During the last few years, millions of people have heard about this phenomenon known as the Bible Codes. However, there are many questions that must be answered. Is it possible that God has actually hidden a series of encoded words within the Hebrew text of the Bible that reveal His supernatural knowledge of historical and current events? But, is this phenomenon genuine? Are the claims about the Bible Codes true?

If this information is accurate, this Bible Codes phenomenon provides powerful new evidence that the Scriptures must truly be the inspired Word of God. However, if this discovery is false, it could easily cause great confusion to millions of interested people, as well as to the Church itself. Numerous articles about the Bible Codes have appeared in major newspapers and magazines throughout the world, including *Time* and *Newsweek*. Millions of people have read several best selling books that explore the Bible Code phenomenon, including my 1996 book, *The Signature of God*, that first introduced the intriguing subject to the North American audience.[1]

Many radio and television shows have discussed this impressive discovery. When I first heard about the codes during a trip to Israel in the late 1980s, I was naturally quite skeptical. However, after more than fifteen years of careful evaluation of the phenomenon, I believe that there is powerful evidence that the code is genuine. Additional research during the last six years has provided more evidence that God placed these codes in the Scriptures. They provide fascinating details about historical events that have come to pass thousands of years after the biblical text was written. The Bible Codes provide a new type of evidence that supplements the many other types of evidence that prove the Scriptures are supernatural. This discovery may provide a last measure of incontrovertible evidence to our skeptical generation that the Bible is the inspired Word of God.

I trust that this in-depth study of the mysterious Bible Codes will help you to understand this phenomenon from a balanced Christian perspective. This book will explore many of the issues raised by this remarkable discovery as well as the numerous legitimate questions and criticisms that have been raised by atheistic, Jewish, and Christian critics who doubt that the Bible Code phenomenon is genuine. I understand the natural reluctance of those who have not spent time exploring this phenomenon to accept the reality of the codes without a detailed examination.

There is no question that the Bible Codes represent an astonishing new claim that demands a high level of validation before we should accept it. By nature I am a skeptic. When I first heard about this, I thought that the claims of the code researchers seemed unbelievable. That is why I am not offended in the slightest when someone tells me that they cannot accept the Bible Codes as genuine. However, after almost a dozen years of research, I am more convinced than ever that God placed the Bible Codes within the text of the Bible to prove to this skeptical generation through this remarkable new evidence that He inspired the human writers to record His revelation to humanity in the Word of God.

A group of mathematicians and computer researchers in both Israel and North America have discovered a series of intriguing Bible Codes about Adolf Hitler and the Holocaust, the Oklahoma City Bombing, the assassination of Yitzchak Rabin, the War in the Gulf, and much more. This book will reveal exactly how Israeli computer scientists recently rediscovered the Bible Codes, which were hidden within the Bible for over three thousand years. In addition, you will learn how Bible students around the world are discovering new codes for themselves, using sophisticated computer programs.

Some of the most fascinating Bible Code research for Christians involves the marvelous discovery by Yacov Rambsel of forty-one encoded words naming Jesus and His disciples, Mary, Joseph, Pilate, and many other people in the life of Christ including King Herod and the High Priest Caiaphas. These names were found encoded in the well known "suffering Messiah" prophecy of Isaiah 53, which predicted the trial, crucifixion, and burial of Jesus Christ more than seven centuries before He was born. This will be explored in detail in chapter 10 of this book.

Many readers will be intrigued by the discovery of remarkable 9/11 Bible Codes that name Osama bin Laden, al Qaeda, the World Trade Center, New York, as well as numerous additional names connected to the tragic Islamic terrorist attack on September 11, 2001, which are fully explored in this chapter.

This chapter will answer your questions about the nature and validity of the Bible Codes and the fascinating scientific evidence that proves the Bible is truly the inspired Word of God. In addition, I will attempt to provide comprehensive answers to the legitimate questions and objections to the Bible Codes raised over the last few years by atheists, Christians, and Jews. It does not surprise me that most people are initially quite skeptical about the codes. As someone who tends to be a skeptic, I waited more than ten years from the time that I first began to gather evidence about this remarkable research before I felt that it was appropriate to write a chapter in my book in 1996 to share the astonishing code discoveries of the Israeli scientists with my readers.

It was vital that I be absolutely convinced of the reliability of this information and that these ELS codes would provide credible evidence supporting the supernatural origin of the Bible. In my opinion, the discovery of the Yeshua Codes about Jesus Christ in the Hebrew Bible provided God's "seal of approval" on this remarkable phenomenon. The new codes revealed Jesus of Nazareth as the true Messiah and acknowledge that He came in the flesh. The codes identifying Jesus as the Son of God provide compelling evidence that God placed these hidden codes within the Bible to be widely shared with this modern generation of skeptics.

The Bible has been studied extensively by hundreds of millions of Jews and Christians over the last thirty-five hundred years. Therefore, some readers have naturally asked how anyone in our generation could possibly discover something new that was not previously known. This is a legitimate question. However, many new archeological, scientific and medical discoveries during the last one hundred and fifty years have provided convincing new evidence regarding the reliability of the ancient biblical text.

Dr. William Albright, the greatest Christian archeologist of the past century, spent his life exploring the land of Israel and the surrounding nations in his search for archeological artifacts. As a result of his and other archeologists' numerous discoveries, Dr. Albright concluded that the Bible was totally accurate in every area where he had examined the archeological evidence. When he summarized the final results of the thousands of archeological discoveries made during the last century, Dr. Albright concluded: "There can be no doubt that archeology has confirmed the substantial historicity of Old Testament tradition."[2]

With powerful apologetic evidence, Christians can challenge the skeptics in our generation to seriously consider the claims of the Bible that it is the supernatural Word of God. The Lord commands Christians, in the words of 1 Peter, to be prepared to explain and defend the reasonableness of our faith in the Bible and in Jesus Christ. We need to be prepared to persuade men and women to turn from their unbelief to seriously consider the claims of Jesus Christ. "But sanctify the Lord God in your hearts: and be ready always to give an answer to every man that asketh you a reason of the hope that is in you with meekness and fear" (1 Peter 3:15). In light of God's command to defend our faith to our generation of unbelievers, I find it natural that we should from time to time discover new types of evidence in both the text of the Scriptures as well as in the world of science and archeology. I found an interesting quotation from the Christian writer, Joseph Butler, in his *The Analogy of Religion* that illustrates this point. "Nor is it at all incredible that a book which has been so long in the possession of mankind, should contain many truths as yet undiscovered."[3]

The Original Discovery of the Bible Codes

Rabbi Michael Dov Weissmandl was a brilliant Czechoslovakian Jewish scholar in astronomy, mathematics, and Judaic studies. In the years before World War I, he found an obscure but intriguing reference to the Bible Codes in a rare book written by a fourteenth-century rabbi known as Rabbeynu Bachayah. The book described a curious pattern of letters encoded within the Torah by skipping an equal number of letters. This discovery inspired Rabbi Weissmandl to begin exploring to see if he could detect other examples of similar codes hidden within the Torah. During the following years, Weissmandl found that he could locate certain meaningful and related words or phrases, such as "hammer" and "anvil" if he examined the letters at sequences that were equally spaced in the Hebrew text. In other words, if he found the first letter of a significant word such as "Torah," and then, by skipping forward seven letters he found the second

Hebrew Alphabet Chart

Hebrew Letter		Phonetics
א		Aleph
ב		Bet
ג		Gimmel
ד		Dalet
ה		Heh
ו		Vav
ז		Za'yin
ח		Chet
ט		Tet
י		Yod
כ	ך	Kaf
ל		Lamed
מ	ם	Mem
נ	ן	Nun
ס		Sa'mek
ע		Ayin
פ	ף	Peh
צ		Tzadai
ק		Qoph
ר		Resh
שׂ	שׁ	Sin Shin
ת		Tav

The second Hebrew letter is the final form.
Hebrew is written and read from right to left

letter of the same word, he would continue to skip forward the same number of letters to see whether or not the complete word "Torah" was spelled out in the text at equally spaced intervals. Rabbi Weissmandl described this unusual phenomenon as "equidistant letter sequences" (ELS).

Weissmandl was amazed to find that numerous examples of significant words were hidden within the Hebrew text of the Torah at equally spaced intervals. These spaced intervals between significant letters varied from every two letters, every seven letters, and numerous other intervals. However, once they found a particular word spelled out at, say every twenty-second letter, the balance of the letters in the encoded words in this group were often spaced at an interval of every twenty-second letter.

Initially, Rabbi Weissmandl could not be certain if this phenomenon was truly significant or whether it was simply due to the great number of possible combinations of words and phrases that could occur by random chance by skipping forward various intervals of letters in the Hebrew text. The proof that this phenomenon was evidence of a supernatural intelligence and design was confirmed almost forty years later in Israel. The invention of sophisticated computers and statistical analysis was finally able to analyze the text of the Bible to prove that these codes could not have been produced by random chance.

Although Rabbi Weissmandl found many coded names by simply manually counting the letters in the text, he did not record his discoveries in writing. Fortunately, some of his students did record several examples of his code discoveries. Over the following decades, students in Israel who had heard about his research began searching the Torah for themselves to ascertain whether or not such codes actually existed. Their discoveries ultimately resulted in the research studies at Hebrew University that have proven the validity of this research. The introduction of high-speed computers allowed Jewish scholars at Hebrew University to explore the text of the Torah in ways that previous generations could only dream about.

Equidistant Letter Sequences

A group of dedicated Jewish scholars in Israel, following up on Rabbi Weissmandl's research, found many additional hidden codes embedded within the text of the Torah. A paper called "Equidistant Letter Sequences in the Book of Genesis" was published in August 1994 in the scholarly journal *Statistical Science*. This academic publication is one of the most prominent mathematical and scientific journals in the world. The study was completed by three eminent Israeli mathematicians Doron Witztum, Yoav Rosenberg, and Eliyahu Rips at the world-renowned Hebrew University and the Jerusalem College of Technology. This study has been republished in several other respected scholarly journals, including *Bible Review*, October 1995, as well as on the Internet. Their discoveries of complex Hebrew codes that reveal supernatural and prophetic knowledge about the future is causing tremendous consternation in the academic community because it challenges the long-held beliefs of liberal scholars who generally reject verbal inspiration of the Bible.

This scientific discovery of the ELS code phenomenon is earthshaking in its potential consequences because it reveals a staggering level of mathematical design and intelligence that could only have been produced by a supernatural mind. This discovery provides compelling mathematical proof that the Bible was inspired by God. The data demolishes the false claim by liberal scholars and skeptics that the Bible was written and edited by uninspired men and that it is full of errors and contradictions. Despite the fact that numerous scholars and scientists have attempted to challenge the validity of this Bible Code research, the evidence for the existence of this phenomenon has not been successfully refuted.

Every Jot and Tittle

Jesus Christ Himself affirmed that the actual letters composing the Scriptures were directly inspired by God and were preserved in their precise order throughout eternity. "For verily I say unto you, Till heaven and earth pass, one jot or one tittle shall in no wise pass from the law, till all be fulfilled" (Matthew 5:18). The English word *jot* is our translation of the Greek word *iota,* the Greek letter *i.* This *iota* is the Greek equivalent of the Hebrew letter *yod,* the smallest letter in the Hebrew alphabet. The word *tittle* is the Greek word *keraia,* derived from the smallest Hebrew grammatical symbol. Jesus Christ stated that even the smallest of the letters and grammatical marks in the original text of the Bible were directly inspired by God.

This intriguing statement by Jesus about the Scriptures has been confirmed two thousand years later by means of an intricate analysis of the Hebrew text of the Bible by mathematicians and computer scientists in Israel. To their total surprise, these researchers discovered that every single letter of the Torah fits into a complicated tapestry of staggering mathematical precision. In this regard, we should remember the provocative words found in Proverbs 25:2, "It is the glory of God to conceal a thing: but the honour of kings is to search out a matter."

This phenomenon of the Bible Codes was placed within the text of the Word of God thousands of years ago; however, God has hidden it successfully until our generation. Many of these codes could not have been discovered by manual examination of the text. The invention of high-speed computers enabled the researchers to examine every possible combination occurring in any of hundreds of possible skip distances (from every second letter to every five hundredth letter, for example) throughout the millions of Hebrew letters in the Old Testament. However, once a meaningful ELS pattern has been detected by the computer program, anyone can personally verify the existence of that particular Bible Code by manually counting out the Hebrew letters to verify that a particular ELS word is spelled out by skipping the appropriate number of letters.

How Do the Bible Codes Work?

The Bible Codes are meaningful Hebrew words spelled out in the biblical text by skipping an equal number of letters. The researchers called this equal skipping of letters "Equidistant Letter Sequence" (ELS). The hidden message is spelled out within the normal surface text by skipping an equal number of letters (say every seventh letter). For example, they discovered that the Hebrew word for Israel, יִשְׂרָאֵל, was spelled out in the opening passage of Genesis by skipping every seven letters and once again by skipping every fifty letters within a short passage of only five verses (Genesis 1:30–2:3). It is interesting to note that these verses where we find "Israel" encoded are known as the *Kiddush* and are recited by Jews around the world every Sabbath.

The practice of hiding an encoded word within a surface text by skipping every tenth, forty-eighth, etc. letter has been used by spies for centuries to send secret messages. For example, an American spy working in a British fort during the Revolutionary War might have written an innocent sounding letter to his mother in which he wrote about his health, the weather, and such. However, the spy created a secret message by encoding his message using every twelfth letter. This requires the spy to carefully choose the words of his surface text to conceal his secret message. When his commander intercepted the letter, he would circle every twelfth letter he found and read the secret message, which might have been: "Four hundred soldiers and twenty-two cannons in fort."

The Central Intelligence Agency would use their computers to create a chemistry professor's treatise that they knew the Russian spies would steal and then distribute to Russian scientists at their secret labs. According to a pre-arranged code, a Russian lab worker who was secretly spying for the CIA would ignore everything else in the treatise, but he would look for the secret message by selecting every seventy-seventh letter to find out which documents he should photograph for the CIA.

Some Jewish rabbis have always known that there were some ELS patterns and words encoded in the Bible, which had been found in the past. Later in this chapter we will examine some of the historical quotes that reveal knowledge of this curious phenomenon long before the creation of computers that could demonstrate the remarkable code patterns running through the Hebrew text of the Bible. However, until the development of high-speed computers, it was impossible to systematically search the biblical text to see if any other coded words might be hidden within the Scriptures.

Almost twenty-five years ago, a group of Israeli researchers developed a computer search program and placed the Hebrew text of the Bible into the computer. Using the ancient Hebrew *Textus Receptus* (the "received text," the ancient Masoretic Hebrew text used by the King James translators) of the Torah, Professors Doron Witztum, Eliyahu Rips, and Yoav Rosenberg began by placing the Hebrew text of the first five books of the Bible into their computers.

The mathematicians initially chose three hundred arbitrary Hebrew word pairs that were logically related in meaning, such as "hammer" and "anvil," or "man" and "woman." They asked the computer program to locate any such word pairs in close proximity within the text of Genesis. Once the computer found the first letter in Hebrew of "hammer," it would search for the second letter at various intervals or spaces between letters (say skipping every second, third, or seventeenth letters). If the program couldn't locate the second letter of the target word "hammer" following the first letter at a two-space interval, it would then search at a three-space interval, then a four-space interval, etc. Once it located the second letter at, say, the twelve-space interval, it would then look forward in the text for the third letter at the same twelve-space interval, and so on through the entire 78,064 Hebrew letters in Genesis. The computer also looked for encoded words by checking in reverse order.

After the program had examined the text for each of the three hundred word pairs, the researchers were astonished to realize that every single word pair had been located in Genesis in close proximity to each other word. As statisticians, they were naturally astounded because they knew it was humanly impossible to construct such an intricate and complicated pattern within a surface text, such as Genesis, which recorded the history of the Jewish people. After calculating the probabilities of this phenomenon occurring randomly by chance alone, they published their conclusions in 1988 as part of another scientist's paper in a highly respected British scientific journal, the *Journal of the Royal Statistical Society*.[4] The odds against the three hundred word pairs occurring by chance in the text of Genesis were phenomenal. The bottom line is that if the phenomenal results reported by the Israeli scientists were genuine, only a supernatural intelligence far beyond our human capacity could have produced the extraordinarily intricate pattern of encoded words they discovered within the Hebrew text of the Bible.

The term "interval" or "skip distance" indicates the number of Hebrew letters that are skipped in the original biblical passage to spell out the encoded word in equally spaced intervals (ELS). If the interval number in brackets is positive (22), then the encoded word begins at the indicated passage and reads right to left (the same direction in which we read a Hebrew text), skipping the indicated number of Hebrew letters. However, if the interval number in brackets is preceded by a minus sign (−13), the encoded word begins at the indicated passage and reads left to right, skipping the indicated number of Hebrew letters.

These ELS word pairs were found compacted together much more closely in the biblical text than random chance would suggest was probable. As they studied these curious patterns further, the scientists discovered that many of the ELS-encoded words related to events and personalities in human history that occurred from ancient times until today. These coded words are interlaced in intricate patterns at evenly spaced intervals in the text, reading both forward and backward. The scientists realized that these ELS-encoded letters formed words and associations of such complexity and design that it was impossible that the letter patterns could have occurred by random chance alone.

Their initial experiment was reported in their contribution to a 1988 paper entitled "Probability, Statistics and Theology" by the mathematician D. J. Bartholomew, which was published by the British *Journal of the Royal Statistical Society.* This article by Bartholomew included the paper on the ELS codes discovered by Doron Witztum, Eliyahu Rips, and Yoav Rosenberg that was read before the Royal Statistical Society on November 11th, 1987.[5]

The Word *Torah*, תורה, Encoded in the Bible

When the researchers looked at the string of Hebrew letters beginning in Genesis 1:1, they counted forward fifty letters from the first appearance of the letter ת, the first letter (tav) of the Hebrew word *Torah* and found the second letter in the word *Torah*, ו. Skipping forward another fifty letters, they found the third letter of the word *Torah*, ר. The last skip forward of fifty letters revealed the fourth letter in the word *Torah*, ה. The Hebrew word תורה, *Torah*, the Law, was spelled out using every fiftieth letter of the text.

To their surprise, they found that in the first verse of Exodus, the second book in the Bible, the same word תורה, *Torah*, was once again spelled out at the same fifty-letter intervals beginning with the first appearance of the letter ת. However, when they examined the opening verses of Leviticus, the third book of the Bible, the ELS word *Torah* was not encoded. The word *God* was spelled out when they skipped forward every eighth letter from the first letter yod, י, that appeared in the book.

When they examined the initial verses of Numbers and Deuteronomy, the fourth and fifth books of the Bible, the scientists again found that the word *Torah* was encoded. In the Book of Numbers, *Torah* was spelled out in reverse at a fifty-letter interval. However, in the Book of Deuteronomy, it appeared in reverse order at a forty-nine-letter interval beginning in the fifth verse of the book.

The mathematician Dr. Daniel Michelson calculated that the odds were more than three million to one against the word *Torah* being encoded four times by chance alone within the opening verses within the first five books of the Bible.[6] Bible students know that the number fifty is very significant in Scripture. For example, God commanded Israel to free their slaves, to cancel all debts, and to return family lands that had been pledged to a lender on the fiftieth Year of Jubilee. In addition, the Bible reveals that God presented Law itself, the Torah, to the Jewish people at Mount Sinai precisely fifty days after their miraculous Exodus from Egypt.

Eden Encoded in Genesis

Israeli Professor Eliyahu Rips discovered that the key word *Eden* was encoded repeatedly sixteen times within the relatively short Genesis 2:4-10 passage (only 379 Hebrew letters) dealing with the Garden of Eden. Professor Michelson calculated that while you would expect to find the ELS word *Eden* five times by random chance, the odds against finding sixteen *Eden*s occurring in ELS codes by random chance in such a short passage were only one chance in ten thousand.[7]

Another fascinating feature of this phenomenon was found by Dr. Doron Witztum in the Genesis 2 passage that deals with the Garden of Eden. Twenty-five different ELS Hebrew names of trees were found encoded within the text of this one chapter in Genesis that records God's creation of vegetation. The mathematicians calculated that the laws of probability suggest the odds against this occurring by chance alone are a hundred thousand to one.[8]

Thousands of detailed and precise ELS patterns and codes such as these were discovered hidden in the Hebrew text of the ancient Scriptures. Mathematicians and statisticians, after exhaustive statistical analysis, concluded that this pattern of coded words could not have occurred by chance, nor could a human writer have purposely produced this complex phenomenon. Their conclusion was that only a divine intelligence could have directed Moses to record this precise Hebrew biblical text containing such complex codes thousands of years ago.

Other Codes Reveal God's Prophetic Foreknowledge

The researchers discovered that some of the words encoded in the text of the Torah concerned events and personalities that occurred thousands of years after Moses wrote the Torah. Naturally, many academics rejected out of hand the very possibility that this Bible Codes phenomenon could be real. However, despite many attempts to deny its validity and numerous false claims that you could find these same complex ELS patterns in other non-biblical texts, no one has successfully refuted the reported ELS data or the Bible Codes phenomenon. The critics have simply denied that the ELS codes are statistically meaning-ful or they have claimed you could find the same phenomenon in other non-biblical texts. In the following chapters we will address these arguments by the code critics and demonstrate that their arguments are not valid.

The Ancestors of King David Named Centuries Before They Were Born

One of the most interesting of the experiments examined the text of Genesis 38, which recorded the history of the great Jewish patriarch Judah and his relationship with his widowed daughter-in-law Tamar, who gave birth as a result of this illicit intercourse to two sons, Pharez and Zerah. The Book of Ruth tells us that King David, the greatest king of Israel, was descended from Pharez, the son of the patriarch Judah as follows: Pharez was the ancestor of Boaz, who married his kinsman Ruth, who gave birth to Obed (*Oved*), who was the father of Jesse (*Yishai*), who was the father of King David. Each of the five Hebrew names of the key ancestors of King David were found encoded at forty-nine-letter intervals, reading left to right, within this Genesis 38 text. Incredibly, these five names (Boaz, Ruth, Oved, Yishai, and David) were encoded at the same forty-nine-letter ELS interval in the precise chronological order they were born, as recorded in the Bible. According to Dr. Moshe Katz, the odds were calculated as only one chance in 800,000 that the five names of David's ancestors would occur in this particular pas-sage and that they would be found in the exact, chronological order in which they lived.[9]

They examined Genesis 28, Jacob's vision of the ladder to heaven, which he received at Mount Moriah, the "place of God." The key words *Temple* and *Torah* were encoded at twenty-six-letter intervals in a continuous sequence of nine Hebrew letters beginning with the מ letter in the word *place* (Genesis 28:16). The occurrence of these two significant words *Temple* and *Torah* in sequence within a biblical passage declaring that "this is none other but the house of God, and this is the gate of heaven" is extraordinary. The researchers calculated the probability of these two key words occurring by random chance in that particular passage at about one chance in 17 billion.[10]

Aaron, Israel's High Priest, Encoded in Leviticus

In another analysis, Israeli mathematician Dr. Eliyahu Rips searched an eleven-verse section of Leviticus chapter 1, which records God's laws of worship concerning the priesthood of the Kohanien, the "sons of Aaron," Israel's High Priest. They found the Hebrew name אהרן, *Aaron*, encoded twenty-five times in this one small section of Leviticus (716 Hebrew letters) instead of eight times, as the laws of probability would suggest. Statisticians calculated that the odds against *Aaron* occurring twenty-five times by chance in this small passage were approximately 400,000 to one.[11]

The Feast of Hanukkah and the Hasmoneans

The wicked Syrian king Antiochus IV slaughtered tens of thousands of Jews who refused to worship him when he conquered Jerusalem. Antiochus IV stopped the Temple sacrifice in 168 B.C. He then defiled the altar by sacrificing a pig upon it, provoking a Jewish rebellion, led by a courageous old man named Mattathias and his five sons. This triggered a spectacular war of religious independence. The Jews, led by is son Judas Maccabaeus ("the Hammer"), defeated the Syrian army against impossible odds in 165 B.C. The Jews reconquered the Temple site on the twenty-fourth day of the ninth month, exactly three years to the day after Antiochus IV had stopped the daily sacrifice.

The Jews cleansed the sacred Temple (1 Maccabees 4:52-54) and reinstituted Temple worship. The Jewish *Talmud* claims that a priest found a one-day supply of the sacred oil hidden in a wall of the Temple. When the oil was used to light the candelabra, it miraculously lasted for the full eight days of the celebration, until new sacred oil could be refined. The Feast of Dedication has been commemorated ever since by the annual eight-day Hanukkah celebration.

The Israeli researchers found the encoded ELS word *Hanukkah*, which refers to the festival (at a −261 interval) in Genesis 36:24-37. Incredibly, this was encoded near the ELS word

Hasmoneans (–524), the name of the family of great warriors led by Judas Maccabee who ruled Israel in the following century. The name *Mattathias*, who led the Jewish rebellion against Syria, was also encoded in Genesis 36:33-40 by skipping every sixty-two letters right to left. In addition, the name of the Jewish general *Maccabee* was found by Doron Witztum, encoded every second letter right to left in Genesis 36:31-32.

King Louis and the French Revolution

Another passage in Genesis reveals a remarkable cluster of encoded words about the French Revolution. The following words are included: *Mapecha HaSarfatit* ("the French Revolution"), "Louis," the name of the French king, and the word *Beit* (house of) *Bourbon*, his royal dynasty. In the same grouping were the following words: *Hamarseille* (the Hebrew name of the French national anthem) and the word *Bastillia* (the Hebrew name of the infamous French prison for political prisoners that was stormed by revolutionaries). Interestingly, this ELS cluster dealing with the French Revolution appears in Genesis 39–41, a passage which describes Joseph's imprisonment in Egypt. The Hebrew word for *Bastillia* is found encoded within the text in Genesis 39:20 that describes "the prison in which the king keeps his prisoners."

They discovered the ELS word *Zedekiah*, who was the last king of Judah when the Babylonian army conquered Jerusalem in 587 B.C. Intriguingly, the encoded name *Matanya* appeared in close proximity within the text. This was the original birth name of King Zedekiah before he ascended the throne (2 Kings 24:17).

The Assassination of Anwar Sadat

Possibly the most fascinating of the codes are those that reveal events that have occurred in our generation. The late Egyptian president Anwar Sadat courageously flew to Israel to meet with the Israeli leaders in an attempt to break the circle of continuous warfare between Egypt and Israel. Tragically, President Sadat was assassinated during a military parade on October 6, 1981, by Islamic fundamentalists from the Moslem Brotherhood who remain bitterly opposed to the peace process. The Israeli researchers found the encoded names *Anwar* and *Sadat* together with *Chaled Islambooli,* חאלד אסלמבלי, the leader of the Moslem Brotherhood assassination team, encoded in Genesis 18. The assassin's name, חאלד, Chaled, appears in ELS code at an interval of six letters, right to left, in Genesis 18:4 beginning with the second letter of the eighth word in that verse. The same code sequence also contained the date *8 Tishri* (October 6) and the year of his assassination, *1981,* together with these encoded words: *president, gunfire, shot, murder,* and *parade.*

Hitler and the Holocaust Bible Codes

One of the most curious of all the hidden ELS codes is the discovery of the words *Hitler, Nazis,* and the names of several of the Holocaust death camps embedded within the text of Deuteronomy. The Israeli researchers naturally wondered if the Bible Codes might reveal anything about the Holocaust, the greatest tragedy in the history of the Jewish people. When they asked the program to search for the target words *Hitler, Nazis,* and *Holocaust,* the computer found that every one of these target words was encoded in a cluster of codes within a small passage in Deuteronomy 10:17–22:

> For the Lord your God is God of gods, and Lord of lords, a great God, a mighty, and a terrible, which regardeth not persons, nor taketh reward: He doth execute the judgment of the fatherless and widow, and loveth the stranger, in giving him food and raiment. Love ye therefore the stranger: for ye were strangers in the land of Egypt. Thou shalt fear the Lord thy God; him shalt thou serve, and to him shalt thou cleave, and swear by his name. He is thy praise, and he is thy God, that hath done for thee these great and terrible things, which thine eyes have seen. Thy fathers went down into Egypt with threescore and ten persons; and now the Lord thy God hath made thee as the stars of heaven for multitude. (Deuteronomy 10:17-22)

They found the word *Hitler,* היטלר, spelled out at a twenty-two-letter interval. Several of the names of concentration death camps were found embedded within this same text, beginning with the second to last appearance of the Hebrew letter bet, ב, in this passage. Counting every thirteenth letter from left to right the coded letters spelled the phrase *b'yam marah Auschwitz*, which means "in the bitter sea of Auschwitz." As they skipped forward another thirteen letters, they came to the letter resh, ר. From the resh they counted every twenty-second letter from left to right and connected to the word *Hitler,* היטלר. Hitler's Nazis ultimately slaughtered over six million Jews and another six million Poles and Russians in the death camps in Eastern Europe. The names of two of the Nazi concentration camps, *Auschwitz* and *Belsen,* were found encoded close to *Hitler* and *Berlin* in a cluster of encoded ELS words: *Germany, Poland, genocide, plagues, cremetoria, an evil house, Fuhrer,* and *Mein Kampf.*

Deuteronomy 33:16 also contained a hidden code about the Nazi Holocaust. Beginning with the first Hebrew letter mem, מ, they counted every 246th letter from left to right and found the encoded word *Melek Natzim,* which means "King of the Nazis." This same passage contained the phrase *kemi bait rah,* "an evil house rose up." In Deuteronomy 32:52, beginning with the letter aleph, א, and counting from left to right every 670 letters spells the name *Aik'man,* a Hebrew variant of the name *Eichmann.* Adolf Eichmann was the Nazi official who designed the Final Solution, the system of concentration death camps used in the Holocaust. He was finally captured after the war in Argentina, abducted to Israel, tried, and executed as a mass murderer.

The series of hidden codes dealing with Nazi Germany and the Holocaust concluded in Deuteronomy 33:21 with a final significant code. Beginning with the letter resh, ר, that appeared in the word *Yisrael,* researchers counted every twenty-second letter from left to right and found the tragic phrase *re'tzach alm,* which means "a people cry murder, slaughter."

Many Jews have asked why the prophecies of the Bible say nothing about the Holocaust, the worst tragedy in the history of God's Chosen People. The discovery of the Bible Codes provides evidence that God encoded prophetic words about the Holocaust within the text of the Bible.

Hitler, the Nazis, and the Death Camps
Were Prophesied in the Bible

Encoded ELS Word	Hebrew	Interval	Begins at:
Hitler	היטלר	(22)	Deut. 10:17
Auschwitz	אושוריץ	(–13)	Deut. 10:21
Holocaust	שׁואה	(13)	Deut. 10:20
Germany	גרמניה	(–933)	Deut. 33:28
Crematorium for my sons	כבשׁן לבני	(134)	Deut. 31:28
The Holocaust	השׁואה	(50)	Deut. 31:16
Plagues	מגפות	(–134)	Deut. 32:32
Eichmann	אייכמן	(9670)	Deut. 32:52
Auschwitz	אושוריץ	(–536)	Deut. 33:24
In Poland	בפולין	(–107)	Deut. 32:22
King of the Nazis	מלך נאצים	(–246)	Deut. 33:16
Genocide	רצח עם	(–22)	Deut. 33:21
The Fuhrer	הפירר	(5)	Deut. 32:50
Hitler	היטלר	(–3)	Num. 19:13
Mein Kampf	מין קאמפ	(9832)	Num. 22:1

17כי י_וה א_היכם הוא א_הי הא_הים וא_ני הא_נים
הא_ הגדל הגבר והנורא אשר לא-ישא פנים ולא יקח
שחד: 18ועשה משפט יתום ואלמנה ואהב גר לתת לו
לחם ושמלה: 19ואאהבתם את-הגר כי-ג_רים הייתם בארץ
מצרים: 20את-י_וה א_היך תירא אתו תעבד ובו תדבק
ובשמו תשבע: 21הוא תהלתך והוא א_היך אשר-עשה
אתך את-הגדלת ואת-הנוראת האלה אשר ראו עיניך:
22בשבעים נפש ירדו אבתיך מצרימה ועתה שמך י_וה
א_היך ככוכבי השמים לרב:

Hebrew Text of Deuteronomy 10:17-22 Passage.

Mathematicians Confirm Their ELS Findings

In 1994 the Israeli scientists wrote a follow-up paper on
their word-pair ELS experiment using the 66 Famous Rabbis
(discussed later in this chapter) for submission to *Statistical
Science*, a scientific journal that insisted that a group of opposing scholars review and challenge their data and examine their
computer program before publication. Despite the fact that all

of the reviewers held previous beliefs against the inspiration of the Scriptures, the overwhelming evidence and the integrity of the data forced the editors to approve the study's scientific accuracy and reluctantly publish the article. Robert Kass, the editor of *Statistical Science*, wrote this comment about the study that was published in August 1994: "Our referees were baffled: their prior beliefs made them think the Book of Genesis could not possibly contain meaningful references to modern day individuals, yet when the authors carried out additional analysis and checks the effect persisted. The paper is thus offered to *Statistical Science* readers as a challenging puzzle."[12]

The study concluded that the peculiar sequences of Hebrew letters appearing in the biblical text at equal spaces from each other forming significant words could not possibly have occurred by simple coincidence or random chance.

The Response from Recognized Experts

I realize that this information about the Bible Code phenomenon will sound almost unbelievable to many readers. However, the well-respected mathematician Professor David Kazhdan, chairman of the Department of Mathematics at Harvard University, and fellow scientists from other universities including Yale and Hebrew University in Jerusalem confirmed that this is "serious research carried out by serious investigators." These recognized experts in mathematics wrote a letter confirming the value of this research in the introduction to a recent Israeli book about this phenomenon called *Maymad HaNosaf* (*The Added Dimension*), written by Professor Doron Witztum of the Jerusalem College of Technology.[13] Dr. David Kazhdan made the following statement during an interview with a newspaper in 1996: "The phenomenon is real; what it means is up to the individual."

Professor Witztum is the leading researcher on these Bible Codes. Realizing that this discovery is extremely controversial in today's academic world, these scientists encouraged additional research on the phenomenon and declared that "the results are sufficiently striking to deserve a wide audience." In light of their known attitude of rejection of the Bible's divine inspiration and the supernatural, their statement is a powerful endorsement that the phenomenon is legitimate and is worthy of continued study.

Scientists who have studied these results state that it would be extremely difficult to create such a Hebrew document containing hundreds of encoded ELS words. They concluded that it would be virtually impossible to reproduce this phenomenon in a Hebrew text, even if they had the help of a group of brilliant linguists or the assistance of the world's most sophisticated supercomputers. In addition, it is impossible to account for the prophetic knowledge regarding future personalities and events found in these codes. The evidence suggests that God inspired Moses to record the precise Hebrew words including the ELS spelled codes in the words of the Torah.

In addition to demonstrating that God inspired the text of the Torah, the evidence of this marvelous design destroys the Documentary Hypothesis, the theory of liberal skeptics that several different "editors" interwove different texts centuries after the death of Moses creating the Book of Genesis. The fact that researchers have found a number of very long ELS patterns extending throughout the first five books of the Bible suggests that only one supernatural mind could have imposed this marvelously complex design upon the Torah. The researchers have since discovered similar codes throughout the whole Old Testament.

The Famous Jewish Sages Experiment

In a 1994 follow-up paper published in the *Statistical Science* journal,[14] the Israeli team of researchers recorded the results of their search for pairs of encoded words that relate to people and events that occurred thousands of years after Moses wrote the Torah. They selected the names of thirty-four of the most prominent rabbis and Jewish sages during the thousand years leading up to A.D. 1900. Interestingly, the researchers simply selected the thirty-four Jewsh sages with the longest biographies in the *Encyclopedia of History of the Great Men in Israel*.[15] They asked the computer program to search the text of the Torah for close word pairs coded at equally spaced intervals that contained both the names of the famous rabbis paired with their date of birth or death, using the Hebrew month and day. (The Jewish people celebrate the memory of their famous sages by commemorating their date of death.) Incredibly, the computer program found every single one of the thirty-four names of these famous rabbis embedded in the text of Genesis paired at significantly close proximity with the actual dates of their birth or death.

Scholars at the *Statistical Science* journal who reviewed this experimental data were naturally amazed. They demanded that the scientists run the computer test program again on a second sample searching for the next thirty-two most prominent Jewish sages listed in a major Jewish encyclopedia. To the astonishment of the skeptical reviewers, the results on the second set of famous sages were equally successful. The staggering result of the combined test revealed that the names and dates of their birth or death of every one of the sixty-six most famous Jewish sages from A.D. 1000 to 1900 were encoded in close proximity within the text of Genesis. The odds against these particular rabbis' names and dates occurring in close proximity by random chance were calculated by the mathematicians as only one chance in 62,500.[16]

In the *Statistical Journal* article in August 1994 Robert Kass made the following statement: "It has been noted that when the book of Genesis is written as two-dimensional arrays, equidistant letter sequences spelling words with related meanings often appear in close proximity. Quantitative tools for measuring this phenomenon are developed. Randomization analysis shows that the effect is significant at the level of 0.00002 [one chance in 50,000]."[17]

Naturally, the researchers attempted to reproduce these results by running the computer program on other religious Hebrew texts outside the Bible. The researchers could not detect significant ELS codes beyond what you would normally find by random chance in any other Hebrew text outside the Bible.

When you carefully consider the ELS phenomenon, you can see that even a minor change of spelling or choice of words would destroy the precise sequence of Hebrew letters that reveals these hidden words encoded at evenly spaced distances throughout a particular text of the Torah. A critic insisted they attempt to find similar complex ELS codes in a Hebrew translation of Tolstoy's famous novel *War and Peace* because it was the same length as the Book of Genesis. However, the phenomenon was not present in *War and Peace*, nor any other modern Hebrew writing. In fact, an exhaustive analysis reveals that no other Hebrew text outside the Old Testament contains these mysterious codes, not even the Hebrew apocryphal books written during the four hundred years before the birth of Christ.

Following the 1994 appearance of the article on the Bible Codes in *Bible Review*, there was a virtual onslaught of letters to the editor in the following monthly issues attacking the article in the strongest terms. Most of the critical letters dismissed the phenomenon without seriously considering the scientific data that was presented. Several critics attacked the author's argument and data in ways that revealed they either failed to grasp the actual statistical method used to detect and analyze the Hebrew codes or they didn't understand the rigorous methodology that eliminated the possibility that this phenomenon had occurred by pure random chance.

After his research was published in *Bible Review* in November 1995, Dr. Jeffrey Satinover responded to the critics who had challenged his assertion that a pattern of elaborate and significant words was encoded within the Torah. Dr. Satinover replied to his critics as follows:

> The robustness of the Torah codes findings derives from the rigor of the research. To be published in a journal such as *Statistical Science*, it had to run, without stumbling, an unusually long gauntlet manned by some of the world's most eminent statisticians. The results were thus triply unusual: in the extraordinariness of what was found; in the strict scrutiny the findings had to hold up under; and in the unusually small odds (less than 1 in 62,500) that they were due to chance. Other amazing claims about the Bible, Shakespeare, etc., have never even remotely approached this kind of rigor, and have therefore never come at all close to publication in a peer-reviewed, hard-science venue. The editor of *Statistical*

Science, himself a skeptic, has challenged readers to find a flaw: though many have tried, none has succeeded. All the 'First Crack' questions asked by *Bible Review* readers—and many more sophisticated ones—have therefore already been asked by professional critics and exhaustively answered by the Israeli researchers. Complete and convincing responses to even these initial criticisms can get fairly technical.[18]

Some critics have suggested that the Israeli scientists simply played with the computer program long enough, that by chance alone "they got lucky." This objection raises the relevant objection that there might be numerous unreported "hidden failures," a common problem in most scientific research today. To prevent this from occurring, editorial observers from the *Statistical Journal* demanded that the Israeli scientists analyze their data by examining a completely new group of personalities that were chosen solely by the *Statistical Journal*'s editorial judges, namely the sixty-six most famous Jewish sages. The results I quoted earlier in this chapter were based on this group of individuals chosen by these judges. In addition, the judges appointed by the *Statistical Journal* analyzed the computer programs to determine that they were both valid and neutral in their design.

We need to keep in mind that the standard text of the five books of the Torah was electronically published years ago in widely available computer programs and printed texts. These texts cannot be modified. In fact, as a result of the production and sale of numerous "Bible Code" computer programs that are now available in North America, anyone with a computer and lots of time can personally verify the existence of these codes within the Hebrew text of the Scriptures. I have personally verified the presence of these fascinating patterns of hidden codes during long hours of examination using the computer programs I acquired several years ago in Jerusalem when this research was just beginning.

Professor Harold Gans, a senior researcher who examined sophisticated foreign government intelligence codes for the U.S. Army, has publicly confirmed the existence of these codes as reported in *Statistical Journal* through the use of advanced analytic techniques and his own sophisticated computer program. Dr. Gans is a brilliant mathematician who has published 180 technical papers. When Gans learned of this discovery by Professor Doron Witztum, as a skeptic and a non-religious Jew, he initially thought that the claims were "ridiculous." Unlike many readers, as an intelligence specialist dealing with complex codes and computers, Gans had the technical ability to test the claims and data for himself. In 1989, he created a complex and original computer program on his computer to check Witztum's data. For nineteen straight days and nights, Gans let his program examine all possible variations and combinations in the 78,064 Hebrew letters in the Book of Genesis. Dr. Gans's computer program checked through hundreds of thousands of possible letter combinations at many different spaced intervals. Finally, Gans was forced to conclude that these codes actually existed and that they could not have occurred by random chance or human design. He had confirmed the absolute accuracy of Professor Witztum's conclusions. As a result of his discoveries, Professor Gans now teaches classes in synagogues throughout the world about the extraordinary evidence proving divine authorship of the Bible.

Dr. Gans's follow-up study found that the text of Genesis also revealed the encoded names of the actual cities where each of these sixty-six sages was born. Gans calculated that the odds against this occurring by chance was one chance in two hundred thousand as recorded in his paper "Coincidence of Equidistant Letter Sequenced Pairs in the Book of Genesis."[19]

Many scientists from other universities and laboratories are now conducting careful investigations that examine the remarkable nature of the phenomenon. After seven years, the critics of the codes finally published an article in *Statistical Science* that attempts to critique the original experiment by the Israeli scientists concerning the methodology used in the experiment concerning the sixty-six great Jewish sages that was first published in 1994 in *Statistical Science*.

Are the Bible Codes Meaningful
or Are They Accidental?

Regardless of the relative merits of the statistical analysis of the presence of the sixty-six rabbis and their dates of death as well as birth cities, the basic phenomenon of the Bible Codes exists as anyone in possession of a Hebrew Bible can confirm. The question that always remains to be answered: Does this phenomenon provide evidence that it was placed there by some supernatural design, or is the presence of these numerous codes regarding future events and people simply the result of random chance? The decision is ultimately a value judgment that each person must make for himself. The mathematician will examine his calculations of statistical probability to determine his answer. The average reader will arrive at his or her own logical and common sense conclusion based on their assessment of the probability or improbability that the ancient Hebrew text of the Bible could contain these ELS patterns naming all of these people, places, and events by random chance as opposed to the supernatural design of God. The decision is yours.

The 9/11 Terrorist Attack Bible Codes

When the tragic, horrific Islamic terrorist attacks took place on September 11, 2001 millions of people throughout the civilized world were stunned to witness such appalling hatred, evil, and the sudden death of over three thousand innocent lives. As people everywhere attempted to process the devastating news that America had been attacked without warning, naturally those students of the Word of God who study the Bible Codes were motivated to begin a rigorous computer search of the Bible to determine if there were any ELS codes that related to this terrible event.

My friends at Bible Code Digest have developed an excellent Web site that seriously examines and explores the existence and significance of the ELS code phenomenon. Dave Swaney of Bible Code Digest has graciously given me permission to use the excellent research completed by his team of code researchers regarding these ELS code discoveries related to the World Trade

Center terrorist attack. I encourage anyone who is interested in exploring the Bible Code phenomenon in more detail to examine their fascinating web site: www.biblecodedigest.com. The following code discoveries relating to the tragic 9/11 terror attack were discovered and reported on their Web site. A statistical analysis of the probabilities of these particular ELS codes occurring in any Hebrew text can be examined in the pages of their site.

In the days following September 11, their team found numerous ELS codes in a very significant passage of the Old Testament—Ezekiel 37, the prophetic passage where Ezekiel saw a vision of "the valley of dry bones" that represented the exiled nation of Israel being reborn in the last days in response to the command of God. Virtually all of the Islamic terrorist proclamations identify America's support for the existence and security of the State of Israel as one of the major reasons they have dedicated themselves to the destruction of the United States of America, the "Great Satan" in their propaganda pronouncements. It is fascinating that this remarkable cluster of significant ELS encoded words related to the 9/11 terrorist attack should be found within this vital prophecy about the rebirth of Israel as a nation in our generation after almost two thousand years of exile.

After a great deal of research, the Bible Code Digest team found the following words that were grouped around the prophecy of Ezekiel 37. While many of these ELS codes have large skip distances, the fact that they cross over each other in close proximity within this key prophecy is quite significant. Where two numbers are given in the ELS skip distance column, that word is encoded twice in this prophecy. Further details are available for your analysis at www.biblecodedigest.com.

Bible Codes About the
September 11, 2001 Terrorist Attack

ELS Encoded Word	ELS Skip Distance
Manhattan	698
World Trade Center	78
Tower Destroyed Toward the Mountain, Oh God	904

Pentagon	65626
Hijackers	29
Ignite the Airliner	267
Terror Hot in me	430
Where are They?	37
And let God not strike Terror	37
Terror of the Sea is There in Them	448
Jihad	210
Arafat	904
Philistines	1406
Bin Laden, Blood of the Poor	93
You will spit at Tradition, Al Kada	1430
Muhammed Omar	37
Taliban	81
Fire from the Heart	267
Saddam Hussein	150684
Saddam	87, 942
Hussein	3714, 3985
This is the King of Babylon	5564
Iraq	195
Severe Illness is spreading, Saddam	87
Saddam, Terminal Illness	141
Terminal Illness, The Days of Saddam are over	139[20]

In my recent book *War on Terror—Unfolding Bible Prophecy*[21] I have documented compelling evidence that President Saddam Hussein of Iraq has supported and directed Osama bin Laden's terrorist attacks on American targets since he vowed his "War of Vengeance" against the U.S.A. following the Gulf War in 1991. Hussein has rebuilt the ancient ruined city of Babylon and proclaims that his destiny is to conquer Israel and her allies as King Nebuchadnezzar did twenty-six centuries ago.

The September 11 Terrorist Attack
Bible Code: Ezekiel 7:2-8

In the first part of Ezekiel chapter 7 the Bible Code Digest researchers found another large group of interesting ELS code words that crossed through or appeared in close proximity to this key Ezekiel prophecy that relate to the terrible events of September 11, 2001.

More Bible Codes Found in Ezekiel 7:2-8
Related to the Sept. 11 Attack

New York
U.S.
An Unheard of Disaster
In the Morning
September 11
2001
bin Laden
Afghan
Taliban
Airliner
Firemen
Saddam
Iraq
Conspiracy
Devastation
Cruelty
Terror
Horrible
Death
Destruction
Butchery[22]

The full list of ELS codes and the analysis of their statistical probability can be downloaded for examination at Bible Codes Digest's Web site. These fascinating ELS codes were found in a very powerful prophecy, Ezekiel 7:2-8, that God proclaimed to the unrepentant people of Israel before the final destruction of their nation, city, and Temple at the hands of the invading Babylonian army of King Nebuchadnezzar in 587 B.C.

> Also, thou son of man, thus saith the Lord God unto the land of Israel; An end, the end is come upon the four corners of the land. Now is the end come upon thee, and I will send mine anger upon thee, and will judge thee

according to thy ways, and will recompense upon thee all thine abominations. And mine eye shall not spare thee, neither will I have pity: but I will recompense thy ways upon thee, and thine abominations shall be in the midst of thee: and ye shall know that I am the Lord. Thus saith the Lord God; An evil, an only evil, behold, is come. An end is come, the end is come: it watcheth for thee; behold, it is come. The morning is come unto thee, O thou that dwellest in the land: the time is come, the day of trouble is near, and not the sounding again of the mountains. Now will I shortly pour out my fury upon thee, and accomplish mine anger upon thee: and I will judge thee according to thy ways, and will recompense thee for all thine abominations. (Ezekiel 7:2-8)

When God judges an unrepentant nation as He did with ancient Israel, He normally uses an evil nation such as the pagan Babylonian empire as His instrument of judgment. However, God will ultimately deliver His righteous judgment upon the pagan nation of Babylon as prophesied numerous times in Isaiah 13:1, 6, 19 and Revelation 18.

Strong Cautions Regarding the Bible Codes

While I believe that many of these ELS codes in the Bible are significant, there are numerous accidental and meaningless ELS words that can be found as well. I also strongly warn readers to consider these vital biblical principles that will keep us from misusing these ELS Bible Codes.

Bible Codes Are Found Only in the
Orthodox Hebrew Text of the Old Testament

No one has been able to locate multiple, detailed, and meaningful Bible codes in clusters within any other Hebrew literature outside the Bible. Experimenters have carefully examined other Hebrew writings for the existence of codes including the Jewish *Talmud*, the *Mishnah*, the apocryphal writings of *Tobit* and *Maccabees*, etc. They even examined modern Hebrew literature such as translations of *War and Peace*. However, the scientists found no significant complex patterns of ELS codes similar to the ones recorded in this book in any other Hebrew literature outside the Old Testament. Several researchers have also found Bible Codes in the Greek text of the New Testament as detailed in my book *The Mysterious Bible Codes*.[23] However, much work remains to be done to verify this phenomenon in the New Testament.

Bible Codes Cannot Accurately Prophesy Future Events

One cannot discover meaningful encoded information about a future event until the event occurs. Obviously, it is impossible to know what target words to ask the program to search for until after an event has happened. However, once an event occurs, such as the Gulf War, we can ask the computer to look in the Bible text for such target words as *Saddam Hussein* or *General Schwarzkopf*. The encoded words related to a future event cannot be discovered in the biblical text in advance of the event because you wouldn't know what ELS words to ask the computer to look for. After a terrible event such as the Sept. 11, 2001, World Trade Center bombing occurs, the Bible Codes can confirm that the Scriptures contain encoded data about that historical event that occurred long after the Scriptures were written.

However, the codes cannot be used to foretell future events. Even if you correctly guessed at the right target words before a future event, such as the assassination of a prominent politician, and you found the name of the person (say, *Peters*) and the word *killed*, you would still not know anything meaningful about the future. Until the event occurs, any suggestion that the occurrence of these two code words means that the politician would be killed would be merely a meaningless guess. The appearance of the words *Peters* and *killed* might suggest an assassination. However, these words without a context might be simply accidental or they might relate to the fact that Peters killed someone else. Since we find ELS words, not sentences, there is no way to determine the meaning of an ELS pattern until the event occurs. Only then can we understand the context and the meaning.

The Bible prohibits us from engaging in foretelling the future. A recent book called *The Bible Code* by agnostic writer Michael

Drosnin claims that he himself discovered codes that allowed him to predict future events. However, a careful examination of his claims reveals that the encoded information he discovered is insufficient to allow anyone to confidently predict any future event. Michael Drosnin may have made a guess about a particular, tragic future event based on his discovery of the encoded name *Yitzchak Rabin*. However, it was simply a guess. There was not enough information in the code he discovered to allow him to confidently affirm that a particular future event, namely the assassination of Yitzchak Rabin, would actually occur. Michael Drosnin claims that he warned the prime minister of Israel about the danger of assassination based on the fact that he found that one of the eight letters of the encoded words *Yitzchak Rabin* happened to appear in the surface text of Deuteronomy 4: 42, which reads in Hebrew "assassin that will assassinate."

However, it was impossible to know in advance of the tragic event what this particular combination actually meant. It could easily have meant that Prime Minister Rabin might order the assassination of some terrorist in the future, or an assassination attempt would fail, or it could easily have meant nothing at all. The point is that the limited information from the encoded individual words can only be accurately interpreted after the fulfillment of an historical event, such as the Holocaust, the Gulf War, or the 9/11 attacks. God did not place these ELS codes within the Bible to enable men to play at becoming prophets of future events. The Bible repeatedly forbids fortune-telling.

The major Israeli code researchers, including Professor Eli Rips, and all of the serious Christian code researchers, including Yacov Rambsel and myself, deny that the Bible Codes can be used to accurately predict future events. The information encoded in the Bible can only be accurately interpreted after a historical event has actually occurred. Then we can compare the details of the historical event with the encoded information in the Bible to determine whether or not God had encoded these prophetic details centuries before the events occurred. In this manner, the Bible Codes give God the glory, not the human researcher. The prophet Isaiah declared these words of God, "I will not give my glory unto another" (Isaiah 48:11).

Bible Codes Do *Not* Reveal Any Hidden Sentences, Teachings, or Doctrines

There are no secret sentences, detailed messages, or theological statements to be found in the encoded ELS words. God's message of salvation and His commandments for holy living are to be found only in the normal, surface text of the Scriptures. The Bible Codes can only reveal key words, such as people's names, places, and occasionally dates (using the Hebrew calendar) that provide confirmation of the supernatural inspiration and origin of the Scriptures. The fact that the ELS patterns reveal words, not complex sentences, prevents anyone from claiming they have found a hidden theological message or making a definite prediction about a future event. Significantly, no one has claimed to discover any new teaching or doctrine in the Bible Codes because there are no sentences; only ELS words.

The Bible Codes have Nothing to Do with Numerology

The phenomenon of the Bible Codes has nothing to do with occult numerology. Numerology is connected with divination or foretelling the future and is clearly forbidden by the Bible. There is nothing occult or secret about the codes. This ELS phenomenon was openly published in scientific and mathematical journals, taught, and broadcast widely since it was first discovered twenty years ago.

The particular interval between the Hebrew letters, the actual number of letters to be skipped, has no importance or significance. The codes have nothing to do with "the occult significance of numbers," as Webster's defines numerology. Obviously, the coded words are found at various intervals (i.e., by skipping two, seven, sixty-one, or more letters). However, the significance or meaning of the encoded ELS word does not relate to the particular interval (the number of letters skipped). Either a particular word is spelled out in Hebrew letters at equal intervals or it is not. Anyone with a Hebrew-English Interlinear Bible can examine a particular encoded word and verify that these words are truly spelled out at ELS intervals. Computer programs such as Bible Codes 2000 are widely available to allow anyone to verify these codes for themselves. The program Bible Code 2000 can be purchased using the order form at the back of the book if you wish to personally research the Bible Codes.

Why Did God Place These Hidden Codes in the Bible?

For almost seventeen centuries, from the time of Emperor Constantine's conversion in A.D. 312 until the beginning of the last century, the Bible was generally accepted by the majority of Western culture as the inspired and authoritative Word of God. However, we have witnessed an unrelenting assault on the authority of the Bible by the intellectual elite, the academic community, liberal theologians, and the secular media during the last one hundred years. Most people in our culture have been exposed to countless attacks on the authority and accuracy of the Scriptures throughout high school, college, and from the mass media. I believe that God has provided this extraordinary new evidence to prove to this generation of skeptics that the Bible is truly the Word of God. The complex nature of these codes means that the phenomenal discovery of many of these encoded words could not have occurred until the development of high-speed computers during the last twenty years.

In a sense, God secretly hid these fascinating codes within the text of the Bible thousands of years ago with a time lock that could not be opened until the arrival of our generation and the development of sophisticated computers. In His prophetic foreknowledge, God knew that our generation would be characterized by an unrelenting attack on the authority of the Scriptures. No previous generation needed the additional scientific evidence provided by the discovery of these codes as much as our present skeptical generation.

Hundreds of years ago, a famous rabbi known as the Vilna Gaon lived and taught in the city of Vilna, Latvia, near the Baltic Sea in northern Europe. This brilliant and mystical Jewish sage taught his students that God had hidden a vast amount of information secretly encoded within the Hebrew letters of the

Torah. Consider the intriguing and suggestive statement about the hidden codes by this famous Jewish sage.

> The rule is that all that was, is, and will be unto the end of time is included in Torah from first word to the last word. And not merely in a general sense, but including the details of every species and of each person individually and the most minute details of everything that happened to him from the day of his birth until his death; likewise of every kind of animal and beast and living thing that exists, and of herbage, and of all that grows or is inert. (Vilna Gaon, Introduction to *Sifra Ditzniut*)

There is a strong tradition that a number of codes were discovered in past centuries by various Jewish sages, including Rabbeinu Bachya, Moses Maimonides, and the Vilna Gaon. Since World War I, Rabbi Michael Weissmandl and others have taught about these codes. There is an interesting statement suggesting knowledge of the codes in the Jewish mystical writing known as the *Zohar*. "The entire Torah is replete with Divine Names. Divine Names run through every single word in the Torah."[24] In approximately A.D. 1200, the brilliant Jewish sage Moses Maimonides, known as Rambam, made a curious comment about this statement in the *Zohar* that indicated he understood that there were complex codes hidden in the Torah. He said that the hidden codes provided another reason why a Torah scroll should be considered as unfit for use if even one single letter was missing from the text. The removal or addition of a single letter from the Hebrew text would eliminate the codes found hidden within that section of text. Also, there is a suggestive statement in the *Talmud* that refers to the codes: "Everything is alluded to in the Torah."[25]

A group called the Discovery Seminar, sponsored by the Aish HaTorah College of Jewish Studies, presents the phenomenon of the Bible Codes to Jewish groups and synagogues throughout the world. This group was created in Israel by a number of scientists, mathematicians, and Judaic scholars. In addition to giving presentations in Israel, Aish HaTorah has adapted the material to English, enabling their teams to share this fascinating information with Jewish audiences throughout the world showing the divine inspiration and authority of the Torah. Numerous agnostic Jews have reportedly returned to their religious roots in Orthodox Judaism as a result of their exposure to the Bible Codes.

The discovery of the Bible Codes revealing information about the life, death, and ministry of Jesus of Nazareth in the prophetic passages of the Old Testament, written centuries before His birth, provides powerful new evidence that Jesus is the true Messiah and the Son of God. The discovery in our generation of the hidden Bible Codes has fascinated millions of Jews, Christians, unbelievers, and skeptics during the last several years. However, a number of Christians have wondered why God would have placed a series of hidden codes within the Hebrew Bible text and not have placed a similar code within the New Testament. Research has been conducted regarding the possibility that the Bible Code phenomenon might be found in the Greek text of the New Testament. I have funded a small team of computer specialists who have developed a computer software program to search the Greek text of the Scriptures. They recently discovered a significant series of Bible Codes about Jesus Christ and various historical events within the Greek New Testament but this is not available for sale. The discovery of the ELS codes in the Greek New Testament is documented in my book *The Mysterious Bible Codes*.[26]

After studying and thinking about the Bible Code phenomenon for many years, I have come to a personal conclusion. The Bible Codes proclaim one message to humanity and have only one purpose: They provide compelling evidence to our generation that the Bible is truly the inspired Word of God.

The Implications of Bible Code Research

Many scholars who are philosophically opposed to the existence of God and the inspiration of the Bible are stunned by this research. Despite many arguments and challenges the data still stands. Several secular scientific journals have declared that the ELS phenomenon in the Bible is real and not a result of fraud or computer error. The simple truth is that this phenomenon could not have occurred by random chance alone. Nor could any group of brilliant human beings, even with supercomputers at their disposal, produce this awesome result of encoding a huge number of significant names about future events within the surface text of the Torah.

Since all scholars agree that the five books of Moses were written thousands of years ago, we have compelling evidence that this ELS Bible Code phenomenon is another clearly authenticated signature of God upon the pages of Scripture. The evidence in the next chapter will reveal that God has encoded the name of His Son, the Messiah, *Yeshua,* throughout the key messianic prophecies in the Hebrew text of the Old Testament.

Notes

1. Grant R. Jeffrey, *The Signature of God* Toronto: Frontier Research Publications, 1996.

2. William F. Albright, *Archeology and the Religions of Israel* (Baltimore: John Hopkins University Press, 1956) 176.

3. Joseph Butler, *The Analogy of Religion, Natural and Revealed* (1736), II, iii.

4. D. J. Bartholomew, "Probability, Statistics and Theology" *Journal of the Royal Statistical Society—A* (1988) 151, Part 1, pp. 137-178.

5. D. J. Bartholomew, "Probability, Statistics and Theology" *Journal of the Royal Statistical Society—A* (1988) 151, Part 1, pp. 137-178.

6. Daniel Michelson, "Codes in the Torah" *B'Or Ha'Torah*, No. 6 (1987), Jerusalem: Shamir.

7. Daniel Michelson, "Codes in the Torah" *B'Or Ha'Torah*, No. 6 (1987), Jerusalem: Shamir.

8. Daniel Michelson, "Codes in the Torah" *B'Or Ha'Torah*, No. 6 (1987), Jerusalem: Shamir.

9. Moshe Katz, *Computorah—Hidden Codes in the Torah.* Jerusalem: Computorah, 1996, p. 120.

10. Daniel Michelson, "Codes in the Torah" *B'Or Ha'Torah*, No. 6 (1987), Jerusalem: Shamir.

11. Daniel Michelson, "Codes in the Torah" *B'Or HaTorah*, No. 6 (1987), p. 7-39. Jerusalem: Shamir.

12. Robert Kass, "Equidistant Letter Sequences in the Book of Genesis," *Statistical Science*, August 1994.

13. Doron Witztum, *HaMeimad HaNosaf* (*The Additional Dimension*) Jerusalem: 1989.

14. Robert Kass, "Equidistant Letter Sequences in the Book of Genesis," *Statistical Science*, August 1994.

15. *Encyclopedia of the History of the Great Men in Israel* Jerusalem: Y. Chachik Publishers, 1940.

16. Robert Kass, "Equidistant Letter Sequences in the Book of Genesis," *Statistical Science*, August 1994.

17. Robert Kass, "Equidistant Letter Sequences in the Book of Genesis," *Statistical Science*, August 1994.

18. Jeffrey Satinover, *Bible Review*, November 1995.
19. Jeffrey Satinover, *Cracking the Bible Code* New York: William Morrow, 1997, p. 224.
20. Internet site: http.www.biblecodedigest.com.
21. Grant R. Jeffrey, *War On Terror – Unfolding Bible Prophecy* Toronto: Frontier Research Publications, 2002.
22. Internet site: http.www.biblecodedigest.com.
23. Grant R. Jeffrey. *The Mysterious Bible Codes* Nashville: Word Publishing, 1998.
24. *Zohar* II, 87a.
25. *Talmud Tan'anis* 9a.
26. Grant R. Jeffrey. *The Mysterious Bible Codes* Nashville: Word Publishing, 1998.

10

Bible Codes Reveal
the Name of Yeshua
in the Old Testament

Of all the codes that I have researched, the following are the most fascinating discoveries that I could share with you. Not only has God included thousands of hidden ELS codes within the text of the Bible, but He has actually placed the encoded name *Yeshua*, ישוע (the Hebrew name of Jesus), in numerous significant prophetic passages from Genesis to Malachi throughout the Old Testament. God has also placed the significant ELS code *Yeshua is My Name*, ישוע שמי, within a key messianic prophecy, Isaiah 53:8-10.

The research conducted during the last several years on the Bible Codes within the text of the Scriptures has given us the strongest possible evidence that the Bible was truly inspired by God. However, once I fully appreciated that the ELS codes revealed significant information about historical events such as Hitler's death camps, the War in the Gulf, and the French

Revolution, I naturally wondered if God had secretly encoded the name of Jesus Christ in the text of the Old Testament.

Providentially, several years ago I received a request from Yacov Rambsel, asking if he could quote from the research material I had written on the laws of probability regarding the messianic prophecies fulfilled in the life, death, and resurrection of Jesus from my 1988 book *Armageddon—Appointment with Destiny*.[1] In discussing this material with Yacov, I realized that he had a real passion for the study of the Hebrew Scriptures and for Jesus Christ as his Messiah. After I completed my chapter on the Bible Codes in the first edition of *The Signature of God* in April 1996, I called Yacov to ask him to review the Hebrew text for accuracy.

Yacov told me that he had just completed his own manuscript on the Bible Codes that focused on a series of extraordinary discoveries about the name of Jesus – Yeshua encoded throughout the Old Testament. His research provided the answer to my question about whether God had encoded the name of Jesus within the Hebrew Scriptures. With Yacov Rambsel's permission, I will share a portion of the phenomenal research that he has completed during thousands of hours of painstaking analysis of the hidden ELS codes. As I mentioned earlier, the Israeli researchers used complex computer programs to explore these codes, and I purchased three Bible Code computer search programs in Jerusalem in 1991 that I used on my Macintosh computer to verify the code research at Hebrew University. However, Yacov completed his detailed analysis by patiently examining the Hebrew text of the Old Testament manually letter by letter and then individually counting the equally spaced intervals between the letters. The amount of work and dedication involved to complete his analysis is staggering. I highly recommend to anyone who is fascinated by this research that they acquire a copy of Yacov Rambsel's book, *Yeshua—The Name of Jesus Revealed in the Old Testament*[2] and his sequel *His Name is Jesus*[3] published by Frontier Research Publications, Inc. You can purchase these books in Christian bookstores; by using the order form at the back of this book; or through our website: www.grantjeffrey.com.

Yacov Rambsel discovered the original Hebrew name of Jesus, *Yeshua,* יֵשׁוּעַ, encoded in Genesis beginning with the very first verse Genesis 1:1, "In the beginning God created the heaven and the earth." Starting with the very first word in the Bible, beginning with the Hebrew letter *yod,* י, the fifth letter in the word, *B'raisheet,* בְּרֵאשִׁית, "In the beginning," the name יֵשׁוּעַ *Yeshua* was found encoded by counting forward every 521st letter. He found the letters that spell *Yeshua Yakhol,* which translates, as "Jesus is able." Some of the Jewish critics who attacked the Yeshua Codes have wrongly claimed that *Yeshua* is *not* the correct Hebrew name of Jesus of Nazareth. However, at the end of this chapter I provide strong historical evidence that *Yeshua,* יֵשׁוּעַ, is the correct Hebrew name of Jesus of Nazareth as used in His lifetime in ancient Israel.

One of the most interesting features is that virtually every one of the major Messianic passages of the Old Testament contains the name *Yeshua,* יֵשׁוּעַ, encoded within the Hebrew text of the ancient prophecies about the coming of the Messiah. As an example, Yacov found the name *Yeshua* embedded in the key messianic prophecy in Isaiah 53:10 that described the trial, death, and burial of Christ. "Yet it pleased the Lord to bruise him; he hath put him to grief: when thou shalt make his soul an offering for sin, he shall see his seed, he shall prolong his days, and the pleasure of the Lord shall prosper in his hand" (Isaiah 53:10).

Yeshua Is My Name

Beginning with the second Hebrew letter *yod,* י, that occurs in the phrase *He shall prolong, ya'arik Kyray,* Yacov counted forward right to left every 20th letter and discovered the Hebrew phrase יֵשׁוּעַ שְׁמִי, *Yeshua Shmi.* "Yeshua [Jesus] is My Name" was encoded in this powerful prophecy that teaches us about the suffering Messiah who died to atone for our sins. The probability that this fascinating ELS combination "Yeshua [Jesus] is My Name" would appear by random chance in this key Messianic prophecy in Isaiah is simply staggering!

A passage in the Book of Genesis declared that the God provided "coats of skin" for Adam and Eve to cover their nakedness after they sinned: "Unto Adam also and to his wife did the Lord God make coats of skins, and clothed them" (Genesis 3:21). This verse revealed that God killed the first animal in history as a blood sacrifice to provide a covering for the sins and nakedness of Adam and Eve. This was a prophetic sign of the Passover Lamb that would be slain in the future as a symbol of the salvation of the Jews every Passover as they annually celebrated their Exodus from Egypt. This also symbolized the perfect sacrifice of the Lamb of God to atone for the sins of all those who would confess their sins and ask Christ to forgive them.

However, this important passage also contains an ELS pattern about Jesus as the true "Lamb of God." Beginning with the last Hebrew letter *heh*, ה, in Genesis 3:20 and counting forward every ninth letter, we find the word *Yoshiah*, meaning "He will save." The name Joshua, *Yoshiah* is a Hebrew equivalent name for *Yeshua* (Jesus). This encoded name *Yoshiah* found in the first few chapters of the Old Testament reminds us of the parallel message given to the young virgin Mary by the angel that declared, "Thou shalt call his name JESUS: for he shall save his people from their sins" (Matthew 1:21).

The Betrayal of Yeshua by Judas Iscariot

One of the most startling of all the Messianic codes Yacov found was hidden within Psalm 41:7-10 which predicted the betrayal of Jesus by His disciple Judas Iscariot: "An evil disease, say they, cleaveth fast unto him: and now that he lieth he shall rise up no more. Yea, mine own familiar friend, in whom I trusted, which did eat of my bread, hath lifted up his heel against me" (Psalm 41:8-9). Yacov noted that verse 8 contained the phrase "they plot evil," *yach' shvu rah'ah*. However, he noticed that beginning with the letter *yod*, י, when he skipped forward right to left every second letter he found it spelled out the word יֵשׁוּעַ, *Yeshua*. In other words, in the exact verse where King David prophesied the tragic betrayal of Jesus the Messiah over one thousand years before it occurred, we also find the name of the person who was betrayed encoded by skipping only two letters at a time within this prophetic passage.

One of the most well known of the messianic prophecies in

the Old Testament describes the exact price of Christ's betrayal, thirty pieces of silver. Over five hundred years before the birth of Jesus, the prophet Zechariah wrote this prediction: "And I said unto them, If ye think good, give me my price; and if not, forbear. So they weighed for my price thirty pieces of silver" (Zechariah 11:12). The phrase reading "my price" is *se'kari*. Beginning with the letter *yod*, י, Yacov counted forward every twenty-fourth letter and found the word *Yeshua*, ישׁוע. The Lord must have inspired Zechariah to choose these specific Hebrew words and this precise spelling to create this remarkable Bible Code. Here, in this key prophecy written five hundred years before Christ's birth, where the prophet described the precise price of our Lord's betrayal, God included a hidden Bible Code to His Chosen People that identified the name of their promised Messiah, *Yeshua*, Jesus.

In the verses that followed this prediction of Christ's first coming, the prophet Zechariah looked forward twenty-five centuries into the future to describe the tremendous emotional upheaval and mourning that will occur when the Jewish people's spiritual eyes will finally be opened to see that the Messiah Jesus of Nazareth whom they have rejected for twenty centuries, is in fact, their Messiah, *Yeshua*, who was crucified two thousand years ago. Zechariah prophetically saw Jesus' Second Coming to save Israel from the Antichrist's armies following the battle of Armageddon. Then the Jewish remnant will see Jesus Christ as their true Messiah: "And I will pour upon the house of David, and upon the inhabitants of Jerusalem, the spirit of grace and of supplications: and they shall look upon me whom they have pierced, and they shall mourn for him, as one mourneth for his only son, and shall be in bitterness for him, as one that is in bitterness for his firstborn" (Zechariah 12:10). Beginning with the letter *chet*, ח, found in the phrase, "an only son," היחיד, Yacov discovered that the word *Mashiach*, משׁיח, meaning "Messiah" was encoded by counting forward every thirty-eighth letter.

Leviticus reveals a fascinating hidden ELS concerning the blood of Jesus Christ that was shed for our sins. We are taught throughout the Scriptures that Jesus Christ is our great High

Priest. "But Christ being come an high priest of good things to come, by a greater and more perfect tabernacle, not made with hands, that is to say, not of this building" (Hebrews 9:11). In Leviticus, Moses revealed God's detailed instructions regarding the rules for the use of the oil of anointing by the holy priesthood and the sacrifices for the sins of the Chosen People.

> And he that is the high priest among his brethren, upon whose head the anointing oil was poured, and that is consecrated to put on the garments, shall not uncover his head, nor rend his clothes; neither shall he go in to any dead body, nor defile himself for his father, or for his mother; neither shall he go out of the sanctuary, nor profane the sanctuary of his God; for the crown of the anointing oil of his God is upon him: I Am the Lord. (Leviticus 21:10-12).

This passage about the anointing of the High Priest prophetically speaks to us of the greater High Priest Jesus the Messiah, who has completed the sacrifice for our sins through His sacrificial death on the Cross once and forever. The anointing of the High Priest of Israel prophetically symbolizes the long awaited anointing of Jesus Christ at His Second Coming, which will be accomplished when the anointing oil (recently found hidden near Qumran by the Dead Sea) as described in Exodus 30:25-35, will be used to anoint Yeshua when He appears as Israel's Messiah-King to usher in the Millennial Kingdom.

Yacov examined this passage and found that, beginning with the first *heh*, ה, in Leviticus 21:10 and counting forward every third letter, it spelled out the phrase *hain dam Yeshua*, which means "Behold! The blood of Yeshua." It is awesome to realize that God secretly encoded these profound words about His Son Jesus in these key messianic prophetic passages throughout the Old Testament over a thousand years before the birth of Jesus.

The study *Statistical Significance Discovered in the Yeshua Codes*[4] was published on the Internet in 1997. This study calculated the probability of this phrase "Behold! The blood of Yeshua" appearing at an ELS interval of every three letters by random chance in a book the size of Leviticus. Their conclusion was that the odds against this happening were so great that you would have to search through 69,711 books the size of Leviticus to expect to discover this phrase appearing only one time at an interval of every three letters.

Another key messianic prophecy, Psalm 72:13-15, includes significant words revealing that Jesus "shall save the souls of the needy. He shall redeem their soul." This significant prophetic passage also contains the ELS encoded word *Yeshua*, יֵשׁוּעַ, which was encoded by skipping every nineteen letters, revealing Jesus Christ as the source of our personal salvation from sin and guilt.

The prophet Isaiah prophesied more than seven centuries before the birth of Jesus Christ that He would come as the great liberator to mankind. Isaiah's prophecy (61:1-2) of the Great Jubilee at the end of this age reminded Israel that their Messiah would finally cancel all their debts and proclaim liberty to all of those who are captives to sin. "The Spirit of the Lord God is on me; because the Lord hath anointed me to preach good tidings unto the meek; he hath sent me to bind up the brokenhearted, to proclaim liberty to the captives, and the opening of the prison to them that are bound; to proclaim the acceptable year of the Lord, and the day of vengeance of our God; to comfort all that mourn" (Isaiah 61:1-2). Starting with the *yod*, י, in the phrase "The Spirit of the Lord God," *Ruach Adonai Yehovah,* and skipping every nine letters from left to right spells *Yeshua.* In addition, Yacov discovered that the word Joshua *Oshiyah,* אׁוֹשִׁיעַ, was also encoded beginning with the last letter aleph, א, in the second verse and counting every thirty-sixth letter from left to right. This word *Oshiyah* means "I will Save" and is a variation of the word *Yeshua* as we saw earlier in Genesis 3:20.

Yeshua Revealed in Daniel's Vision
of the Seventy Weeks

Of the many discoveries made by Yacov Rambsel, one of the most significant findings concerns Daniel's great prophecy of his vision of the seventy weeks recorded in Daniel 9:25-27.

Yeshua Coded in the Old Testament Prophecies

יֵשׁוּעַ

גִּילִי מְאֹד בַּת־צִיּוֹן הָרִיעִי בַּת יְרוּשָׁלַם
הִנֵּה מַלְכֵּךְ יָבוֹא לָךְ צַדִּיק וְנוֹשָׁע הוּא
עָנִי וְרֹכֵב עַל־חֲמוֹר וְעַל־עַיִר בֶּן־אֲתֹנוֹת:

Rejoice greatly, O daughter of Zion; shout, O daughter of Jerusalem

Behold, thy King cometh unto thee: he is just, and having salvation;

lowly, and riding upon an ass, and upon a colt the foal of an ass. Zechariah 9:9

יֵשׁוּעַ

כַּמַּיִם נִשְׁפַּכְתִּי וְהִתְפָּרְדוּ כָּל־עַצְמוֹתָי
הָיָה לִבִּי כַּדּוֹנָג נָמֵס בְּתוֹךְ מֵעָי
יָבֵשׁ כַּחֶרֶשׂ כֹּחִי וּלְשׁוֹנִי מֻדְבָּק מַלְקוֹחָי
וְלַעֲפַר־מָוֶת תִּשְׁפְּתֵנִי כִּי סְבָבוּנִי כְּלָבִים
עֲדַת מְרֵעִים הִקִּיפוּנִי כָּאֲרִי יָדַי וְרַגְלָי:

My strength is dried up like a potsherd; and my tongue cleaveth

to my jaws; and thou hast brought me into the dust of death.

For dogs have compassed me: the assembly of the wicked have

enclosed me: they pierced my hands and my feet.

I may tell all my bones: they look and stare upon me. Psalms 22:15-17

יֵשׁוּעַ

וְתֵדַע וְתַשְׂכֵּל מִן־מֹצָא דָבָר לְהָשִׁיב וְלִבְנוֹת יְרוּשָׁלַם
עַד־מָשִׁיחַ נָגִיד שָׁבֻעִים שִׁבְעָה וְשָׁבֻעִים שִׁשִּׁים וּשְׁנַיִם
תָּשׁוּב וְנִבְנְתָה רְחוֹב וְחָרוּץ וּבְצוֹק הָעִתִּים וְאַחֲרֵי
הַשָּׁבֻעִים שִׁשִּׁים וּשְׁנַיִם יִכָּרֵת מָשִׁיחַ וְאֵין לוֹ וְהָעִיר
וְהַקֹּדֶשׁ יַשְׁחִית עַם נָגִיד הַבָּא וְקִצּוֹ בַשֶּׁטֶף וְעַד
קֵץ מִלְחָמָה נֶחֱרֶצֶת שֹׁמֵמוֹת:

Know therefore and understand, that from the going forth of the commandment to

restore and to build Jerusalem unto the Messiah the Prince shall be seven weeks,

and threescore and two weeks: the street shall be built again, and the wall, even

in troublous times. And after threescore and two weeks shall Messiah be cut off,

but not for himself: and the people of the prince that shall come shall destroy the

city and the sanctuary. Daniel 9:25,26

Yeshua Coded in the Old Testament Prophecies

יֵשׁוּעַ

מֵעֹצֶר וּמִמִּשְׁפָּט לֻקָּח וְאֶת־דּוֹרוֹ מִי יְשׂוֹחֵחַ כִּי נִגְזַר
מֵאֶרֶץ חַיִּים מִפֶּשַׁע עַמִּי נֶגַע לָמוֹ: וַיִּתֵּן אֶת־רְשָׁעִים
קִבְרוֹ וְאֶת־עָשִׁיר בְּמֹתָיו עַל לֹא־חָמָס עָשָׂה וְלֹא מִרְמָה
בְּפִיו וַיהוָה חָפֵץ דַּכְּאוֹ הֶחֱלִי אִם־תָּשִׂים אָשָׁם נַפְשׁוֹ
יִרְאֶה זֶרַע יַאֲרִיךְ יָמִים וְחֵפֶץ יְהוָה בְּיָדוֹ יִצְלָח:

He was taken from prison and from judgment: and who shall declare his generation?
for he was cut off out of the land of the living: for the transgression of my people was
he stricken. And he made his grave with the wicked, and with the rich in his death
because he had done no violence, neither was any deceit in his mouth.
Yet it pleased the Lord to bruise him; he hath put him to grief: when thou shalt make
his soul an offering for sin, he shall see his seed, he shall prolong his days, and the
pleasure of the Lord shall prosper in his hand.   Isaiah 53:8-10

יֵשׁוּעַ

לָכֵן יִתֵּן אֲדֹנָי הוּא לָכֶם אוֹת הִנֵּה הָעַלְמָה   7:14

הָרָה וְיֹלֶדֶת בֵּן וְקָרָאת שְׁמוֹ עִמָּנוּ אֵל:

חֶמְאָה וּדְבַשׁ יֹאכֵל לְדַעְתּוֹ מָאֹס בָּרָע וּבָחוֹר בַּטּוֹב: 7:15

Therefore the Lord himself shall give you a sign;
Behold, a virgin shall conceive, and bear a son,
and shall call his name Immanuel.
Butter and honey shall he eat, that he may know
to refuse the evil, and choose the good.   Isaiah 7:14, 15

יֵשׁוּעַ

יַחַד עָלַי יִתְלַחֲשׁוּ כָּל־שֹׂנְאָי עָלַי וַחְשְׁבוּ רָעָה לִי: 41:8

דְּבַר־בְּלִיַּעַל יָצוּק בּוֹ וַאֲשֶׁר שָׁכַב לֹא־יוֹסִיף לָקוּם: 41:9

An evil disease, say they, cleaveth fast unto him:
and now that he lieth he shall rise up no more.
Yea, mine own familiar friend, in whom I trusted,
which did eat of my bread, hath lifted up his heel against me   Psalms 41:8, 9

Know therefore and understand, that from the going forth of the commandment to restore and to build Jerusalem unto the Messiah the Prince shall be seven weeks, and threescore and two weeks: the street shall be built again, and the wall, even in troublous times. And after threescore and two weeks shall Messiah be cut off, but not for himself: and the people of the prince that shall come shall destroy the city and the sanctuary; and the end thereof shall be with a flood, and unto the end of the war desolations are determined. And he shall confirm the covenant with many for one week: and in the midst of the week he shall cause the sacrifice and the oblation to cease, and for the overspreading of abominations he shall make it desolate, even until the consummation, and that determined shall be poured upon the desolate. (Daniel 9:25-27)

Serious students of the Bible are familiar with the controversy during the last century among theologians about the correct identity of the "Messiah the Prince" referred to in Daniel 9:25. Those who deny that Daniel's prophecy prophesies Jesus Christ's first coming have claimed that "Messiah the Prince" was a reference to King Hezekiah or some other historical individual. However, Yacov Rambsel made a wonderful discovery when he found the name ישוע, *Yeshua*, in Daniel 9:26 starting with the letter *yod*, י, in the phrase "the city," *v'ha'iry*, by counting left to right every twenty-sixth letter. In addition, he found the name *Nazarene*, נצרת, encoded every 112 letters together with the encoded words: *King,* מלך (46), *Branch,* נצר (50), *Jesse,* ישי (10), and *Messiah,* משיח (52), all found within Daniel's prophecy of the seventy weeks.

Word	Hebrew	Interval	Reference begins
Yeshua	ישוע	(−26)	Dan. 9:26
Nazarene	נצרת	(112)	Dan. 9:23-27
King	מלך	(46)	Dan. 9:24-25
Branch	נצר	(50)	Dan. 9:24-25
Jesse	ישי	(10)	Dan. 9:25
Messiah	משיח	(52)	Dan. 9:25-26

King David's Psalm 22 Prophecy:
Yeshua, the Crucified Messiah

A thousand years before Jesus of Nazareth was born, King David wrote his prophetic Psalm 22, which clearly predicted the death of Jesus by crucifixion in these key words "they pierced my hands and my feet." The method of execution known as crucifixion was not even invented when King David made his remarkable prediction. In addition, David's prophecy revealed that the soldiers would gamble for the garments of Jesus of Nazareth in these words, "For dogs have compassed me: the assembly of the wicked have enclosed me: they pierced my hands and my feet. I may tell all my bones: they look and stare upon me. They part my garments among them, and cast lots upon my vesture" (Psalm 22:16-18). The clear fulfillment of David's prophetic psalm in the death of Jesus of Nazareth on the Cross is confirmed by an intriguing group of ELS words found clustered together in this important prophetic passage about the crucified Messiah.

The word *Yeshua*, יֵשׁוּעַ, was found encoded right to left beginning with the letters of the first verse of this psalm, which contains one of the most important messianic prophecies in the whole of the Old Testament. The following words are encoded within this significant messianic and prophetic Psalm 22. In addition to revealing the name *Yeshua* connected to the one who would fulfill the prophecy; it reveals that He would be the "anointed" one, descended from "Jesse," and that He would be the "King of the Jews." Jesus of Nazareth fulfilled the prophecies of the "Branch" and was named *Yeshua* by the angel Gabriel's pronouncement to Mary because "He will save His people from their sins."

Word	Hebrew	Interval	Reference begins
Yeshua	יֵשׁוּעַ	(50)	Ps. 22:1
King	מֶלֶךְ	(8)	Ps. 22:10-11
Branch	נֵצֶר	(3)	Ps. 22:11
Jesse	יִשַׁי	(14)	Ps. 22:12-13
Messiah	מָשִׁיחַ	(8)	Ps. 22:14-15
Salvation	יֵשַׁע	(49)	Ps. 22:24-26

Jesus' Life and Death in the Bible Codes

Naturally, the Orthodox Jewish researchers from Israeli strongly reject the significance of the Yeshua Codes discovered by Yacov Rambsel. In their public criticism against these codes they are forced by the evidence to admit that these ELS word patterns do exist, but they reject our conclusion that these ELS patterns are genuine and meaningful ELS codes because they are clustered together in such prophetically significant passages. However, the recent *Statistical Significance Discoveries in the Yeshua Codes* proves that some of these Yeshua codes cannot be explained by random chance.[5] Several of our critics challenged us to find a complex series of ELS words revealing the name of Yeshua together with His apostles in one location in the Hebrew text. The next section will reveal the results of our experiment, which we believe validates that these ELS Yeshua codes are purposeful.

Yeshua Found in Isaiah's Prophecy about the "Suffering Messiah"

One of the most interesting subjects mentioned in the first edition of my book *The Signature of God* was Yacov Rambsel's incredible discovery of the name of *Yeshua* Jesus encoded in the major messianic prophetic passages throughout the Old Testament. I verified by my computer and through manual examination of my Hebrew-English Interlinear Bible that Yacov had found the name *Yeshua* encoded in Isaiah 53:10. This famous messianic prophecy foretold the grief of the suffering Messiah and His atoning sacrifice when He offered Himself as the Lamb of God, a perfect sacrifice for our sins through His death on the Cross: "Yet it pleased the Lord to bruise him; he hath put him to grief: when thou shalt make his soul an offering for sin, he shall see his seed, he shall prolong his days, and the pleasure of the Lord shall prosper in his hand" (Isaiah 53:10).

The words *Yeshua Shmi* (Yeshua [Jesus] is My Name), שְׁמִי יֵשׁוּעַ, are encoded in this messianic verse beginning with the second Hebrew letter yod (י) beginning in the phrase "He shall prolong," *ya'arik*, יַאֲרִיךְ, and counting every twentieth letter left to right. Yacov's discovery of the name *Yeshua* encoded in

Isaiah 53 and in dozens of other well-known messianic prophecies has thrilled thousands of readers of my book *The Signature of God* as well as Yacov's bestselling book *Yeshua*.[6]

However, I challenged Yacov to continue his code research and complete an in-depth investigation of possible additional codes related to the life of Jesus in the text of Isaiah 53. As a result of hundreds of hours of further detailed research, I would like to share his additional discoveries. Over forty ELS names of individuals and places associated with the crucifixion of Jesus of Nazareth were found encoded in Isaiah's "Suffering Servant" passage, which was written seven centuries before the birth of Jesus. I hope that you will be as thrilled with this astonishing discovery as I am. Yacov's complete research on this project is documented in his book *His Name Is Jesus*, published by Frontier Research Publications Inc. I highly recommend his book to anyone who is interested by the phenomenon of the Bible Codes. With Yacov's permission, I will share a portion of his research on the incredible codes found in Isaiah 53.

Within these key chapters of Isaiah, God has secretly encoded the names of the people, the locations, and key events in the life of Jesus Christ that were historically recorded in the New Testament seven centuries later. God clearly is in charge of human history. The Lord has revealed His supernatural prophetic knowledge of future events to our generation through the extraordinary discovery of the Bible Codes. This unprecedented phenomenon is a forceful reminder of the words recorded by Moses thousands of years ago: "The secret things belong unto the Lord our God: but those things which are revealed belong unto us and to our children for ever, that we may do all the words of this law" (Deuteronomy 29:29). Let us examine the details of this remarkable series of Bible Codes about Jesus Christ and His crucifixion found in the prophecy of Isaiah.

First, we need to review the words of Isaiah's remarkable prophecy about the coming Messiah who would suffer for the sins of mankind. The full passage from Isaiah 52:13 through chapter 53 reads as follows:

Behold, my Servant shall deal prudently, he shall be

exalted and extolled, and be very high. As many were astonied at thee; his visage was so marred more than any man, and his form more than the sons of men: So shall he sprinkle many nations; the kings shall shut their mouths at him: for that which had not been told them shall they see; and that which they had not heard shall they consider.

Who hath believed our report? and to whom is the arm of the Lord revealed? For he shall grow up before him as a tender plant, and as a root out of a dry ground: he hath no form nor comeliness; and when we shall see him, there is no beauty that we should desire him. He is despised and rejected of men; a man of sorrows, and acquainted with grief: and we hid as it were our faces from him; he was despised, and we esteemed him not. Surely he hath borne our griefs, and carried our sorrows: yet we did esteem him stricken, smitten of God, and afflicted. But he was wounded for our transgressions, he was bruised for our iniquities: the chastisement of our peace was upon him; and with his stripes we are healed.

All we like sheep have gone astray; we have turned every one to his own way; and the Lord hath laid on him the iniquity of us all. He was oppressed, and he was afflicted, yet he opened not his mouth: he is brought as a lamb to the slaughter, and as a sheep before her shearers is dumb, so he openeth not his mouth. He was taken from prison and from judgment: and who shall declare his generation? for he was cut off out of the land of the living: for the transgression of my people was he stricken. And he made his grave with the wicked, and with the rich in his death; because he had done no violence, neither was any deceit in his mouth.

Yet it pleased the Lord to bruise him; he hath put him to grief: when thou shalt make his soul an offering for sin, he shall see his seed, he shall prolong his days, and the pleasure of the Lord shall prosper in his hand. He shall see of the travail of his soul, and shall be satisfied: by his knowledge shall my righteous servant justify many; for he shall bear their iniquities. Therefore will I divide him a portion with the great, and he shall divide the spoil with the strong; because he hath poured out his soul unto death: and he was numbered with the transgressors; and he bare the sin of many, and made intercession for the transgressors. (Isaiah 52:13–53:1–12)

Some of the critics of the Yeshua Codes have challenged our conclusion that the name *Yeshua* is purposely encoded in Isaiah 53 and that this ELS actually refers to the historical Jesus of Nazareth. However, if the critics examine the encoded ELS words discovered in this messianic prophecy, they will find over forty encoded names identifying virtually everyone who was present at the crucifixion of Jesus Christ. The mathematical odds against finding forty words naming each of these key individuals, places, and events in the life and death of Jesus of Nazareth by random chance alone in a similar sized non-biblical Hebrew text are simply astronomical. The following section will reveal remarkable ELS code words found encoded in Isaiah's prophecy about the Suffering Messiah (Isaiah 52:12 to 53:13).

Yeshua the Nazarene

In Isaiah 53:6, starting with the third letter in the eleventh word and counting every forty-seventh letter from right to left, we find the word *Nazarene,* נזיר, near the name *Yeshua,* ישוע, in the same messianic prophecy. Jesus lived with his family in the town of Nazareth in northern Galilee where Joseph, the husband of Jesus' mother Mary, pursued his occupation as a carpenter. The word "Nazarene" was also used to describe a special person who was chosen for a sacred purpose and dedicated at birth to the service of God. A Nazarite was totally dedicated when born to the worship of the Lord and was willing to take the serious vow of the Nazarene.

Another vital identification of Jesus with the word Nazarene appears in the life of Jesus the Nazarene, as described in the Gospel of Matthew: "And [Jesus] came and dwelt in a city called Nazareth: that it might be fulfilled which was spoken by the prophets, He shall be called a Nazarene [נזיר]" (Matthew 2:23).

Galilee

The codes reveal the place where Jesus lived for most of his life — Galilee. In Isaiah 53:7, starting with the second letter in the first word and counting every thirty-second letter from left to right spells "Galilee" גליל. There are two ways to spell "Galilee" in Hebrew. The first is with the hen ה at the end of the word, and the second is without the hen ה letter. Jesus was raised in Nazareth, in a region of northern Israel called Galilee, as confirmed in Matthew 21:11: "And the multitude said, this is Jesus [Yeshua] the prophet of Nazareth of Galilee." In addition, much of His ministry was conducted at various locations surrounding the beautiful Sea of Galilee.

Three Marys and the Disciple John at the Cross

The Gospel of John records that three women named Mary (*Miryam,* מרים) were present at the crucifixion of Jesus, together with His beloved disciple, John (*Yochanan,* יוחנן). The gospel of John says:

> Now there stood by the cross of Jesus his mother, and his mother's sister, Mary the wife of Cleophas, and Mary Magdalene. When Jesus therefore saw his mother, and the disciple [John] standing by, whom he loved, he saith unto his mother, Woman, behold thy son! Then saith He to the disciple [John], Behold thy mother! And from that hour that disciple took her unto his own home. (John 19: 25–27)

This moving passage reveals the profound love of Jesus for His mother Mary and His loyal friend John. We find that the names of the three Marys and the disciple John are encoded beside the name Jesus (*Yeshua,* ישוע), which is spelled out at a twenty-letter interval reading left to right beginning in Isaiah 53:10.

In Isaiah 53:11, starting with the fifth letter in the ninth word and counting every twentieth letter from left to right spells *Ma 'al Yeshua Shmee ohz,* מעל ישוע שמי עז, a phrase which means "exceedingly high, Yeshua is my strong name." From the *yod,* י, in Yeshua's name, counting in reverse every twenty-eighth letter spells *John,* יוחנן. Isaiah 52:13 says, "Behold, my Servant [Yeshua] shall deal prudently, he shall be exalted and extolled, and be very high." In Isaiah 53:11, starting with the first letter in the first word and counting every forty-second letter from left to right spells "Messiah," *Mashiach,* משיח. From the *mem,* מ, in the word "Messiah," counting every twenty-third letter from left to right spells "Mary," מרים.

Remarkably, in Isaiah 53:10, all three of the ELS names of Mary use the same letter *yod,* י, in the word *ya'arik,* יאריך. This is the same letter that forms the first letter in the encoded names *Yeshua* and John. In Isaiah 53:10, starting with the third letter in the seventh word and counting every sixth letter from right to left spells "Mary," *Miryam,* מרים. In Isaiah 53:12, starting with the fifth letter in the fourth word and counting every forty-fourth letter from left to right again spells Mary מרים. It is interesting to find the names of three Marys encoded in these verses beside the encoded names *Yeshua* and John when we remember that John's Gospel records that these four individuals were all present at the crucifixion of Jesus Christ. In addition to naming Mary, the mother of Jesus, we also find in Isaiah 53:2, starting with the second letter in the first word and counting every 210th letter from right to left spells "Joseph," *Yoseph,* יוסף, the name of Mary's husband.

"Disciples" Found in Isaiah 53

In Isaiah 53:12, starting with the third letter of the second word and counting every fifty-fifth letter from left to right spells *limmudim ahnan,* למדרים אנן, which means "the disciples mourn." Sometimes, the letter *tav,* ת, precedes this word. In this same count of fifty-five, but adjacent to "disciples," we find the word "priest." In Isaiah 53:5, starting with the second letter in the first word and counting every fifty-fifth letter from left to right spells "the Kohanim" (the priestly tribe) *ha'kohain,* הכהן.

It is fascinating to discover that the names of almost every one of Jesus' disciples (Judas Iscariot is excluded) are encoded within Isaiah's messianic prophecy, written seven centuries before Jesus was born.

The disciple's names are encoded as follows:

1. *Peter*. In Isaiah 53:3, we find the name "Simon Peter," starting with the second letter in the fifth word and counting every nineteenth letter from right to left, the ELS code spells "Peter," *Kepha*, כפה.

2. *James*, the son of Zabbadai. In Isaiah 52:2, starting with the third letter in the ninth word and counting every thirty-fourth letter from left to right, the ELS code spells "James," *Ya'akov*, יעקב.

3. *John*. In Isaiah 53:10, starting with the fourth letter in the eleventh word and counting every twenty-eighth letter from left to right, the code spells "John," *Yochanan*, יוחנן.

4. *Andrew*. In Isaiah 53:4, starting with the first letter in the eleventh word, which is "God" *Elohim*, אלהים, and counting every forty-eighth letter from left to right, we find the encoded word "Andrew," *And'drai*, אנדרי.

5. *Philip*. In Isaiah 53:5, starting with the third letter in the tenth word and counting every 133rd letter from left to right spells "Philip," *Pilip*, פילף.

6. *Thomas*. In Isaiah 53:2, starting with the first letter in the eighth word and counting every thirty-fifth letter from right to left the encoded word spells "Thomas," *Toma*, תומא.

7. *Matthew*. There are three ways to spell the name of the disciple Matthew: *Mati*, מתי; *Mattai*, מתתי; and *Mattiyahu*, מתתיהו. The encoded word *Mattai*, מתתי, is an accepted abbreviated form of *Mattiyahu*, מתתיהו. In Isaiah 53:8, starting with the first letter in the twelfth word and counting every 295th letter from left to right we find the encoded word "Matthew," *Mattai*, מתתי.

8. *James*, son of Alphaeus. *Ben Chalipi Ya'akov*, חלפי יעקב בן. In Isaiah 52:2, starting with the fourth letter in the third word and counting every twentieth letter from left to right the encoded word spells the word *Ya'akov*, יעקב. Two of Christ's disciples were known by the name James. It is fascinating that

we found the name "James" *Ya'akov* יעקב encoded twice within Isaiah 53.

9. *Simon*, (Zelotes) the Canaanite. *Shimon hakanai* הקני שמעון. In Isaiah 52:14, starting with the first letter in the second word and counting every forty-seventh letter from right to left we find the encoded word "Simon," *Shimon,* שמעון.

10. *Thaddaeus*. In Isaiah 53:12, starting with the first letter of the eighth word and counting every fiftieth letter from left to right the encoded word spells the name "Thaddaeus," *Taddai,* תדי.

11. *Matthias*. In Isaiah 53:5, starting with the fourth letter in the seventh word and counting every eleventh letter from left to right spells "Matthias," *Mattiyah,* מתיה. It is fascinating to note that this name Matthias is the name of the last disciple who was chosen by lot by the elders of the early Church to replace the dead traitor Judas Iscariot, whose guilt in betraying Jesus Christ caused him to commit suicide. Luke, the writer of the book of Acts, records how Matthias, the replacement disciple, was chosen: "And they gave forth their lots; and the lot fell upon Matthias [מתיה]; and he was numbered with the eleven apostles" (Acts 1:26).

It is noteworthy that in the early Church an essential qualification for choosing a disciple to replace the deceased Judas Iscariot was that the person must have personally witnessed the three and one half year ministry of Jesus Christ as well as His resurrection (Acts 1:21–26). This eyewitness requirement was established to assure that Matthias could also personally testify to everyone about his personal, eyewitness experience of the life and ministry of Christ from His baptism to His death and resurrection from the dead, and finally, His ascension to heaven. It is interesting to note that the names of virtually every one of Christ's disciples were found encoded near the name *Yeshua* within Isaiah's prophecy. Significantly, the name of Judas Iscariot, the Lord's betrayer, was not found encoded in this passage.

Jesus' Trial and the Names of the Two High Priests

The codes reveal the names of Israel's two high priests at the time of Jesus' trial. Starting with the third letter in the seventh word in Isaiah 52:15 and counting every forty-first letter from right to left spells "Caiaphas," *Kayafa,* כיפה, the name of the high priest of Israel named in the Gospel account of the trial of Jesus. In Isaiah 53:3, starting with the fifth letter in the sixth word and counting every forty-fifth letter from right to left spells "Annas," *Ahnan,* ענן, who was the former high priest and the influential uncle of Caiaphas. The New Testament reveals the names of these high priests in Luke 3:2: "Annas and Caiaphas being the high priests, the word of God came unto John the son of Zacharias in the wilderness." The high (chief) priests were leaders in the Sanhedrin trial in the Temple that lead to Christ's crucifixion, according to John 19:15: "But they cried out, Away with him, away with him, crucify him. Pilate saith unto them, Shall I crucify your King? The chief priests answered, We have no king but Caesar."

The Pharisees, the Levites, King Herod, Rome, and Caesar

The Pharisees and King Herod were also involved in the crucifixion. We find their names encoded in Isaiah 53:9. Starting with the second letter in the fourteenth word and counting every sixty-fourth letter from left to right, we find the word "Pharisee," *pahrush,* פרוש. These Jewish religious leaders were a strong influence in both the Temple and in the broader Israeli society. They encouraged people to follow the strict religious laws of the Scriptures and the written and oral traditions based on the teachings of their rabbis over the centuries. In Isaiah 53: 6, starting with the first letter in the fourth word and counting every twenty-ninth letter from left to right, we find the encoded words "the man Herod," *ish Herod,* איש הורד. The fact that both the names Pharisees and Herod are encoded in Isaiah's messianic prophecy is remarkable.

In Isaiah 53:11, starting with the first letter of the second word and counting every fourteenth letter from left to right, we find the Hebrew word "Levis," *Levim,* לוים, clearly identifying the Temple priests, chosen from the Jewish tribe of Levi, who joined in the conspiracy against Jesus. In addition, starting with the second letter in the thirteenth word in Isaiah 53:9 and counting every seventh letter from left to right, the encoded letters spell "the evil Roman city," *rah eer Romi,* רע עיר רומי, the power ruling the known world at that time that actually ordered the death of Jesus. The Jewish authorities did not possess the legal power to inflict a death sentence upon any offender found guilty in their Sanhedrin Court in the Temple. The only way a death sentence could be legally carried out by the Jewish authorities in Judea at that time was to find a Roman law that the prisoner had also broken and to then appeal to the Roman governor to sentence the person to death under the laws of Rome.

The Gentile soldiers of the Roman Empire who were present at the crucifixion spiritually represented the Roman emperor and the entire Gentile world who also rejected the claims of Jesus as Messiah, the Son of God, and thus spiritually the Gentiles shared the responsibility for the execution of God's Messiah. In this sense, all of humanity, Jews and Gentiles, was represented at the crucifixion of the Lamb of God, Jesus Christ. In Isaiah 53:11, starting with the fourth letter in the seventh word and counting every 194th letter from left to right, we find the encoded words *Kaisar ahmail ovaid,* קיסר עמל אבד, which mean "wicked, Caesar wretched [perish]," or alternatively phrased as "wicked Caesar, to perish." The wicked Roman emperor Tiberius died within five years following the death of Jesus Christ.

Jesus Christ: The Atonement Lamb
and the Light of the World

The Gospel of John records that John the Baptist received a profound revelation of Jesus Christ as the Atonement Lamb of God when He came to be baptized in the Jordan River. "The next day John seeth Jesus coming unto him, and saith, Behold the Lamb of God, which taketh away the sin of the world" (John 1:29). In

Isaiah 52:12, starting with the second letter in the twelfth word and counting every nineteenth letter from left to right spells "from the Atonement Lamb," *me'kippur tela,* מכפר טלא.

In Isaiah 53:5, starting with the seventh letter in the fifth word and counting every twentieth letter from right to left, "lamp of the Lord" *ner Adonai,* נר יהוה, is spelled out. This encoded word is adjacent to *Yeshua,* ישוע, at a twenty-letter interval. The Gospel of John affirms repeatedly that Jesus Christ is the true light of the world. This is confirmed in the following passage: "Then spake Jesus again unto them, saying, I am the light of the world: he that followeth me shall not walk in darkness, but shall have the light of life" (John 8:12).

The Messianic Title "Shiloh," "Messiah" and "Passover"

In Isaiah 53:9, starting with the second letter in the eleventh word and counting every fifty-fourth letter from right to left spells *Shiloh,* שילה. Both Jewish and Christian scholars acknowledge that the word *Shiloh* is a clear prophetic title of the coming Messiah. In Genesis 49:10, Moses recorded the deathbed prophecy of the patriarch Jacob: "The sceptre shall not depart from Judah, nor a lawgiver from between his feet, until Shiloh come; and unto him [Yeshua] shall the gathering of the people be." This famous prophecy clearly identified the coming Messiah as "Shiloh." The discovery of the word *Shiloh* encoded beside the name *Yeshua* in the powerful messianic prophecy of Isaiah 53 provides compelling evidence of the identity of Jesus of Nazareth as God's Messiah in this passage.

In addition, the word *Yeshua* was found together with the word *Messiah* encoded in this key passage. In Isaiah 53:8, starting with the third letter in the second word and counting every sixty-fifth letter from left to right spells "Messiah," *Mashiach,* משיח. In this same count, but starting with the third letter in the tenth word of verse 10, which is the *ayin,* ע, and counting every sixty-fifth letter from left to right spells *Yeshua,* ישוע. It is fascinating that the words *Jesus* and *Messiah* are both encoded in this prophecy of Isaiah sharing the same 65-letter ELS interval. Also, the word *Passover* was found encoded in Isaiah 53:10.

Beginning at the third letter of the thirteenth word at an interval
of every sixty-two letters in reverse spells "Passover," *Peh'sakh*,
פסח.

The Bread and Wine

In Isaiah 53:1, starting with the fifth letter in the eighth word
and counting every 210th letter from right to left spells "the
bread," *ha'lachem*, הלחם, which may refer to the symbol of
bread that Jesus used at the Last Supper to refer to His body,
which was broken for our sins. Another group of Hebrew letters
at the same 210-letter interval beginning with the second letter
in the eleventh word spells the word "wine," *yeyin*, יין, which
was the other key symbol used by Jesus at His last Passover
Supper in the Upper Room to symbolize His blood, which was
shed for our sins.

The names "Jonah" and "water" were also encoded close
together in this passage. In Isaiah 52:4, starting with the fourth
letter in the sixth word and counting every nineteenth letter from
left to right spells "Jonah," יונה. A few verses later, in Isaiah 52:
7, starting with the first letter in the ninth word and counting
every nineteenth letter from left to right spells "water," מים.
The prophet Jonah was thrown in the water to awaken him to
God's command to preach to his enemies, the Ninevites. These
codes revealing "Jonah" and "water" remind us of the history
of the prophet Jonah, who was "three days and three nights in
the whale's belly." Jesus used Jonah's experience as a prophetic
symbol of His own death and resurrection.

Those Who Watched the Crucifixion from Afar

Mark 15:40 says, "There were also women looking on afar off:
among whom was Mary Magdalene, and Mary the mother of
James the less and of Joses, and Salome." In Isaiah 52:15, starting with the third letter in the sixteenth word and counting
every 113th letter from right to left spells "Salome," *Shalomit*,
שלמית. In verse 13, starting with the fourth letter in the second
word and counting every 149th letter from right to left spells
"Joses," *Yosai*, יוסי. The man Joses was apparently another
son of Mary, the mother of Jesus, and therefore was Jesus'

half-brother. According to Mark 15:40, both Marys were weeping at the crucifixion of Jesus. Encoded in Isaiah 52:15, starting with the fifth letter in the eighteenth word and counting every thirteenth letter from left to right spells the words "the Marys weep bitterly," *na'ar Miryam be'ku abhor,* נאר מרים בכו. In Isaiah 53:9, starting with the first letter in the third word and counting every twenty-eighth letter from right to left spells "tremble Mary" *rahal Miryam,* רעל מרים. The letters adjacent to the above spell "the blessed" *habarucha,* הברוכה. Mary, the mother of Jesus, was called "blessed" in the Gospel of Luke: "And the angel came in unto her [Mary], and said, Hail, thou that art highly favoured, the Lord is with thee: blessed [הברוכה] art thou among women" (Luke 1:28).

Thus far, we have found ELS encoded words naming virtually every one of the people involved with the crucifixion of Jesus, in addition to many others who were present during His remarkable life of ministry.

The Cross and the Passover Feast

In Isaiah 53:10, starting with the third letter in the second word and counting every fifty-second letter from right to left spells "cross," צלב. From the same word, taking the first letter and counting every 104th letter from right to left spells "Passover," פסח, as mentioned earlier. In Isaiah 52:14, starting with the third letter in the sixth word and counting every twenty-sixth letter from left to right spells "My Feast (my sacrifice)," *Chaggai,* חגי. The Feast of Passover, the Chaggai, when Jesus was crucified, occurred the day following the evening Passover Supper, when the Last Supper occurred.

The Time and Place of Christ's Crucifixion

Jesus was crucified on the day of the Passover Feast, which took place annually on the fifteenth of the Jewish month Nisan (also known as the month of Aviv). Mount Moriah, the Temple Mount, is the place where God supernaturally provided a ram as a substitute sacrifice in the place of Abraham's son Isaac. This was also the place where God commanded King David to prepare the site for the building of the Temple, which was ultimately built by his son Solomon. However, Mount Moriah is a long mountain ridge that begins in the south of Jerusalem and continues northward past the northern city walls to the site of Golgotha, the "place of the skull," where Jesus was crucified outside the city walls, just north of the Damascus Gate. The Book of Hebrews confirms the Gospel account that Christ's death took place outside the city walls: "Wherefore Jesus also, that he might sanctify the people with his own blood, suffered without the gate" (Hebrews 13:12). In Isaiah 52:1, starting with the third letter in the eighth word and counting every twenty-seventh letter from right to left spells *aviv ve'moriah,* אביב ומריה, which means "Aviv of Mount Moriah." This is an intriguing Bible Code discovery naming the actual month of Passover, "Aviv," and "Mount Moriah," the place of Christ's sacrifice for our sins as written by Isaiah centuries before the event. The adjacent letters spell *rosh,* ראש, which means "the first" or "the head of the year" (the first month of the religious year was the month Nisan-Aviv, the month of Passover), when Jesus was crucified.

"Let Him Be Crucified"

Two thousand years ago, the Gentile Romans and the Jewish leaders joined together to crucify Jesus of Nazareth. Every human being on earth was morally represented by the Gentile Romans and the Jewish leadership because Jesus died on the Cross for all of our sins. Matthew records the terrible moment when the Roman governor agreed to Christ's death. "Pilate saith unto them, What shall I do then with Jesus which is called Christ? They all say unto him, Let him be crucified" (Matthew 27:22). The prophet Isaiah foretold this tragic series of events seven centuries earlier. "He was taken from prison and from judgment: and who shall declare his generation? for he was cut off out of the land of the living: for the transgression of my people was he stricken" (Isaiah 53:8). Perhaps the most interesting code discovery in this passage is the fact that this exact phrase was encoded in Isaiah's prophecy. Starting with the second letter in the sixth word of Isaiah 53:8 and counting every fifteenth letter right to left spells "let Him be crucified" *yitz'tzahlaiv,* יִצְלַב.

Over one thousand years before the birth of Jesus, the psalmist David wrote his prophetic Psalm 22, which foretold the tragic crucifixion of Christ. David wrote of the future death of the Messiah: "The assembly of the wicked have inclosed me: they pierced my hands and my feet" (Psalm 22:16). Incredibly in Isaiah 52:10, we find the word "pierce" encoded. Starting with the third letter in the fifteenth word, which is "in His hands" בידו, and counting every ninety-two letters from left to right spells "pierce," *dahkar,* דקר in reverse.

Can any reader have any remaining doubt that the Bible Codes identify Jesus of Nazareth as the prophesied Messiah who died for our sins as the Son of God?

The following is a chart summarizing the most important codes found in Isaiah's prophecy that name virtually everyone associated with the crucifixion of Jesus. This summary list was prepared as a convenience for the reader and as an aid for those students of the Scripture who wish to check out these Bible Codes for themselves.

Jesus and His Disciples Found Encoded in Isaiah 53

ELS Word	Begins	Word	Letter	Interval
Yeshua Shmi –				
Jesus is My Name	Isa. 53:10	11	4	(−20)
Nazarene	Isa. 53:6	11	3	(47)
Messiah	Isa. 53:11	1	1	(−42)
Shiloh	Isa. 53:12	21	4	(19)
Passover	Isa. 53:10	13	3	(−62)
Galilee	Isa. 53:7	1	2	(−32)
Herod	Isa. 53:6	4	1	(−29)
Caesar	Isa. 53:11	7	4	(−194)
Evil Roman city	Isa. 53:9	13	2	(−7)
Caiaphas—High Priest	Isa. 52:15	7	3	(41)
Annas—High Priest	Isa. 53:3	6	5	(−45)
Mary	Isa. 53:11	1	1	(−23)
Mary	Isa. 53:10	7	3	(6)
Mary	Isa. 53:9	13	3	(44)

The Disciples	Isa. 53:12	2	3	(−55)
Peter	Isa. 53:10	11	5	(−14)
Matthew	Isa. 53:8	12	1	(−295)
John	Isa. 53:10	11	4	(−28)
Andrew	Isa. 53:4	11	1	(−48)
Philip	Isa. 53:5	10	3	(−133)
Thomas	Isa. 53:2	8	1	(35)
James	Isa. 52:2	9	3	(−34)
James	Isa. 52:2	3	4	(−20)
Simon	Isa. 52:14	2	1	(47)
Thaddaeus	Isa. 53:12	9	1	(−50)
Matthias	Isa. 53:5	7	4	(−11)
Let Him Be Crucified	Isa. 53:8	6	2	(15)
His Cross	Isa. 53:6	2	2	(−8)
Pierce	Isa. 52:10	15	3	(−92)
Lamp of the Lord	Isa. 53:5	5	7	(20)
His Signature	Isa. 52:7	8	4	(49)
Bread	Isa. 53:12	2	3	(26)
Wine	Isa. 53:5	11	2	(210)
From Zion	Isa. 52:14	6	1	(45)
Moriah	Isa. 52:7	4	5	(153)
Obed	Isa. 53:7	3	2	(−19)
Jesse	Isa. 52:9	3	1	(−19)
Seed	Isa. 52:15	2	2	(−19)
Water	Isa. 52:7	9	1	(−19)
Levites	Isa. 54:3	3	6	(19)
From the Atonement Lamb	Isa. 52:12	12	2	(−19)
Joseph	Isa. 53:2	1	2	(210)

When my book *The Signature of God* and Yacov Rambsel's book *Yeshua* were published in 1996, hundreds of thousands of readers were thrilled with this new discovery about the Bible Codes. Many students of the Scriptures were especially fascinated with Yacov's research that revealed the encoded name of Jesus found in well-known messianic prophecies. However, a number of Bible Code researchers in Israel and North America, as well as Orthodox Jewish rabbis, have disputed the significance of this discovery of Yeshua's name. They have pointed out that the name *Yeshua*, יֵשׁוּעַ, is a relatively small word with only four Hebrew letters.

Some of these critics have contemptuously rejected the significance of the Yeshua Codes and declared that one could find the name *Yeshua* יֵשׁוּעַ in virtually any passage in Hebrew literature (from a novel to the Israeli phone book). However, these critics ignore the fact that the name *Yeshua* appears at very small ELS intervals (i.e., every fifth, ninth, or twentieth letter, etc.) in dozens of well known messianic prophecies. No one has found significant names of any other historic personalities (such as Mohammed, Napoleon, Alexander the Great) encoded repeatedly at small ELS intervals within dozens of Old Testament messianic prophecies.

One critic claimed on the Internet that the name of a false messiah "Rev. Sung Yung Moon" appears by accident frequently in these same messianic prophecies where Yacov found the ELS *Yeshua*. However, this is not true. While the three letter Hebrew word for "moon" naturally appears by accident frequently including a few occasional places near some of these messianic prophecies, the ELS word "moon" does not identify the Rev. Sung Yung Moon of South Korea, who formed the Unification Church. The encoded words do not reveal "Rev. Sung Young Moon" as the critics falsely imply; it is only the three-letter Hebrew ELS word for "moon" that appears frequently by accident as you would expect with any three letter word. This particular criticism is without merit.

A Challenge to the Critics of the Yeshua Codes

Yacov's discovery of more than forty names of individuals and places associated with the crucifixion of Jesus of Nazareth in Isaiah's "Suffering Servant" messianic passage is unprecedented. In my 1997 book *The Handwriting of God*[8] I issued a challenge to the critics who reject the Yeshua Codes to find any other passage of similar length (only fifteen sentences as in Isaiah 52:13 to 53:12) in Hebrew literature outside the Bible that contains forty meaningful ELS codes, including the names of Jesus, the Nazarene, Messiah, Passover, Herod, Mary, and the names of Christ's disciples, etc. If they cannot discover these names encoded in any passage outside the Bible, and we believe it will be impossible, we will have additional evidence that these codes about *Yeshua* the Nazarene, and His disciples, are truly unprecedented. To make the task easier for our critics, we challenge them to find any fifteen-sentence passage in any language or literature outside the Bible that contains forty or more ELS words related to people, places, and events concerning a historical event. If our critics can accomplish this feat, I will be willing to admit that our discoveries in Isaiah 53 are not as significant as we claim. Over six years ago I made this challenge. I am still waiting for their answer.

Is the Hebrew Name of Jesus
Yeshua, יֵשׁוּעַ, or Yeshu, יֵשׁוּ?

Some Jewish critics have claimed that the name *Yeshua*, יֵשׁוּעַ, is not the true name that Jesus of Nazareth used during His lifetime. They have claimed that the three-letter name *Yeshu*, יֵשׁוּ, which is often used by Jews today when referring to Jesus is the correct Hebrew name. Several Israeli critics of the Yeshua Codes have claimed on the Internet, "Yeshua is a recent, manipulative invention used to facilitate the proselytization of Jews." Some readers have written, "Jews say *Yeshu* and Messianic Jews say *Yeshua*."

Obviously, it is vital that we determine the correct and authentic Hebrew name of Jesus as used in the first century by Jews in Israel. The Jewish linguist Eliezer Ben-Yehuda was the man who recreated the ancient Hebrew language in the last century in Palestine. He began with the ancient Hebrew words used in the Bible and Temple worship and began to expand the vocabulary with new, modern words based on biblical Hebrew forms and rules of grammar. It is interesting to note that Ben-Yehuda discusses the name Jesus in the prolegomena to his Thesaurus to the Hebrew language, *Thesaurus Totius Hebraitatis*. According to a study on this subject by Prof. Kai Kjoer-Hansen in the magazine *Mishkan*, Ben-Yehuda refers to Jesus eight times, using the spelling *Yeshua* every time. While most Hebrew writing today in Israel uses the shorter name

Yeshu, through centuries of long habit, the historical evidence strongly supports the claim that the original Hebrew name of Jesus was *Yeshua,* יֵשׁוּעַ.

The great Jewish rabbi Moses Maimonides, known as Rambam (A.D. 1200), wrote about Jesus using the name *Yeshua,* יֵשׁוּעַ, in his *Epistle to Yemen* as well as in his monumental fourteen-volume study *Mishnah Torah,* which codified all of the religious laws from the Torah. In his volume entitled *The Laws of Kings and Their Wars,* which deals with the qualifications of the true Messiah, Rabbi Maimonides wrote about Jesus of Nazareth and spelled His name twice as *Yeshua,* יֵשׁוּעַ. He wrote: "Jesus of Nazareth who aspired to be the Messiah and was executed by the court was also [alluded to] in Daniel's prophecies."[9] The Hebrew word "Jesus" was spelled as follows: *Yeshua* יֵשׁוּעַ. I acquired an uncensored edition of Rambam's *Mishnah Torah* in a Jewish bookstore in Jerusalem several years ago. Most editions of the *Mishnah Torah* have been censored during the last eight hundred years and have the relevant passages that deal with Jesus of Nazareth removed. However, when the Jews of Yemen flew back to Israel in the 1950s they carried with them their rare uncensored copies of the Mishnah Torah that dated back to the original eleventh-century writings of Maimonides. Rabbi Eliyahu Touger translated and edited this volume, which was published by the Maznaim Publishing Corporation in New York and Jerusalem in 1987. Rabbi Touger wrote this footnote: "Though most published texts of the *Mishnah Torah* conclude this chapter with this paragraph, a large portion of the Rambam's text was censored and left unpublished. We have included the original text, based on the Yemenite manuscripts of *Mishnah Torah* and early uncensored editions."[10]

In light of this overwhelming evidence I believe we can have confidence that the name *Yeshua,* יֵשׁוּעַ, is the genuine Hebrew name of Jesus of Nazareth. The name of Jesus of Nazareth found in the Bible Codes is also spelled with four letters יֵשׁוּעַ *Yeshua.* In conclusion, the Bible Codes are a fascinating discovery that points to the divine inspiration of the Holy Scriptures. They are worthy of further study.

Notes

1. Grant R. Jeffrey, *Armageddon—Appointment with Destiny,* Toronto: Frontier Research Publications, Inc., 1988.

2. Yacov Rambsel, *Yeshua—The Name of Jesus Revealed in the Old Testament,* Toronto: Frontier Research Publications, Inc. 1997.

3. Yacov Rambsel, *His Name Is Jesus,* Toronto: Frontier Research Publications, Inc. 1998.

4. Statistical Significance Discovered in the Yeshua Codes Internet site: http://www.yfiles.com/yeshuacodes.html.

5. Statistical Significance Discovered in the Yeshua Codes Internet site: http://www.yfiles.com/yeshuacodes.html.

6. Yacov Rambsel, *Yeshua—The Name of Jesus Revealed in the Old Testament,* Toronto: Frontier Research Publications, Inc. 1998.

7. Yacov Rambsel, *Yeshua— The Name of Jesus Revealed in the Old Testament,* Toronto: Frontier Research Publications, Inc. 1998.

8. Grant R. Jeffrey, *The Handwriting of God,* Toronto: Frontier Research Publications, Inc. 1997.

9. Moses Maimonides, *The Laws of Kings and Their Wars,* translated by Eliyahu Touger, New York: Maznaim Publishing Corp., 1987, pp. 234-235.

10. Moses Maimonides, *The Laws of Kings and Their Wars,* translated by Eliyahu Touger, New York: Maznaim Publishing Corp., 1987, p. 235.

11

The Phenomenon of "Undesigned Coincidences"

Compelling evidence that the Scriptures are absolutely reliable and inspired by God is revealed in the phenomenon called "undesigned coincidences" found in the pages of the Bible. This phenomenon cannot be explained unless these inspired writings are completely true. The evidence of undesigned coincidences was first noted in 1738 by Dr. Philip Doddridge in his *Introduction to the First Epistle to the Thessalonians*. Doddridge wrote:

> Whoever reads over St. Paul's epistles with attention . . . will discern such intrinsic characters of their genuineness, and the divine authority of the doctrines they contain, as will perhaps produce in him a stronger conviction than all the external evidence with which they are attended. To which we may add, that the exact coincidence observable between the many allusions to particular facts, in this as well as in other epistles, and the account of the facts themselves, as they are recorded

in the history of the Acts, is a remarkable confirmation of the truth of each.[1]

Dr. William Paley, the author of the noteworthy book *Horæ Paulinæ,* was the first writer to fully develop this evidence regarding these undesigned coincidences in great detail as proof that no man could have created these Epistles of Paul without the divine aid of God Himself.[2] However, the greatest evidence of this type was researched by Rev. J. J. Blunt as detailed in his book, *Undesigned Coincidences in the Writings of the Old and New Testament.*[3] As Rev. Blunt declared in his fascinating manuscript, the evidence from "instances of coincidence without design" provide an incredibly strong proof that the Scriptures were inspired by God.

The evidence from coincidence is so strong in the mind of the average person that juries have often convicted people to the death penalty upon this kind of evidence. The value of this evidence is that it establishes a strong proof that the individual authors of the books of the Bible acted as independent witnesses to the facts that they observed and recorded in the Scriptures. Furthermore, these coincidences are such as could not possibly have arisen as a result of mutual understanding among the biblical writers or artificial arrangement. Often the facts and evidence that coincidentally prove the accuracy of the Bible's narrative are found in obscure passages unconnected with the main passage describing the story.

The Rebellion of Absalom Against King David

One of the saddest and most tragic stories found in the pages of the Scriptures concerns the revolt of David's son Prince Absalom toward the end of David's reign and the agony experienced by the king when his beloved and rebellious son was killed. Absalom was the third son born to David as a result of his marriage with Maacah, the daughter of Talmai, the king of Geshur. This story has often been preached from the pulpit to remind us of the consequences of pride and blind ambition in the inevitable judgment of God upon Absalom's rebellion and his ultimate death. Many preachers have reminded parents about David's complacency in failing to discipline his favorite son as he grew to manhood, full of pride and arrogance.

The Scriptures record that "Absalom prepared him chariots and horses, and fifty men to run before him" (2 Samuel 15:1) and stirred rebellion against his father by promising the people that he would rule in their favor when he became king of Israel. David's unwillingness to deal with the growing rebellion of his son ultimately set the stage for Absalom's revolt against his father's throne, David's flight from Jerusalem, and the bitter war against the rebels. Finally, the tragic moment came when David heard of his loyal army's victory over the rebels. He cried out in anguish, "Is the young man Absalom safe?" (2 Samuel 18:29). When the servants of the king finally had the courage to tell the truth they admitted that Absalom was dead. King David wept bitterly for the loss of his beloved son, crying out, "O my son Absalom, my son, my son Absalom! Would God I had died for thee, O Absalom, my son, my son!"

In the midst of the rebellion the Bible records that, "Absalom sent for Ahithophel the Gilonite, David's counsellor, from his city, even from Giloh, while he offered sacrifices. And the conspiracy was strong; for the people increased continually with Absalom." Ahithophel had been King David's faithful counsellor or prime minister for many decades giving the king the benefit of his great wisdom. The Book of Samuel tells us that Ahithophel was considered a brilliant counselor. "And the counsel of Ahithophel, which he counselled in those days, was as if a man had inquired at the oracle of God: so was all the counsel of Ahithophel both with David and with Absalom" (2 Samuel 16:23). In fact, when David learned that his trusted friend and counselor had betrayed him, he was so afraid of the danger from Ahithophel that he prayed, "O Lord, I pray thee, turn the counsel of Ahithophel into foolishness" (2 Samuel 15:31). Years earlier King David had prophesied a double prophecy in his Book of Psalms that foresaw the betrayal by his friend Ahithophel. However, David's words also predicted the ultimate betrayal a thousand years later of Jesus of Nazareth by His friend and disciple Judas Iscariot. "Yea, mine own familiar friend, in whom I trusted, which did eat of my bread, hath lifted up his heel against me" (Psalm 41:9).

The question that has troubled many Bible students and writers of commentaries is this. Why did Ahithophel, David's trusted counselor, immediately join Absalom's rebellion against his father's throne after a lifetime of faithful service? Furthermore, why would Ahithophel ask the young prince to allow him to personally lead the army of rebels to immediately attack and kill King David before the king could escape? "Moreover Ahithophel said unto Absalom, 'Let me now choose out twelve thousand men, and I will arise and pursue after David this night . . . and I will smite the king only' " (2 Samuel 17:1,2). Finally, why would Ahithophel advise Absalom to openly have sexual relations with his father's wives on the roof of the palace? "And Ahithophel said unto Absalom, 'Go in unto thy father's concubines, which he hath left to keep the house; and all Israel shall hear that thou art abhorred of thy father: then shall the hands of all that are with thee be strong.' So they spread Absalom a tent upon the top of the house; and Absalom went in unto his father's concubines in the sight of all Israel" (2 Samuel 16:21,22). The Bible does not openly record the motivation for this incredible betrayal of King David as if the reason was so obvious to people living in that day that there was no need to comment on it.

The answer to this great mystery is found in several of the passages in the Old Testament that often cause readers to skip forward because the list of names recorded in the chapter seems to have little relevance to us. However, the solution to this puzzle about Ahithophel's motive does exist in the Word of God and it reveals a very important lesson that every single follower of Christ needs to learn. To find the solution to the mystery of the betrayal surrounding Absalom's rebellion, we need to go back almost thirty years to the incident when David committed adultery with Bathsheba, the beautiful wife of Uriah the Hittite. Most commentators and preachers have discussed the sin of David as if it was the result of a momentary weakness when he happened to observe the woman Bathsheba bathing. The truth is somewhat different.

When David was supposed to be at war leading his troops against the enemy, the Scriptures record that he had stayed home in his palace in Jerusalem. "And it came to pass, after the year was expired, at the time when kings go forth to battle, that David sent Joab, and his servants with him, and all Israel; and they destroyed the children of Ammon, and besieged Rabbah. But David tarried still at Jerusalem" (2 Samuel 11:1). David's first mistake was that he was not in the place God had called him to be, leading his nation against their enemies as their king. As the evidence unfolds about this biblical mystery we will also find that Bathsheba was no stranger to the king.

When you read the Scriptures carefully you will note that the passage describing Bathsheba tells us that she was the "daughter of Eliam" and "the wife of Uriah the Hittite" (2 Samuel 11:3). Another significant passage in the Book of Samuel lists the great military heroes that guarded King David throughout his many battles against Saul, the Philistines, and many enemy nations. This list of the thirty-seven "mighty men" of David records that "Uriah the Hittite" and "Eliam, the son of Ahithophel the Gilonite" were part of this elite force that fought for the king (2 Samuel 23:34,39). Now we can begin to understand what was occurring behind the scenes in this famous biblical story. Uriah the Hittite, the husband of Bathsheba, and Eliam, the father of Bathsheba, are not strangers to David. They are friends who had fought back-to-back against their enemies over many years. They had sat together around the campfire at night during many military campaigns. Bathsheba is the wife of Uriah, David's loyal bodyguard, and the daughter of Eliam, another faithful bodyguard. David viewed Bathsheba while she was bathing because Uriah and his wife had a house close to King David's palace as a probable reward for his years of loyal service. It is very likely that Bathsheba, Uriah, and her father Eliam had attended royal banquets in David's palace.

The story of David's sin with Bathsheba takes on a very different complexion in light of these scriptural facts that have been unnoticed for centuries. When David committed adultery with Bathsheba he took the wife of Uriah, a loyal friend and the daughter of another friend. Then when she becomes pregnant

David tried to get Uriah to visit his wife to provide confusion about when and how she became pregnant. When Uriah refused to visit his wife, David conspired with his general Joab to murder Uriah to cover up his shameful betrayal and adultery. Later, the prophet Nathan came to David and proclaimed God's anger against David's sins of adultery and the murder of Uriah. Nathan warned that David would be afflicted by warfare the rest of his life in punishment for his sins. Furthermore the prophet foretold that "by this deed thou hast given great occasion to the enemies of the Lord to blaspheme, the child also that is born unto thee shall surely die" (2 Samuel 12:14). Throughout history this prophecy was fulfilled as the skeptics and critics attacked the Bible and King David's character by referring to his great sin with Bathsheba.

Yet, there is still more to the story. Note carefully that 2 Samuel 23:34 told us that Eliam, the father of Bathsheba, was also the son of Ahithophel, David's counselor. Therefore, Ahithophel, David's prime minister, was the grandfather of Bathsheba. After David sinned with Bathsheba and killed Uriah, many people in the palace and the army would have realized that David was the father of the child born to Bathsheba after the death of her husband. People living at that time knew the length of a woman's pregnancy was nine months and therefore knew that the king must be the father of the widow Bathsheba, whom he later married. As David's counselor in the palace, Ahithophel must have burned with rage to know his king had betrayed his granddaughter's honor and killed Uriah, her husband, who was a fellow soldier with his son Eliam, Bathsheba's father. However, there was nothing he could do at that time to exact his revenge. If he had risen in anger against the king he would have lost his life. So he remained silent, keeping his thoughts of revenge secretly to himself all of the years that followed until he saw an opportunity to destroy King David. The Arabs have an expression, "That a man who seeks his revenge before forty years has past, has moved in haste."

Finally, after decades of waiting, King David's rebellious son Absalom revolted against his aged father. This was Ahithophel's chance to get revenge for the wrongs committed years earlier against his family. He joined Absalom's conspiracy and offered to kill David personally. Finally, we can understand Ahithophel's strange advice to Absalom to have sexual relations with David's wives "in the sight of all Israel." He was attempting to get his revenge by encouraging Absalom to do the same thing to David's wives as the king had done to his granddaughter. Significantly, as David fled from Jerusalem, a man named Shimei cursed the king and cast stones at him saying, "Behold, thou art taken in thy mischief, because thou art a bloody man" (2 Samuel 16:8). When David's men wanted to kill this man, the king stopped them, and stated that the man was right and that God had told him to curse the king. Obviously, King David knew very well, as did the people around him, why Ahithophel had joined Absalom's revolt.

These verses provided clues and evidence that finally allowed us to solve the mystery of Ahithophel's betrayal of David. More importantly, these clues scattered in passages throughout the Old Testament provide overwhelming evidence in support of the truthfulness of the Bible's report about the life of King David. No one writing a story like this as fiction would hide the clues so well that the mystery of Ahithophel's motive for betrayal could not be discovered for thousands of years. However, someone truthfully recording a contemporary series of events will often pass over in silence the motive for a person's actions because that motive is so obvious and well known to the writer and those who were living at the time of the events. The presence of coincidental evidence such as we find in this analysis provides very strong proof that the biblical record is a faithful and reliable account of the events in question. As Paul Harvey often says when he completes his radio program, "Now you know the rest of the story!"

There is one further detail that should not be overlooked. Consider how David responded to his sin and God's punishment in the death of his child born to Bathsheba. While the baby was sick, King David fasted and prayed that God would allow the child to live. However, after his child died, David stopped fasting and said, "But now he is dead, wherefore should I fast? Can I bring him back again? I shall go to him, but he shall not return to me" (2 Samuel 12:23). In this touching scene, where the Bible assures us that children who die will go to heaven, we can see the difference between the way a man thinks about his sin and the way God deals with our sins. King David had sinned in his weakness. He sincerely repented of his sins as witnessed by his touching words of deep repentance in his Psalms. His son had died as God warned through his prophet Nathan's words. David stopped fasting and prepared to carry on with the rest of his life, believing that his sin and its consequences were over forever.

This is the way most Christians think about their sins. When convicted of our sin, we sincerely repent and ask God to forgive us. The Lord forgives our sin and we believe, like King David, that the consequences of our sins are removed. We believe that it's all over. However, although God truly forgives our sins, it's not over. God will not stop the natural consequences of our sin from affecting our lives and the lives of those around us. When we sin, it is similar to throwing a pebble on a pond. The ripples on the pond are like the effects of our sinful actions that will affect many things in our lives and those we know. Often the consequences will cause great problems many years later. King David thought his sin with Bathsheba was dealt with forever, but the tragic consequences caught up with him years later and almost caused him to lose his life and throne. At a time in his life when David should have been enjoying his victories and honors, the consequences of his sin from years before almost destroyed him. David was forced to flee from his royal city, up the side of the Mount of Olives in fear after the betrayal of his son and his closest counselor. It was the worst moment is his long life.

The true and lasting consequences of our sins are often underestimated by Christians. Sometimes Christians, when they are tempted to sin, begin to think like King David. They feel that they can sin, then ask God to forgive their sin and that He will make everything perfect as if their sin had never occurred. But our sins have consequences that will continue to destroy our body, our friendships, our families, and our career, years after God has forgiven us if we truly repent of our rebellion.

We need to realize that, when we choose to sin against God, the
effects of our choice will continue to affect our life as long as
we live. While God does forgive He does not change the law of
cause and effect that will inevitably produce the consequences
of our sins.

David and Goliath

The story of David and Goliath is one of the most well known of
the Bible stories. During that time the Jews were under the brutal
domination of the Philistines. Finally, the Lord raised up a hero
to stand against the Philistines and defeat their great champion,
Goliath. The army of Israel faced the army of the Philistines but
King Saul could not find an Israelite brave enough to engage
the Philistine's giant warrior in hand-to-hand combat that
would determine who would dominate the land. There are a
number of small details or coincidences in this biblical story that
provide very strong proof that it is a genuine account. Consider
that the Bible mentions that Goliath comes from the village of
Gath. "And there went out a champion out of the camp of the
Philistines, named Goliath, of Gath, whose height was six cubits
and a span" (1 Samuel 17:4). This is significant because Gath
was one of the villages where the giant race of Anakims lived.
When the twelve spies entered Canaan they were fearful of the
giant races that lived in the land. "And they brought up an evil
report of the land which they had searched unto the children of
Israel, saying, 'The land, through which we have gone to search
it, is a land that eateth up the inhabitants thereof; and all the
people that we saw in it are men of a great stature' " (Numbers
13:32).

Another passage in the Book of Joshua tells us that Gath was
one of the few places where the giant race of Anakim still survived. "And at that time came Joshua, and cut off the Anakims
from the mountains, from Hebron, from Debir, from Anab, and
from all the mountains of Judah, and from all the mountains of
Israel: Joshua destroyed them utterly with their cities. There was
none of the Anakims left in the land of the children of Israel: only
in Gaza, in Gath, and in Ashdod, there remained" (Joshua 11:
21,22). There were only three cities in Israel where the remnants

of the giants survived. This coincidence that, four hundred years after the conquest of Canaan, we find Goliath living in Gath, one of those three villages, is a marvelous confirmation of the truthfulness of the biblical record about David and Goliath. In this coincidence we find that three separate biblical books, Numbers, Joshua, and Samuel, confirm the accuracy of one of the elements in this famous biblical account.

One other feature in the story of David and Goliath always fascinated me as a young boy. Why did David pick up five smooth stones for his sling when he knew that God would guide his aim to kill the Philistine giant with only one stone? Did David lack faith in God's supernatural power to destroy Israel's great enemy? The answer to this mystery appeared to me one night when I was reading the Book of 2 Samuel, chapter 21. To my surprise I found that Goliath was not the only giant in his family. The father of Goliath was a giant who had five sons, all of whom fought for the Philistines. Every one of these four brothers were also giants who ultimately died in combat with the brave soldiers of David. Summarizing the story of their death in combat with David's men, the prophet Samuel recorded: "These four were born to the giant in Gath, and fell by the hand of David, and by the hand of his servants" (2 Samuel 21:22). When David picked up five smooth stones for his sling he was simply being prudent in preparing for the possibility that Goliath's four brothers might have joined the battle when Goliath was killed. He might have needed the additional four stones to defeat the four other giants.

Why Did Israel Not Use Horses?

I believe the horse is the most noble and beautiful animal on earth. As a young boy I grew up on a ranch in Canada where my family ran a western-style Christian summer camp for young people, Frontier Ranch, where we raised over a hundred quarter horses. Some of my fondest memories are those when I would ride my horse along old abandoned logging trails and camp out overnight in the forest. As one who loves horses I always thought it strange that the Israelites never used horses in their many battles against the pagan armies in their conquest of the Holy Land prior to the reign of King Solomon.

Why did Israel never use horses to defend themselves against the cavalry and war-horses of their enemies? There are one hundred and eighty-eight references to horses throughout the Old Testament proving that the horse was well known to the Jews. The Book of Job describes the glory and bravery of the horse in the following passages: "Hast thou given the horse strength? hast thou clothed his neck with thunder? Canst thou make him afraid as a grasshopper? The glory of his nostrils is terrible. He paweth in the valley, and rejoiceth in his strength: he goeth on to meet the armed men. He mocketh at fear, and is not affrighted; neither turneth he back from the sword. The quiver rattleth against him, the glittering spear and the shield. He swalloweth the ground with fierceness and rage: neither believeth he that it is the sound of the trumpet" (Job 39:19-24).

Archeology has revealed that horses were commonly used in the armies and societies of all of the ancient nations of the Middle East, with the exception of Israel, until the reign of King Solomon approximately 970 B.C. For example, the Ten Commandments prohibited the Jews from coveting an ox or ass, but there was no mention of horses. "Thou shalt not covet thy neighbour's house, thou shalt not covet thy neighbour's wife, nor his manservant, nor his maidservant, nor his ox, nor his ass, nor any thing that is thy neighbour's" (Exodus 20:17). In the Book of Judges we find evidence that donkeys were the normal mode of transportation for Israel rather than horses. As an example, according to Joshua 15:18, when the daughter of Caleb, a leader of Israel, came to visit Othniel she used an ass, or donkey, not a horse. The Book of Judges revealed that the governors of Israel rode upon white asses.

Later, we read of Saul searching for the lost asses of his father. In the passages of the Old Testament dealing with this period before the reign of King Solomon, although the Jewish state trained very effective armies and won numerous wars in their conquest of Canaan, they never used horses for cavalry nor for their war chariots. The only horses mentioned were those of the enemies of Israel such as the nine hundred chariots of the cavalry of King Jabin of Canaan. In the Bible's description of the battle with the Philistines, when they seized the Ark of God, Israel lost thirty thousand infantry, but there was no mention of horsemen, proving they had no cavalry. The Scriptures describe the battle against King David, when his son Absalom was killed by riding his mule under the branches of a tree, proving that even royal princes did not ride horses in that time.

Why did Israel refuse to use horses for their cavalry when the foreign armies had the advantage of horses in their cavalry and war chariots? The answer is found in a single command of God forbidding the use of horses as recorded in Deuteronomy 17:16. "But he shall not multiply horses to himself, nor cause the people to return to Egypt, to the end that he should multiply horses: forasmuch as the Lord hath said unto you, 'Ye shall henceforth return no more that way.' "

The primary reason for God's prohibition of horses for Israel was the fact that Egypt was the world's premier source of breeding farms to produce war-horses. God knew that Israel would be tempted to enter into alliances with Egypt to acquire horses for their army. Therefore, the Lord gave a prohibition against the use of horses to ensure that Israel would not depend on an alliance with Egypt to obtain war-horses. Egypt used its virtual monopoly on war-horses to enforce a series of alliances. Just as America and Russian use the supply of advanced weapons they offer to client states to lock them into defensive treaties, nations could only purchase Egyptian war-horses if they entered into defensive treaties with Egypt. Therefore, if Israel had acquired horses from Egypt, she would have been entangled in foreign alliances rather than trust in the power of God to save her.

However, there is another reason. Israel was a nation of valiant soldiers who won remarkable battles against the overwhelming armies of her pagan enemies through the supernatural power of God. When they won such battles against the more powerful armies of her pagan enemies they knew that it was only through the supernatural power of their God. When they acknowledged that they won such battles through God's miraculous intervention, the Lord received the glory. War chariots with horses and cavalry were the equivalent of modern tanks in terms of warfare. By forbidding the Jewish state to acquire horses, God assured that the Israelites would be forced to fight defensive battles to protect the territory of the Holy Land that the Lord had given to them. If the aggressive armies of Israel had access to highly mobile horses, they would have been tempted to use their increased mobility with horses and war chariots to conquer foreign lands and nations far beyond the borders of the Promised Land. The coincidence that Israel never used horses in its many battles until the apostasy that followed King Solomon's reign, without the writers ever explaining their motive, provides a strong indication that the narrative is genuine and accurate.

The coincidences discussed in this chapter form a subtle kind of proof for the inspiration of the Scriptures. I have just touched the tip of the iceberg of those that we could examine. However, if you think about this evidence carefully, you will appreciate that these undesigned coincidences are absolutely consistent with God's direct inspiration of the Bible.

Notes

1. Philip Doddridge, *Introduction to the First Epistle to the Thessalonians* (London: Matthew and Leigh,1738).
2. William Paley, *Horæ Pauline* (London: Baldwin and Co., 1820).
3. J. J. Blunt, *Undesigned Scriptural Coincidences* (London: John Murray, 1876).

12

The Evidence of the Men who Wrote the New Testament

The Bible itself is a standing and an astonishing miracle. Written, fragment by fragment, throughout the course of fifteen centuries, under all different states of society, and in different languages, by persons of the most opposite tempers, talents, and conditions, learned and unlearned, prince and peasant, bond and free: cast into every form of instructive composition and good writing, history, prophecy, poetry, allegory, emblematic representation, Judicious interpretation, literal statement, precept, example, proverbs, disquisition, epistle, sermon, prayer-in short all rational shapes of human discourse; and treating, moreover, of subjects not obvious, but most difficult-its authors are not found, like other writers, contradicting one another upon the most ordinary matters of fact and opinion, but are at harmony upon

the whole of their sublime and momentous scheme
(Professor Maclagan).

Aside from the pages of the Scriptures we know almost nothing
about the lives of the Jewish patriarchs, priests and prophets
who were chosen by God to record His revelations to mankind
in the Old Testament. However, one of the unusual features of
the Scriptures that proves it was inspired by God is that the
writers of the Bible wrote as no men have ever written, before or
since. The normal tendency of writers in literature is to protect
their reputations by disguising or minimizing their weaknesses
and failures. In total contrast to normal human motivations, the
writers of the Bible reveal themselves "warts and all" throughout their manuscripts. Rather than minimize their mistakes and
weaknesses, these writers revealed their total character; both
weaknesses and strengths. This characteristic of the Scriptures
provides compelling evidence that these men were inspired
by God to record these words for eternity in the Word of God.
The apostles who wrote the Gospels admit that they hid in fear
when their leader was arrested and crucified. They admit to
many human weaknesses and failures, yet they changed their
world through the supernatural power of God's Holy Spirit.

The Lives of the Apostles

On the other hand, when we examine the lives of the writers of
the New Testament, we find that there is a considerable amount
of historical evidence about the lives of the disciples and
apostles revealed within the writings of the early Church. Jesus
Christ chose the twelve apostles whose role was to confirm by
their words and their lives the reality of the life, death, and
resurrection of Jesus Christ. As a new faith, Christianity needed
reliable eyewitness accounts who would personally verify the
facts regarding the life of Jesus of Nazareth. He commanded
these fishermen and tax collectors to abandon their previous
lives and follow Him to a destiny beyond that of any other
men in the history of mankind. To this day, two thousand years
later, millions of parents still name their sons by the names of

the apostles who followed Jesus Christ and turned their world upside down.

Jesus Christ's choice of disciples was not based on their previous character or accomplishments because none of them had risen to prominence in the society of Israel in the first century. It is interesting to note that Jesus did not choose the type of men most modern leaders would choose for such an overwhelming task of preaching a revolutionary message to the world. None of the twelve disciples were religious scholars or professional men of distinction before Christ chose them. None of the disciples were wealthy; none were professionals or natural leaders within the Jewish society during that first century. None of the revealed personal qualities of the disciples at the time Jesus chose them suggested that they would ultimately prove to be great men of faith who would stand the test of time. However, after only three-and-a-half years in the daily presence of Jesus, these men were transformed into great men of God who would stand unflinching against the imperial power of Rome, the greatest power on earth in their lifetime.

Jesus apparently chose His disciples in the same manner that the sculpture Michelangelo chose the rough marble material for His projects, because he saw the possibilities hidden within the uncut stone. A story about Michelangelo tells about a young girl who watched the sculptor as he produced his masterpiece in his workshop in Rome. As she watched him chisel into the huge block of marble she asked Michelangelo how he knew that the figure of David lay hidden within the huge block of uncut marble. The answer, of course, was that Michelangelo, the master sculptor, saw in his imagination the possibility of what the marble could reveal if he removed the unnecessary material that surrounded and hid the potentially beautiful sculpture from the eyes of anyone but the master sculptor.

Jesus Christ chose His band of disciples, not for what they were in themselves before He met them, but for what they could become after the touch of the Master's Hand. The truth of this statement is found in the Gospel of John which recorded Christ's words: "And when Jesus beheld him, he said, Thou art Simon the son of Jona: thou shalt be called Cephas, which is by interpretation, A stone" (John 1:42). The transformation of the character of the apostles was possibly the greatest miracle performed by Jesus Christ during his years of ministry. These simple disciples, after living in the presence of Jesus Christ, turned the world upside down. The result of their teaching the words of Jesus Christ was to turn their world right side up.

When Jesus entered history two thousand years ago, the Roman Empire held over half of the population of the known world as slaves, subject to the vilest abuse of their masters. Most of humanity lived as slaves or serfs under the cruel brutality of Rome's mighty legions. Yet the life and teaching of Jesus, as expressed in the lives of these twelve men and those who took up the cross to follow Him, would ultimately transform this wicked Roman Empire into the first society in history that would proclaim and uphold the rights of men and women to live in freedom and liberty. In a similar manner, Jesus is still transforming the lives and characters of countless men and women who are still turning their world right side up. When we encounter Jesus Christ, the most important thing is not our previous personal history of sinful rebellion, but the transformation that Jesus Christ will produce in us when we surrender our lives to His power and authority. Through His grace and power He can transform every one of us into someone who can make a true difference in our world as witnesses of His power to save and transform the lives of His followers.

One of the criteria by which we can judge the trustworthiness of the testimony of the apostles is whether or not they held firmly and consistently throughout their life to their testimony about Christ's miracles, His claims to be God, and His death and resurrection. The combined testimony of their teachings, the history of their lives, and their martyrdom provides the strongest witness to the truthfulness of their story. After the arrest, trial, and death of Jesus, these men initially fled in fear. However, these same men were totally transformed in their characters by the power of the Holy Spirit only three days after the resurrection of Christ. The historical records of the first century clearly prove that every one of these men later faced a martyr's death without denying their faith in Jesus Christ as their Savior. What could possibly account for their transformation from defeated cowards to mighty men of God within a few days of the death of their leader? Obviously, the only answer that makes sense is that these men were transformed in their character and motivation by their personal knowledge of the facts surrounding the resurrection of Jesus Christ.

Some atheists have suggested that the disciples, during the decades following His death, simply invented their accounts of Jesus. These Bible critics say that the disciples, in an attempt to enhance His authority, then published the story that Jesus claimed to be God and was resurrected. Any fair-minded reader should consider the historical evidence. First, the apostles were continually threatened and pressured to deny their Lord during their ministry; especially as they faced torture and martyrdom. However, none of these men who spent time with Jesus chose to save their lives by denying their faith in Him. Consider this hypothetical situation: Suppose these men had conspired to form a new religion based on their imagination. How long would anyone continue to proclaim something they knew was a lie when faced with lengthy torture and an inescapable, painful death? All they had to do to escape martyrdom was to admit they had concocted a lie and simply deny their faith and claims about Jesus as God. It defies both common sense and the evidence of history that anyone, let alone a group of twelve men, would persist in proclaiming a lie when they could walk away by admitting that it was a fraud.

Yet, history reveals that not one of these men, who knew Jesus personally, ever denied their testimony about Him despite the threat and reality of imminent death. This proves to any fair-minded observer that these men possessed an absolute, unshakable personal knowledge about the truth of the life, death, and resurrection of Jesus. Each of the apostles were called upon to pay the ultimate price to prove their faith in Jesus, affirming with their life's blood that Jesus was the true Messiah, the Son of God, and the only hope of salvation for a sinful humanity.

The Martyrdom of the Apostles

Most of our information about the deaths of the apostles is derived from early church traditions. While tradition is unreliable as to small details, it very seldom contains outright inventions. Eusebius, the most important of the early church historians wrote his history of the early church in A.D. 325. In his *Church History* Eusebius wrote, "The apostles and disciples of the Savior scattered over the whole world, preached the Gospel everywhere." The Church historian Schumacher researched the lives of the apostles and recounted the history of their martyrdoms.

Matthew suffered martyrdom in Ethiopia, killed by a sword wound.

Mark died in Alexandria, Egypt, after being dragged by horses through the streets until he was dead.

Luke was hanged in Greece as a result of his tremendous preaching to the lost.

John faced martyrdom when he was boiled in a huge basin of boiling oil during a wave of persecution in Rome. However, he was miraculously delivered from death. John was then sentenced to the mines on the prison island of Patmos. He wrote his prophetic Book of Revelation on Patmos. The apostle John was later freed and returned to serve as Bishop of Edessa in modern Turkey. He died as an old man, the only apostle to die peacefully.

Peter was crucified upside down on an x-shaped cross, according to church tradition because he told his tormentors that he felt unworthy to die in the same way that Jesus Christ had died.

James the Just, the leader of the church in Jerusalem, was thrown over a hundred feet down from the southeast pinnacle of the Temple when he refused to deny his faith in Christ. When they discovered that he survived the fall, his enemies beat James to death with a fuller's club. This was the same pinnacle where Satan had taken Jesus during the Temptation.

James the Greater, a son of Zebedee, was a fisherman by trade when Jesus called him to a lifetime of ministry. As a strong leader of the church, James was ultimately beheaded at Jerusalem. The Roman officer who guarded James watched amazed as James defended his faith at his trial. Later, the officer walked beside James to the place of execution. Overcome by conviction, he declared his new faith to the judge and knelt beside James to accept beheading as a Christian.

Bartholomew, also known as Nathanael, was a missionary to Asia. He witnessed to our Lord in present day Turkey. Bartholomew was martyred for his preaching in Armenia when he was flayed to death by a whip.

Andrew was crucified on an x-shaped cross in Patras, Greece. After being whipped severely by seven soldiers they tied his body to the cross with cords to prolong his agony. His followers reported that, when he was led toward the cross, Andrew saluted it in these words: "I have long desired and expected this happy hour. The cross has been consecrated by the body of Christ hanging on it." He continued to preach to his tormentors for two days until he expired.

The apostle Thomas was stabbed with a spear in India during one of his missionary trips to establish the church in the sub-continent.

Jude, the brother of Jesus, was killed with arrows when he refused to deny his faith in Christ.

Matthias, the apostle chosen to replace the traitor Judas Iscariot, was stoned and then beheaded.

Barnabas, one of the group of seventy disciples, wrote

the Epistle of Barnabas. He preached throughout Italy and Cyprus. Barnabas was stoned to death at Salonica.

The apostle Paul was tortured and then beheaded by the evil Emperor Nero at Rome in A.D. 67. Paul endured a lengthy imprisonment which allowed him to write his many epistles to the churches he had formed throughout the Roman Empire. These letters, which taught many of the foundational doctrines of Christianity, form a large portion of the New Testament.

The details of the martyrdoms of the disciples and apostles are found in traditional early church sources. These traditions were recounted in the writings of the church fathers and the first official church history written by the historian Eusebius in A.D. 325. Although we can not at this time verify every detail historically, the universal belief of the early Christian writers was that each of the apostles had faced martyrdom faithfully without denying their faith in the resurrection of Jesus Christ.

The Transformed Lives of Men and Women

J. W. Alexander wrote, "The study of God's Word for the purpose of discovering God's will, is the secret discipline which has formed the greatest characters."[1] Some of the greatest evidence proving the truth of the Bible is found in the transformed lives of men and women who placed their faith and trust in Jesus Christ. An abiding faith in the revealed truth of God in the Scriptures strengthens people to rely on God in the face of the greatest trials and tribulations of their life. An unshakable faith in the Bible's revelation will enable us to stand against the greatest persecutions as Hebrews 11 records how great heroes of the Bible stood against the opposition of Satan.

The Scriptures have fascinated and held the undying attention of the most brilliant men of each age. An anonymous writer once wrote, "He who teaches the Bible is never a scholar; he is always a student." An early church father living in the second century, Tertullian, devoted his life to the study of Scripture each day and night. By the end of his life Tertullian had memorized most of the Bible by heart, including the punctuation! A profound love of the Scriptures motivated the Christians in those early centuries of persecution to walk in obedience to their Savior, Jesus Christ.

Eusebius, the greatest historian of the early church, wrote about one persecuted Christian whose eyes were burned out during one of the ten great waves of persecution against the early church. Despite the loss of his eyes, this Christian saint could repeat to assembled Christians large portions of the Bible from memory. Thomas Beza, the brilliant translator of the Scriptures in A.D. 1585, had such a profound love of the words of his Savior that, at the age of eighty, he could still repeat from memory in the Greek language all of the New Testament Epistles. Two of the leading reformers during the Protestant Reformation, Cranmer and Ridley, found their faith immeasurably strengthened as both memorized the entire New Testament during the time of their persecution. Those who love the Bible will never find themselves without a faithful friend, a wholesome and wise counselor, the most cheerful companion, and the most effectual comforter of their soul.

Dr. A. T. Pierson suggested in one of his books about the Scriptures, that we should approach spiritual discovery much as the ancient Jews approached the Temple in Jerusalem. The outer Court of the Gentiles is analogous to the letter of Scripture. The Inner Court of the Israelites, a much holier place, is similar to the inner truth of Scripture; the Holy of Holies, the most holy place in the Temple is equivalent to the person of Jesus Christ Himself. It is only when we pass through the veil into the innermost Holy of Holies that we come to meet Him face to face.

The great men who founded the United States of America, including George Washington, were strongly influenced by their faith in the Word of God. President Washington once declared, "It is impossible to rightly govern the world without God and the Bible." Abraham Lincoln, America's most beloved president, wrote about the Bible.[2] "Read this book for what you can accept and take the rest on faith, and you will live and die a better man." The great writer, Charles Dickens, stated that the Bible is the Word of God. "The New Testament is the very best book that ever was or ever will be known in the world."[3] Another great writer, Lord Francis Bacon, was the finest scientist in England in the sixteenth century and contributed much to the scientific study of nature. Bacon wrote a pivotal book, *The Advancement of Learning,* in which he called for a study to be made of Bible prophecy to systematically show how God had precisely fulfilled the predictions made over thousands of years. Filled with wonder at the creation of the world, Francis Bacon wrote: "Thy creatures, O Lord, have been my books, but thy Holy Scriptures much more. I have sought thee in the courts, fields and gardens; but I have found thee, O God, in thy sanctuary, thy temples." Although Bacon acknowledged the awesome evidence about God revealed by science and nature, he discovered that the most profound knowledge of God was found in his detailed study of the inspired Word of God.

Many Christians have personally studied the Scofield Reference Bible. However, very few are aware of the spiritual motivation that encouraged C. I. Scofield to embark upon the production of a study Bible complete with cross references and study notes to help the student explore the biblical text. When he was a young Christian, Scofield met a friend, C.E. Paxson, in his office and noted that his friend had marked his Bible with notes and underlined related passages. Scofield was initially angry at the idea that his friend had defaced his Bible with these personal markings. However, he soon realized that these markings were extremely helpful to his friend and assisted in his understanding of the relation between various passages. In his later life Scofield would declare that the inspiration of his friend's Bible markings would lead him to prepare the exhaustive study notes and research presented in the now-famous Scofield Reference Bible with its helpful footnotes, maps and cross-references. Truly, the Bible is a deep well that can never be exhausted by a student of the Scriptures. Those who preach constantly from the depths of God's Word will always have something fresh and meaningful to say to their hearers.[4]

The Seven Wonders of the Word of God

We have all heard of the Seven Wonders of the World that have intrigued mankind throughout history. Yet, for those who will examine the evidence, the Scriptures should hold an equal fascination. The Bible also manifests Seven Wonders of the Word of God.

The wonder of its formation

The marvelous manner in which the Scriptures grew from the first five books of Moses to include all thirty-nine books of the Old Testament and, then, the addition of the twenty-seven books of the New Testament in the first century of our era, is one of the greatest mysteries of the ages.

The wonder of its unity

The Bible is a complete library composed of sixty-six books written by forty-four different authors over a period of sixteen hundred years. The authors came from different backgrounds-including kings of Israel, warriors, shepherds, poets, a physician and fishermen. However, the Bible is the most unified book in the world, containing a progressive revelation of the message of God without any real contradictions.

The wonder of its age

The Bible is without doubt the oldest and most ancient book in the world, beginning with its first section of five books written by Moses thirty-five centuries ago. What other ancient writing is read daily by hundreds of millions of people who find answers to their most immediate problems and concerns?

The wonder of its sales

Despite the fact that it is the oldest and most popular book in the world, its continuing sales year after year are the greatest wonder in the field of book publishing. Scholars have estimated that there are far more than two billion Bibles published throughout the globe. Incredibly, the American Bible Society printed its two billionth Bible in 1976 and presented it to President Ford. Despite the phenomenal number of Bibles that exist, it continues to outsell every other book with several hundred million in annual sales worldwide.

The wonder of its popularity

Despite the fact that the Bible was written over two thousand years ago by ancient inhabitants of the Middle East in an oriental form of literature, the Bible remains the most fascinating and intriguing book on earth. Every year the Bible is read by over a billion adults and young people representing every nation and class of people on the planet.

The wonder of its language

The Scriptures were written in three languages, Hebrew, Aramaic and Greek, by forty-four writers. Most of these writers were not well educated, nor did most of them know each other. Yet the wisest men of every age have acknowledged the Bible as the world's greatest literary masterpiece.

The wonder of its preservation

There is no other book in history which has suffered more opposition, hatred, persecution and outright burning. Yet, after thousands of years of opposition, the Bible has not only survived, it has triumphed over emperors, kings and dictators who sought to silence its message of salvation through the blood of Jesus Christ.

The Bible's Transformation of Society

Did the Bible actually change society? The answer is Yes! The early Christians startled the pagan world of Rome by their altruism and unselfish care for the poor, the sick, and the dispossessed. Despite the overwhelming wealth of the powerful Roman Empire and other pagan empires of Egypt, Babylon and Assyria, there is no evidence from inscriptions or archeology that these societies ever developed hospitals, housing for the poor, or any other provision for the unfortunate people in great need. However, early Christians manifested the love of Christ by caring for both the sick and the needy out of a pure altruism that shocked the jaded Romans.

Let us examine the social situation in England before the Evangelical Revival led by John and Charles Wesley that saved England from a moral abyss. The situation faced by England in the early 1700s was virtually the same as the current moral collapse we see in North America every day. Bishop George Berkeley wrote in his 1738 book, *Discourse Addressed to Magistrates and Men in Authority,* that the level of public morality and religion had collapsed in Britain "to a degree that has never been known in any Christian country. . . . Our prospect is very terrible and the symptoms grow worse from day to day." Berkeley spoke of a torrent of evil in the land "which threatens a general inundation and destruction of these realms. . . . The youth born and brought up in wicked times without any bias to good from early principle, or instilled opinion, when they grow ripe, must be monsters indeed. And it is to be feared that the age of monsters is not far off."

Many different writers and observers, including Daniel Defoe, Alexander Pope and Samuel Johnson confirm that England was on the point of moral collapse in the early part of the 1700s. In the previous century the official Church of England had severely suppressed other Christians through strict laws, such as the Act of Conformity, forbidding Nonconformist (independent pastors who were not endorsed by the Church of England) from teaching or preaching. Many of the greatest preachers in England were driven out of their churches for refusing to accept these laws.

When the Great Plague of 1665 killed one in every five people in London, everyone who could, fled London, including most of the leaders of the official Church of England and the government. Many of the Nonconformist pastors ignored the laws and returned to help their dying congregations by preaching that the only hope for mankind was by trusting in Jesus Christ. Then the apostate government of England passed the infamous Five Mile Act which prohibited any of the expelled clergy from approaching within five miles of their former church. As a result of this continuing persecution, the Puritans and other nonconforming pastors were driven from their churches and from society. Over four thousand pastors were thrown into prison. Finally, in 1714, the Schism Act prohibited anyone from teaching anywhere without a special license from his bishop. The result of the suppression of the free preaching of the Word of God was the descent of England into a morass of immorality, perversion, and a widespread moral collapse.

The writer Thomas Carlyle wrote his verdict on this society which could easily fit the condition of North America today, "Stomach well alive, soul extinct." The writer Mark Pattison wrote about the state of morals in this period as follows, "Decay of religion, licentiousness of morals, public corruption, profaneness of language-a day of rebuke and blasphemy." As the moral code broke down, with the teaching of the Gospel repressed, and the crime rate rising, the ruling classes naturally responded by fearfully demanding severe laws to restrain criminals. The moral debasement of England in this century can be illustrated by its savage laws which showed no mercy to those who violated them.

At a time when the writer William E. Blackstone was proudly writing about the glory of England's "unmatched Constitution" both adults and children were subject to one hundred and sixty different laws that resulted in hanging. If anyone shoplifted more than one shilling, stole one sheep, harmed a tree, gathered fruit from someone's property, or snared a rabbit on someone's estate, they would be hanged until dead. The evangelist Charles Wesley reported in his Journal that he preached in one jail to fifty-two people on death row including one child of ten years. Public drunkenness was so widespread that many adults and children died as alcoholics. Millions of children and women were working in appalling conditions in factories and mines with unbelievably low wages and no safety rules whatsoever. In other words, England was a moral and spiritual wasteland. Truly, the name Ichabod, "the glory of the Lord hath departed," was the epitaph that should be written over this tragic and most shameful century of England's history.

Yet, into this cesspool, God sent the only hope for England; His Holy Scriptures as preached by the greatest evangelists of that age, John and Charles Wesley. In 1769 John Wesley began the Sunday School movement that ultimately flourished throughout England teaching the Bible to millions of young English children. The preaching of the Wesley brothers brought about a spiritual revolution in England and the return to a true faith in the Word of God and its laws. John Wesley's preaching of the whole Bible transformed an immoral state into a reformed nation based to a great extent on the Word of God. As Rev. Wesley addressed three thousand people on one occasion, he declared these words from the prophet Isaiah 61:1-2: "The spirit of the Lord is upon me, because he hath appointed me to preach the Gospel to the poor; he hath sent me to heal the broken-hearted; to preach deliverance to the captive, and recovery of sight to the blind; to set at liberty them that are bruised, to proclaim the acceptable year of the Lord."[5]

The incredible spiritual energy of this renewed preaching of the Gospel of Christ produced a remarkable series of Christians including John Milton and John Bunyan who collectively transformed the soul of that nation. Their faithful preaching of the Word of God produced a marvelous passion for righteousness and freedom that became the central principle of the Evangelical Renewal that saved England from moral corruption. John Wesley preached, "We know no Gospel without salvation from sin. . . . Christianity is essentially a social religion; to turn it into a solitary religion is indeed to destroy it." The revival of Christianity under the Wesleys and other great preachers of the Gospel produced a practical religion that transformed every aspect of their world. Wesley declared that "a doctrine to save sinning men, with no aim to transform them into crusaders against social sin, was equally unthinkable."[6] The Christian revival in England spread across the English speaking world causing innumerable souls to turn to personal faith in Jesus Christ. The brilliant writer, Thomas Macaulay, wrote about the Scriptures in the *Edinburgh Review*, "The English Bible, a book which, if everything else in our language should perish, would alone suffice to show the whole extent of its beauty and power."[7]

In addition to the personal transformations, this evangelical revival based on the Word of God transformed all of society.

Many features of modern western society that we take for granted today, were the result of the great move of God produced by the Wesleyan Revival. The imprisonment of debtors and children was made illegal. Schools were opened to every child who wanted to learn in every parish in the nation. Harsh penal laws and child labor in mines and factories ended as a result of new laws based on the Scriptures. The evangelical movement created the first hope for prosperity and self-respect that the forgotten masses of England had ever known. Finally, the return to the Bible brought about the greatest religious transformation known to mankind. England was restored to greatness. Universal free schools, charities and free hospitals were formed by Christians who found their motivation in following the Savior, who said, "And ye shall know the truth, and the truth shall make you free" (John 8:32).

Bishop Davidson declared that Wesley was "one of the greatest Englishmen who ever lived" and stated that "Wesley practically changed the outlook and even the character of the English nation." In truth, it was the return to the Bible, the Word of God, that transformed England from a moral wasteland into a land based on the Bible and the faith of Jesus Christ. The only hope for North America today is a similar spiritual revival based on a return to the unchanging Word of God.

Notes

1. J. W. Alexander, *Leaves of Gold* (Brownlow Publ. Co.).
2. Frank S. Mead, Ed., *The Encyclopedia of Religious Quotations* (Westwood, New Jersey: Fleming Revell Company, 1965).
3. Frank S. Mead , ed., *The Encyclopedia of Religious Quotations* (Westwood, New Jersey: Fleming Revell Company, 1965).
4. Paul Lee Tan, ed., *Encyclopedia of 7700 Illustrations* (Hong Kong: Bible Communications,1991).
5. John Wesley, *Wesley's Journal* (1739).
6. Henry Carter, *The Methodist.* (p. 174).
7. Thomas Macaulay, *Edinburgh Review.* Jan. 1828.

13

The Final Decision Is Yours

In the final analysis the evidence presented in this book regarding the authority and inspiration of Scripture should prove to any fair-minded reader that there is overwhelming proof that the Bible was truly inspired by God. This fact brings us to the place where there is one basic choice that each of us must make. For those who still reject the Bible, there are only two possibilities: either Jesus Christ is wrong or you are. The suggestion that neither is wrong or that it doesn't really matter is untenable because you are simply avoiding the real issue. The evidence presented in this book and the history of the last two thousand years proves that Jesus Christ is not mistaken about the truths He articulated. Each of us must decide if we will personally accept or reject the truth about Jesus Christ expressed in the inspired Word of God. Our answer to this question will determine our happiness in this life and our eternal destiny in either heaven or hell in the next life.

Our personal determination about whether or not the Bible

is the inspired Word of God will depend on our evaluation of the Scriptures and the evidence we have explored in this book *The Signature of God*. However, God never told us, "Believe in the Bible and you shall be saved." The demons of hell know that the Scriptures are true, but this knowledge does not save them. It is significant that the Bible tells us: "Believe on the Lord Jesus Christ, and thou shall be saved, and thy house" (Acts 16:31). The clear message of the Scriptures is that our personal relationship to Jesus Christ will determine our eternal destiny-heaven or hell.

The Coming Kingdom of God

The ancient Scriptures tell us that there will be a generation of men at the end of this age living in the tribulation period who will endure the greatest evil ever unleashed by Satan. The wrath of God will be poured out on unrepentant sinners during that unprecedented seven-year period. Satan himself will be unleashed to attempt his final rebellion against Almighty God in his relentless campaign to establish his satanic kingdom throughout the earth under the rule of his personal representative, the Antichrist. However, these same Scriptures assure us that Jesus Christ will return from heaven at the moment the earth faces it final crisis to defeat the armies of the Antichrist and save mankind from certain destruction. The Lord will defeat Satan after a terrible seven-year period of trial known as the Tribulation. The prophets reveal that two-thirds of mankind will die in horrific judgments, wars, famines, and plagues during this terrible seven-year period.

However, this final trial of mankind in this age will end triumphantly with the glorious return of Jesus Christ from heaven with an army of powerful angels and the saints of all the ages. When Christ finally defeats the evil leaders of the world, He will establish His righteous government throughout the world from His throne in Jerusalem. Ultimately, the sound of gunfire will be silenced forever, the terror of torture chambers will be destroyed, the horror of starvation and plague will be removed, the fear of violence and abuse will be lifted from the hearts of men and women. Mankind will finally experience true peace under the kingdom of the Messiah, Jesus Christ.

The Nature of God

What is the nature of God who inspired the writers of the Bible? For thousands of years men have attempted in every culture and society to imagine the nature of God. They have created God in their own image, in the image of the sun, moon, stars, the earth and a hundred other objects. Regardless of their philosophical speculations about the divine intelligence that created our universe, man will never be able to find the truth about God unless he is willing to accept God's written revelation regarding His nature and commands to mankind. The Bible, from Genesis to Revelation, reveals the nature of God as a loving, holy, powerful personality who is vitally interested in the lives and destiny of men.

Years ago, philosophers assigned the name First Cause to describe the intelligent supernatural power that must have created our universe. Someone once analyzed the nature of the First Cause by comparing the nature of the First Cause, the Creator, and the nature of the universe.

The First Cause of limitless Space must be infinite in extent.

The First Cause of endless Time must be eternal in duration.

The First Cause of perpetual Motion must be omnipotent in power.

The First Cause of unbounded Variety must be omnipresent in phenomena.

The First Cause of infinite Complexity must be omniscient in intelligence.

The First Cause of Consciousness must be personal.

The First Cause of Feeling must be emotional.

The First Cause of Will must be volitional.

The First Cause of Ethical values must be moral.

The First Cause of Religious values must be spiritual.

The First Cause of Beauty values must be aesthetic.

The First Cause of Righteousness must be holy.

The First Cause of Justice must be just.
The First Cause of Love must be loving.
The First Cause of Life must be alive.

This analysis reveals that the First Cause of all things, the Creator, must be infinite, eternal, omnipotent, omnipresent, omniscient, personal, emotional, volitional, moral, spiritual, aesthetic, holy, just, loving, and alive. However, when we examine the nature of God as revealed throughout the Holy Scriptures we discover that the Holy nature of God is precisely that as described above.

Your Final Decision

The decision as to whether or not the Bible is truly the inspired Word of God is vital for every person because it will affect every other area of their lives. If the Bible is true then we are accountable to Jesus Christ who will judge each of us at the end of our life. However, if the Bible is not the inspired Word of God, we can safely ignore its commands and warnings about heaven and hell. In the absence of the Word of God those who search for ultimate truth are like a man searching in a strange country for a hidden treasure without the assistance of a map or a guide.

In light of the overwhelming evidence presented in this book for the inspiration and authority of the Bible any fair-minded reader can see that only a supernatural intelligence could have produced the Scriptures. The Signature of God proves that the Bible contains scientific, archeological and historical information that could not have been produced by human beings unless God directed their writing. However, there are many people, including some readers of this book, who will still claim they can't accept that the Bible is the inspired Word of God. The problem with those readers who still refuse to acknowledge the evidence for inspiration is not a problem of belief, rather it is their lack of willingness to accept information that challenges long-held positions. While such people can see the strong evidence supporting the Bible, they cannot bring themselves to accept the inevitable conclusion because they would have to abandon their previously held agnostic position to which they are emotionally and intellectually committed. In other words, the problem is not that they can not believe the evidence before their eyes; the problem is that they will not believe the evidence pointing to the Bible's divine inspiration, no matter how powerfully the evidence points to the authorship of the Scriptures by God Himself.

Many individuals who have rejected God and the Bible have a huge "investment" in their declared position of rejection of the Scriptures. When they are faced with the evidence that proves the Bible is inspired by God, they are threatened by this information because it requires them to think seriously about God and their responsibility to Him. Many people have avoided thinking seriously about Jesus Christ and eternity by hiding behind their denials of the authority of the Bible and its demands for a decision about Jesus Christ. However, in light of the fascinating evidence provided in this book, every one of us needs to carefully consider the implications. If the Bible is truly the Word of God, then every one of us will stand before Jesus Christ at the end of our life to answer for our sins. On that day, Christians, who accepted Christ's payment of our debt to God through His sacrifice on the cross, will know that their sins have been forgiven by God. Their destiny will be to live with God forever in heaven. However, those who rejected Christ's salvation and the hope of heaven as presented in the Scriptures will have to bear their own punishment for their sinful rebellion when they are exiled to hell forever.

The powerful evidence in this book that proves the Bible is truly the Word of God provides us with a confidence that we can believe the words of the apostle Paul when he spoke about the necessity of faith in Jesus Christ: "Neither is there salvation in any other: for there is none other name under heaven given among men, whereby we must be saved" (Acts 4:12). This declaration of Paul runs counter to the natural inclination of mankind to believe that all religions are equally true and that all roads lead to Rome. Many in our society today believe that, if a person is sincere, God will allow them to enter heaven. However, the Word of God declares that sincerity is not enough. If you are sincere in your faith, but have chosen to place your faith in a false religion, then you are sincerely wrong.

There is only one way to reconcile ourselves as sinners to a holy God. The true path to salvation according to the Bible is through personal repentance of our sins, and placing our total faith in Christ's sacrificial death on the cross. Every one of us has rebelled against God through our personal sins: "For all have sinned, and come short of the glory of God" (Romans 3: 23). The Scriptures declare that our sinful rebellion has alienated each of us from the holiness of God and prevents us from ever entering heaven unless our sins are forgiven by God. "For the wages of sin is death; but the gift of God is eternal life through Jesus Christ our Lord" (Romans 6:23). The death of Jesus Christ on the cross is the key to bringing us to a place of true peace in our heart. The death of our old nature when we identify with Christ's death is the key to finding true peace with God. The only way we can be filled with the grace of God is to approach Him as we would bring a container to a well. It must be empty. It is only then that God can begin to fill us with His grace and spirit.

God cannot simply ignore our sin and allow an unrepentant sinner into heaven despite their rejection of God. God's absolute justice makes it impossible for Him to ignore our sins. God's holiness demands that "death," as the "wages of sin," must be paid for our sins in order for His justice to be satisfied (Romans 6:23). If unrepentant sinners actually entered heaven without repenting of their sins, their presence in the Holy New Jerusalem would actually turn that portion of heaven into hell. If you think carefully about it, sinners who reject the forgiveness and worship of Christ would not want to live in heaven. They would despise the holy living and glorious worship of God. The sacred nature of a holy heaven and the evil nature of sin make it absolutely impossible for God to forgive men's sins unless they wholeheartedly repent and turn from them. Only then can God forgive and transform us into sinners saved by the grace of Jesus Christ who cleanses us from our sinful rebellion against His laws. Although we can cleanse our bodies with water, the cleansing of our souls requires the spiritual application of the blood of Christ to our heart.

The Gospel of John records the answers Jesus gave to Nicodemus, one of the religious leaders of Israel, who asked Him about salvation. He told him that, "Ye must be born again" (John 3:7). Jesus explained to Nicodemus, "Whosoever believeth in him should not perish, but have eternal life. For God so loved the world, that he gave his only begotten Son, that whosoever believeth in him should not perish, but have everlasting life" (John 3:15,16). Every sinner stands condemned by God because of our sinful rebellion against His commandments as revealed in the Scriptures. Jesus said, "He that believeth on him is not condemned: but he that believeth not is condemned already, because he hath not believed in the name of the only begotten Son of God" (John 3:18).

Your decision to accept Christ as your personal Savior is the most important one you will ever make. It will cost you a great deal to live as a committed Christian today. Many people will challenge your new faith in the Bible and in Christ. The British writer John Stuart Mill wrote about the importance of our belief in Christ: "One person with a belief is equal to ninety-nine people who only have opinions." However, the Lord Jesus Christ asks His disciples to "follow Me." That decision and commitment will change your life forever. Your commitment to Christ will unleash His supernatural grace and power to transform your life into one of joy and peace beyond anything you have ever experienced. While the commitment to follow Christ will cost a lot, it will cost you everything if you are not a Christian at the moment when you die. Jesus challenges us with these words, "For what shall it profit a man, if he shall gain the whole world, and lose his own soul?" (Mark 8:36).

If you are a Christian, I challenge you to use the evidence in this book when you witness to your friends about your faith in Christ. The proof that the Bible is inspired by God will not convince anyone to place their faith in Jesus Christ. Nevertheless, this evidence proving the Bible's inspiration may remove the intellectual barriers that many people in modern society have raised against seriously considering the claims of Jesus

Christ. Once they acknowledge the Scripture's authority, they can begin to consider whether or not they want to accept Christ as their Savior.

If you have never accepted Christ as your Savior, the evidence in The Signature of God provides proof that God inspired the writers of the Bible to record His message to mankind. The Scriptures reveal that every one of us will be judged by God as to what we have done with His Son, Jesus Christ. Will you accept Him as your personal Savior and find peace with God throughout eternity; or will you reject Him forever?

You have seen the evidence. The final decision is yours.

Appendix

William A. Dembski is a well-respected mathematician and philosopher and is a fellow of the Center for Renewal of Science and Culture at the Seattle-based Discovery Institute. He is now associated with Baylor University in Texas. His review of Dr. Jeffrey Satinover's excellent book *Cracking the Bible Code* provides an intriguing analysis of the Bible Code phenomenon from the viewpoint of a mathematician.

First Things: A Journal of Religion and Public Life

Books in Review
Cracking the Bible Code
**Copyright © 1998 First Things 85
(August/September 1998): 61-64.**
The Bible by Numbers
Cracking the Bible Code. **By Jeffrey Satinover.
Morrow. 346 pp. $23.
Reviewed by William A. Dembski**

The "Bible Code" is the name for computer-generated sequences of letters taken from the Hebrew Bible. Researchers string all the letters together, deleting spaces between words. Then, instead of running through the text letter by adjacent letter (as we do in ordinary reading), they run through the text by skipping a fixed number of letters. The resulting sequences, known as equidistant letter sequences (or ELSs), are then inspected for patterns that cannot reasonably be attributed to chance. The Bible Code comprises such equidistant letter sequences.

The Bible Code is controversial because some have presented it as a preprogrammed time capsule set to go off once humans invent computers. The human authors of the Bible, writing well before the advent of computers, would have been incapable of consciously introducing into the Bible the patterns that Bible Code researchers are finding by means of computers. Hence these patterns, if not attributable to chance, must stem from a nonhuman intelligence. Moreover, if the patterns contain information about subsequent events in world history, this nonhuman intelligence would also have to possess preternatural foreknowledge. And since the Bible claims to be inspired by precisely such a being, the most obvious solution to the identity of this nonhuman intelligence is the God of the Hebrew Scriptures, to wit, YHWH. Here, in broad strokes, is the logic underlying the Bible Code.

Jeffrey Satinover's *Cracking the Bible Code* is the place to begin for anyone interested in the subject. It is engagingly written, well-informed, and generally sober. In particular, it avoids the statistical fallacies too commonly associated with coverage of the Bible Code. Even so, it is an uneven text. It is superb in describing the history leading up to today's investigations. Indeed, the window it provides on Jewish intellectual life from the Middle Ages through the present is itself worth the price of the book. It is also very good at making intelligible the mathematics needed for deciding whether the Code is genuine. On the other hand, its speculative portions about the significance of the Bible Code are often diffuse and controversial.

The best known example of the Bible Code, and one Satinover treats in detail, is the Great Sages experiment. Several Israeli mathematicians took thirty or so prominent rabbis from the *Encyclopedia of Great Men of Israel*, and looked among the equidistant letter sequences of Genesis for a juxtaposition of rabbi names with their dates of birth or death. They found some. On calculating the improbability of so close a match between names and corresponding dates, the mathematicians concluded that the match couldn't have happened by chance (the probability was less than 1 in 60,000). The journal *Statistical Science* tacitly agreed. After an arduous review, its editors finally decided to publish the results of this experiment. Suddenly the Bible Code had a measure of academic respectability.

Nevertheless, one paper in a prestigious journal is hardly enough to settle so controversial a topic. The Bible Code raises a number of sticking points. For instance, even if a nonhuman intelligence can convincingly be shown to have introduced information into the Bible, the identity of that intelligence remains controversial. That's not to say that the Orthodox Jewish preference for identifying this intelligence with YHWH wouldn't be the most plausible one. But New Age adherents will be sure to have their own preferences. Moreover, if other sacred books exhibit codes, we may enter a new form of theological disputation: My code is better than yours.

Another sticking point concerns how to use the Bible Code should it prove genuine. There are roughly two approaches, one modest, the other extravagant. The modest approach uses the Bible Code simply to authenticate the Bible, showing that there is a nonhuman intelligence behind the text. For example, Satinover describes how Bible Code researchers looked among the equidistant letter sequences of Leviticus 1:1-13 and found an overwhelming number of references to the high priest Aaron. What led the Bible Code researchers to look for Aaron's name were the persistent references throughout this passage to the Aaronic priesthood, yet no references to Aaron himself. In this passage of thirteen verses one would expect on average to find eight references to Aaron among the equidistant letter sequences. There are actually twenty-five. The probability of this happening by chance is less than 1 in 2,000,000.

This approach to the Bible Code as a scheme for authenticating the Bible is modest and seems to me the most promising course for deciding the genuineness of the Code. There is, however, also an extravagant approach. It uses the Code for divination, retrodicting the past as well as predicting the future.

Satinover explicitly adopts the modest approach, stressing that the Bible Code's only legitimate function is to authenticate the Bible. Nevertheless, Satinover and most of the Bible Code advocates find the lure of the extravagant approach hard to resist. Thus Satinover describes, without criticism, how Israeli intelligence during the Gulf War used the Bible Code to predict Iraq's first Scud attack on Israel.

The key problem confronting the Bible Code, at least for now, however, is whether the patterns found in the Bible's equidistant letter sequences decisively preclude chance. Throughout *Cracking the Bible Code* one finds references to "p-values," some of which are quite small. "P-value," short for "probability value," refers to the probability that a given pattern might be present in the equidistant letter sequences by chance. The smaller this probability, the more compelling the inference that a nonhuman intelligence influenced the writing of the Bible. There is, however, a catch.

A small p-value by itself isn't enough to preclude chance. In addition, the pattern for which one calculates a p-value must be independently given. The Bible Code researcher can't just willy-nilly search through equidistant letter sequences until something interesting or unusual turns up. Statisticians call this cherry picking or data snooping, and it vitiates any statistical analysis. Patterns must be given independently of the search, and only then can small p-values indicate the finger of God.

To Satinover's credit, he is fully aware of the dual requirement that p-values be small and that patterns be given independently. Moreover, despite his enthusiasm for the Bible Code, he never loses sight of this requirement. By keeping to a sound statistical methodology throughout, Satinover earns the credibility that others writing on the Bible Code fail to achieve.

If all that is required to demonstrate divine agency is to find an independently given pattern that also has a small p-value, why does the Bible Code remain controversial? One problem is that Bible Code research is stretching what statisticians mean by "independently given patterns." Moreover, the p-values are not always easy to calculate. The Bible Code is forcing statistics to extend its research frontiers, an unprecedented case of biblical studies advancing statistical research.

Although it's too early to decide whether the Bible Code is genuine, Satinover makes a good argument for taking it seriously. The credibility of the key players is significant. The main figures involved in this debate, whether critics or advocates of the Bible Code, are top rung, well-credentialed mathematicians. All the fundamental research on the Bible Code has been done openly, and without a hint of deception. It is notable that advocates of the Bible Code have jeopardized their careers, converted to Orthodox Judaism, refocused their research, and in some cases changed disciplines.

Statistical analyses, though yet to decide this debate, have at least been suggestive. Highly improbable, independently given patterns seem to occur in the Hebrew Bible with an obstinacy displayed in no other text. What's more, if this phenomenon had to occur reliably in some ancient text, there would be no better candidate than the Hebrew Bible, especially its first five books, known as the Torah.

The textual transmission of the Hebrew Bible, and especially of the Torah, is far more accurate than anything else in antiquity. Because the Bible Code is sensitive to copying errors, the Hebrew Bible satisfies a crucial necessary condition for possessing such a code. Indeed, if the Bible Code ultimately proves genuine, we can credit its discovery to generations of obsessive-compulsive scribes who meticulously transcribed the Hebrew Bible. We might then even regard their obsessive-compulsiveness as a divine grace.

The philosopher Bertrand Russell was once asked why he didn't believe in God. He replied, "Not enough evidence." Satinover's fascination with the Bible Code is that it may provide evidence for God's existence that would have convinced even a Bertrand Russell. There has been a long dismal trend of science eroding faith in God. In the Bible Code Satinover sees a unique wedding of science and theology, wherein each reinforces the other.

But perhaps that wedding is not unique. At the same time that research in the Bible Code has taken off, research in a seemingly unrelated field has taken off as well, namely, biological design. These two fields are in fact closely related. Indeed, the same highly improbable, independently given patterns that appear as the equidistant letter sequences in the Bible Code appear in biology as functionally integrated ("irreducibly complex") biological systems, of the sort Michael Behe discussed in *Darwin's Black Box*.

The relevant statistical methodology is identical for both fields. As a result, the two fields stand to profit from each other. For instance, my forthcoming book, *The Design Inference*, gives a thorough account of universal probability bounds, i.e., how small a p-value one needs to eliminate chance decisively. (Although the literature on universal probability bounds dates back to the French probabilist Emile Borel, it seems not to have been engaged by the Bible Code researchers.)

This convergence of the Bible Code and biological design should not seem surprising. There is a tradition within both Judaism and Christianity of speaking of two "books" where God reveals himself—the Book of Scripture, which is the Bible, and the Book of Nature, which is the world. I commend Jeffrey Satinover for his efforts to read both books.

William A. Dembski, a mathematician and philosopher, is a fellow of the Center for Renewal of Science and Culture at the Seattle-based Discovery Institute. His new book, The Design Inference, *will be published by Cambridge University Press this August.*

Selected Bibliography

Anderson, Sir Robert, *Human Destiny*. London: Pickering & Inglish, 1913.

Aviezer, Nathan, *In The Beginning . . . Biblical Creation and Science*. Hoboken: KTAV Publishing House, Inc., 1990.

Ball, Rev. C. J., *Light From The East*. London: Eyre and Spottiswoode, 1899.

Bentwich, Norman, *Fulfilment in the Promised Land*. London: The Soncino Press, 1938.

Blomberg, Craig, *The Historical Reliability of the Gospels*. Leicester: Inter-Varsity Press, 1987.

Blunt, Rev. J. J., *Undesigned Coincidences in the Old and New Testament*. London: John Murray, 1876.

Bready, J. Wesley, *England: Before and After Wesley*. London: Hodder and Stoughton Ltd., 1939.

Bright, John, *The Authority of the Old Testament*. Grand Rapids: Baker Book House, 1967.

Burrows, Millar, *The Dead Sea Scrolls of St. Marks Monastery*. New Haven: The American Schools of Oriental Research, 1950.

Canton, William, *The Bible and the Anglo-Saxon People*. London: J. M. Dent & Sons, Ltd., 1914.

Cobern, Camden M., *The New Archeological Discoveries*. London: Funk & Wagnalls Co., 1929.

Duncan, J. Garrow, *Digging Up Biblical History*, Vol. I & II. London: Society For Promoting Christian Knowledge, 1931.

Ebers, Georg, Egypt: *Descriptive, Historical, and Picturesque*, Vol. i & II. London: Cassell, Petter, Galpin & Co., 1878.

De Haan, M. R., *The Chemistry of the Blood*. Grand Rapids: Zondervan Publishing House, 1943.

Finegan, Jack, *Light From the Ancient Past*. Princeton: Princeton University Press, 1946.

Finegan, Jack, *Archeological History of the Ancient Middle East*. New York: Dorsett Press, 1979.

Forster, Rev. Charles, *Sinai Photographed*. London: Richard Bentley, 1862.

Flavius, Josephus, *Antiquities of the Jews*. Grand Rapids: Kregal Publications, 1960.

Gaussen, L., *The Divine Inspiration of the Bible*. Grand Rapids: Kregel Publications, 1971.

Geikie, Cunningham, *The Holy Land and the Bible*. New York: James Pott & Co. Publishers, 1891.

Greenblatt, Robert B., *Search The Scriptures*. Toronto: J. B. Lippincott Co., 1968.

Keith, Alexander, *Evidence of the Truth of the Christian Religion*. London: T. Nelson and Sons, 1846.

Keith, Alexander, *Christian Evidences: Fulfilled Bible Prophecy*. Minneapolis: Klock & Klock Christian Publishers, Inc., 1984.

Layard, Austen H., *Discoveries Among the Ruins of Nineveh and Babylon*. New York: Harper & Brothers, 1853.

Little, Paul, *Know Why You Believe*. Downers Grove: Inter-Varsity Press, 1988.

Loftus, William Kennett, *Travels and Researches in Chaldea and Susiana*. London: James Nisbet & Co., 1857.

Manniche, Lise, *An Ancient Egyptian Herbal*. London: British Museum Press, 1993.

Maspero, G. *History of Egypt*. London: The Grolier Society, 1900.

McDowell, Josh, *Evidence That Demands a Verdict*. Arrowhead Springs: Campus Crusade For Christ, 1972.

McMillen, S.I., *None of These Diseases*. Grand Rapids: Fleming H. Revell, 1984.

Morris, Henry M., *Many Infallible Proofs*. El Cajun: Master Books, 1974.

Morris, Henry M., *The Bible and Modern Science*. Chicago: Moody Press, 1968.

Morris, Henry M., *The Biblical Basis for Modern Science*. Grand Rapids: Baker Book House, 1984.

Morris, Henry M., *Scientific Creationism*. El Cajon: Master Books, 1985.

Morris, Henry M., *Remarkable Record of Job*. Santee: Master Books, 1988.

Morris, Herbert W., *Testimony of the Ages*. St. Louis: William Garretson & Co., 1884.

Panin, Ivan, *The Writings of Ivan Panin*. Agincourt: The Book Society of Canada, Ltd., 1972.

Petrie, Flinders, *Seventy Years in Archeology*. New York: Henry Holt and Co., 1932.

Ragozin, Zenaide A., *Chaldea from the Earliest Tmes to the Rise of Assyria*. London: T. Fisher Unwin, 1886.

Rambsel, Yacov A., *Yeshua – The Name of Jesus Revealed in the Old Testament*. Toronto: Frontier Research Publications, Inc., 1996.

Rappaport, S., *History of Egypt*. London: The Grolier Society, 1904.

Rawlinson, George, *History of Herodutus*, 4 vol. London: John Murray, 1875.

Richards, Lawrence O., *It Couldn't Just Happen*. Fort Worth: Word, Inc., 1989.

Robinson, Gershon, *The Obvious Proof*. London: CIS Publishers, 1993.

Rosner, Fred, *Medicine in the Bible and the Talmud*. Hoboken: KTAV Publishing House, Inc., 1995.

Rule, William Harris, *Biblical Monuments*. Croydon: Werteimer, Lea and Co., 1873.

Sayce, A. H., *Records of the Past*, 5 vol. London: Samuel Bagster & Sons, Ltd., 1889.

Sheppard, Lancelot C., *Prophecy Fulfilled – The Old Testament Realized in the New*. New York: David McKay Co. Inc., 1958.

Siculus, Diodorus, *Library of History*. Cambridge: Harvard University Press, 1989.

Smith, George Adam, *The Historical Geography of the Holy Land*. London: Hoddr and Stoughton, 1894.

Smith, William, *A Dictionary of the Bible*. Boston: D. Lothrop & Co., 1878.

Stanley, Arthur Penrhyn, *Sinai and Palestine*. London: John Murray, 1905.

Stoner, Peter W., *Science Speaks*. Chicago: Moody Books, 1963.

Stone, Michael, *The Armenian Inscriptions From the Sinai*. Cambridge: Harvard University Press, 1982.

Thompson, J. A., *The Bible and Archeology*. Grand Rapids: Eerdmans Publishing Co. 1972.

Thompson, William M., *The Land and the Book*. Hartford: The S. S. Scranton Co., 1910.

Tiffany, Osmond, *Sacred Biography and History*. Chicago: Hugh Heron, 1874.

Unger, Merrill, F., *Archeology and the Old Testament*. Grand Rapids: Zondervan Publishing Co., 1954.

Varghese, Roy Abraham, *The Intellectuals Speak Out About God*. Chicago: Regnery Gateway, 1984.

Vermes, Geza, *The Dead Sea Scrolls In English*. London: Penguin Books, 1988.

Vermes, Geza, *Discovery in the Judean Desert*. New York: Desclee Co., 1956.

Vincent, Rev. J. H., *Curiosities of the Bible*. Chicago: R. C. Treat., 1885.

Vos, Howard, *Can I Trust The Bible?* Chicago: Moody Press, 1963.

Wilson, Bill, *A Ready Defense – The Best of Josh McDowell*. San Bernardino: Here's Life Publishers, Inc., 1990.

Wood, Percival, *Moses – The Founder of Preventative Medicine*. London: Society For Promoting Christian Knowledge, 1920.